Already Home

"This book is a testament to the healing power of connection with ourselves and with the world around us."
—Sharon Salzberg, author of *Lovingkindness* and *Faith*

"So many of us have been uprooted, scattered across continents, disconnected from our geographic, cultural, and family origins—Barbara Gates's book is a profound and lyrical exploration of our common homelessness."
—Wes Nisker, author of *Essential Crazy Wisdom* and *Buddha's Nature*

"Self and home, garden and neighborhood, are continually reborn, with each shift of attention, into the vibrant particular-ness that is never apart from the sacred ground of all place and all time."
—Sylvia Boorstein, author of *Pay Attention for Goodness' Sake*

"This is the sort of book one is homesick for after finishing it. Honest, searching, and as engrossing as a mystery, it pulled me onward. It's a marvelous meditation on how the fear of change and mortality has led us to destroy in the name of preserving."
—Annie Gottlieb, author of *Do You Believe in Magic?* and *The Cube*

"I felt the vastness of what Gates took on. She is a detective, honest and committed in her search for meaning, uncovering the many layers of home."
—Sue Bender, author of *Plain and Simple*

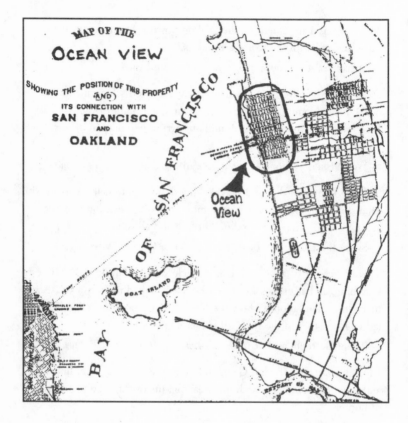

Already Home

a topography of spirit and place

Barbara Gates

Shambhala
BOSTON
2003

Shambhala Publications, Inc.
Horticultural Hall
300 Massachusetts Avenue
Boston, Massachusetts 02115
www.shambhala.com

9 8 7 6 5 4 3 2 1

First Edition
Printed in the United States of America

⊗ This edition is printed on acid-free paper that meets
the American National Standards Institute z39.48 Standard.
Distributed in the United States by Random House, Inc.,
and in Canada by Random House of Canada Ltd

Library of Congress Cataloging-in-Publication Data
Gates, Barbara, 1946–
Already home: a topography of spirit/by Barbara Gates.—1st ed.
p.   cm.
ISBN 1-57062-490-9
1. Gates, Barbara, 1946—Homes and haunts. 2. Berkeley
(Calif.)—Biography. I. Title.
CT275.G2958 A3 2003
979.4'67053'092—dc21
2002014200

For Patrick, Caitlin, and Cleo
and all of the neighbors—
past, present, and future

When we inhale, the air comes into the inner world. When we exhale, the air goes out to the outer world. The inner world is limitless, and the outer world is also limitless. We say "inner world" or "outer world," but actually there is just one whole world.

—Shunryu Suzuki

contents

AUTHOR'S NOTE   xiii

PROLOGUE   xv

Part One: Running

Escaping What's Here and Now

   1. On the Run   3

   2. Circling the Yard   1 2

      Dawn Redwood   2 2

Part Two: Stopping

Here and Now Is All We've Got

   3. Take More Risks   2 7

   4. Nocturnal Mind   3 5

   5. Mama Raccoon   4 0

      Mother Mammal   4 8

Part Three: Looking

Inhabiting the Uninhabitable

   6. No Inner/No Outer   5 3

   7. Skunk Practice   6 1

   8. Homeless: Through the Fence   7 0

9. Skunk Practice: Through Deep Time   77
10. Homeless: In the Street   88
11. Skunk Practice: In the Industrial Zone   97
12. Homeless: In the Yard   107
13. On Inhabiting   116
     Geology   121

Part Four: Seeing
Letting Go of Hope
14. Vital Statistics: Exhaustion   125
15. Homeless: An Interlude with Dogs   136
16. Vital Statistics: Safety   143
17. Homeless: A Second Interlude with Dogs   153
18. Vital Statistics: Turning to the Fathers   159
19. Homeless and Home: With the Grandmothers   164
     Bay and Creeks   174

Part Five: Settling
Before and Beneath
20. Beneath the Pavement   179
21. Shellmound: Original Use: Home   189
22. Shellmound Mind: Dump and Cemetery   197
23. Owner? Guardian?   209

Epilogue
Already Home   225

Acknowledgments   231
Resources   239
Epigraph Credits   247

author's note

PEOPLE OFTEN ASK ME, "Are you writing fiction or nonfiction?" I usually say, "According to my family and neighbors, fiction!" Certainly, it is through my particular lens that the events from our intertwining lives are seen and re-visioned to make the stories in this book. This might not be easy at times for those who recognize exchanges that seem somewhat like, but different from, their own versions. And I am sorry for that. To protect privacy, I have sometimes changed the names of streets and businesses, places, and people; often characters are composites. I have compressed conversations and occasionally changed the sequence of events. At the same time, *Already Home* is the result of seven years of research into the evolution of this place. It has been my intention to tell the story true, but that may mean "true" to my underlying understanding of what has gone on, true to something I hope to convey about places, people, and the relationship between them.

Prologue

Formed by the collision of tectonic plates lifting the hills as the creeks eroded them, the San Francisco East Bay terrain was divided into hills and flatlands long before the appearance of human beings. As generations of Native American families traveled back and forth across the flatlands parallel to what we now call the San Francisco Bay, they may well have worn the path later named the Contra Costa Road by the Spanish rancheros. This road became a stagecoach route for the next wave of European settlers and is now called San Pablo Avenue. Crossing one alluvial fan after another, San Pablo extends where 150 years ago marshes and grasslands teemed with geese, elk, and bobcats. Now it is an urban strip of auto repair shops, car dealerships, fast food restaurants, and gas stations. Below San Pablo Avenue, down in the flatlands of Berkeley, crossed by the tracks of the Southern Pacific Railroad, and bordered by U.S. Interstate 80, is the Ocean View neighborhood.

At the mouth of Strawberry Creek, where it feeds into the San Francisco Bay, the land that is now Ocean View was for forty-five hundred years the site of a Native American shellmound. Following the abandoning of the shellmound, the Ohlone Indian culture continued to evolve its customs into those that are still recognizable today by native descendants. After the Spanish invasion and the founding of missions along the Pacific coast, this same terrain was home to the rancheros and, beginning in the mid-1800s, to a new European settlement, the first established in the East Bay by miners returning from the goldfields in the western foothills of the Sierra Nevada. These new immigrants chose to settle in Ocean View close to the booming markets of San Francisco yet across the Bay, where land was still cheap and water plentiful.

Up Strawberry Creek, toward the hills, the University of California was established, while below in the flatlands, Ocean View grew into a city neighborhood—a mix of industry and residence, suffering from factory emissions, drugs, and crime. Now this neighborhood is being remade again. Warehouses have been turned into artists' studios, shops, and cafés, ramshackle Victorian houses have been renovated.

As the movement of tectonic plates slowly tears apart California along the San Andreas fault and, more slowly, tears apart the San Francisco East Bay along the Hayward fault, which underlies it, people from across the globe—Latin America, Europe, Africa, South Asia— migrate to the West coast of the United States and settle in the Ocean View neighborhood.

I am one of the many migrants to Ocean View and live in one of the Victorian houses with my husband, Patrick; our daughter, Katy; and our mixed Australian shepherd, Cleo.

EARLY IN THE MORNING when most of the world around me is asleep, I find myself most awake. As the fog thins into a coal blue sky, I pause at the top of the steps on our front landing. The street below is empty except for a homeless wanderer pushing a shopping cart of cans past the run-down fourplex on the corner, past Pioneer and Italianate Victorian houses, and down across the tracks in the direction of the Bay.

Toward the hills, Carmen's house is silent, the windows dark. Carmen must have just returned from her night shift as a nurse in the emergency room. On the Bay side, Grandma Darlene's house is also dark and still. It wasn't until two this morning that some neighborhood kids, Donna, and young Michelle, as well as their mother, Dee (drinking once again), finished the party on their front stoop. Through the attic skylight, we heard the beat of rap music until the firm words of Grandma Darlene sent everyone home and Donna and Michelle to bed. Dee, who has been kicked out and homeless now for years, headed off to find someplace to sleep, perhaps at a friend's or in the street.

Upstairs in our attic bedroom, Patrick is still asleep; in her bunk bed off the living room, Katy is also asleep, while Cleo is curled up in her basket. Downstairs, our tenants—one of a series of young couples—paced long into the night lulling the cries of their new baby. At last, their flat is quiet.

I love to listen to the silence, to open in that way, beyond the ups and downs of daily life to fundamental ground. What sounds like silence this morning is the continuous rush of cars on the freeway. And as I begin to pay attention to that, I hear the call of the train. The first two hoots are so tender I can barely discern them—harmonic puffs dissolving into the fog, then again louder, and louder still. This is followed by the clatter of metal on metal and a great rushing (toward who knows where) that gradually subsides into a hushed rumble once again.

Descending the steps, I retrieve the newspaper from the recesses of the "ugly hedge." That old hedge was in place when we bought our house. From the start, I've lobbied to pull it out and Patrick's been adamant that we really do need it. It's the kind some people clip in geometric precision to resemble the outer battlements of a medieval fortress. Maybe it serves that function here: to protect our inner sanctum from the noise and dangers outside.

Following a sudden yen, I step from the confines of the sidewalk to the broad blacktop of the street. From here, if I squint west through the late winter fog, I can make out two opposing streams of glittering light. There, three miles from the Berkeley Hills, at the very base of the flatlands, cars and trucks rush along the freeway where there was once tideland, marsh, and bay. I enjoy this wide view.

Five years ago, the shock of a breast cancer diagnosis jolted me to open up the view. I stretched my mind to find a more inclusive identity than my narrow mortal self. This involved a reversal of figure with ground (of the usually featured character with the often ignored background). I began to teach myself to attend to the precious particulars of life in the context of a spacious landscape, to see the players (featuring me) in my daily drama as a few of the multitude of expressions of a big sweep evolving through the millennia. What a relief it was to include trees and creeks, trains and streets in a sense of who or how I conceived myself to be. Indeed, in my death, whenever it came, the terrain would continue and a more limited me would somehow be part of that.

Thus I embarked on an exploration of this place I'm learning to call home. Home has never been something that came easily to me. As I taught myself to settle into my body with all its blemishes and struggles, I committed to settling into the place where I lived—conflicts and commerce, fumes, all of it. Confronted so rudely by the impermanence of my body and an endangered world, I insisted on seeing true. Now or never.

Over the years, mine has become an unexpectedly all-consuming quest involving daily walks or runs, friendships, research, and imagination. I am continuing to find out not only about the terrain, but about myself. And not only about myself, but about what some call my "not-self," or to put it differently, about how self and terrain are inseparable.

FROM THE SECOND STORY of our house, the kitchen windows provide a wide vista of our yard and those of our neighbors. Rising above all else is our dawn redwood, whose ancient heritage serves as a reminder of the vast reaches of evolutionary time, in keeping with the big view.

As I prepare Katy's breakfast, I appreciate the panorama. Everything begins to brighten, shiver, stretch, and sing. House finches flit in the willow. One, two, three cats leap the fence. Landing in Roy and Sheryl's yard just to our north, the cats scale Roy's newly dug trench. That's Roy's way—refurbishing his Craftsman bungalow, doing his own electrical work, planting trees, digging trenches—heartening for someone practicing law, Roy's trade. I watch the cats congregate in front of Roy's three-car garage as Sheryl joins them to fill the cat bowls. Rumor has it that Sheryl offers medical attention and neck rubs to any cat in need. Their own cat family includes two indoor and seven outdoor by the latest count. It's through Sheryl and Roy that we've met other inhabitants of this corner (feline and other-wise), like Genevieve and Paul, who live one house farther north; they came to Sheryl and Roy's joint birthday party.

Out the east window, I watch a passerby pause by the For Sale sign in front of Carmen's. It's hard to imagine this corner without Carmen. With her bright cheeks and auburn hair, she squats in her gardening apron amid abundant bloom—weeding, pruning her vines, planting bulbs. But over the years, Carmen has completed her fence, her roof, her foundation, and a new paint job and now is ready to sell her house so she can move somewhere more rural.

Down the block, a Guatemalan family I barely know heaves their belongings into a pickup truck; mattresses, an ironing board, a red velveteen couch, and a box of toys are all strapped to the truck. Word has it they're moving somewhere less expen-sive; they've been driven out by rising rent as the neighborhood changes.

Across the street from Carmen's, in the backyard of the cor-ner house, Joaquin climbs a tall painting ladder and takes down the party lanterns. It must have been the extended Lopez clan who gathered this past weekend, joining Claudia and Joaquin and their four children for the gala party. Joaquin and his broth-ers helped Roy dig his trench and replace his front window, which had been shattered by BBs. On weekend evenings, I see

Claudia and Joaquin's many relatives crisscrossing the neighborhood carrying tamales and burritos and (I hazard a guess) potato tacos, the dish I've enjoyed at neighborhood parties at Roy and Sheryl's and a specialty of the small village from which Claudia hails in Mexico.

A sudden burst of action interrupts my scan of the yards: a soccer ball just misses my head and lands in Cleo's bowl, sending dry dog food scattering. Katy scoots into the kitchen, retrieves the ball, and dribbles out, setting off Cleo in a rush of barks and pounces, black plume tail waving. As Cleo bounds out the back door, I hear a high whistle—a signal, I've been told, to do with drug transactions.

At the bathroom sink, I nudge Patrick's shower-wet shoulder, winning room to brush my teeth and spit. The mirror reflects back Patrick's ruddy face (bleary with shaving foam) next to mine (blue eyes apologetic, silver hair askew). Patrick arches a wry brow at me and perhaps at his own predicament as well. With scant interest in dressing up—or, for that matter, in appearances in general—he shaves each morning and dons the straitjacket of tie and suit, all for looking lawyerly as he heads across the Bay to work.

Over breakfast dishes, I look west out the window above the kitchen sink toward the spire of the Pilgrim's Rest Church. A glint of teal and russet. Just there, from a broken shingle above the nave, a kestrel soars out from the crevice where he and his family have recently found refuge. In back of the church, on the wheelchair ramp to the parish hall, a sleeping bag starts to wiggle. People, too, have found refuge by this church over the years, until someone notices and kicks them out.

A police siren blares on San Pablo Avenue. Up and down the block, dogs begin to bark.

MANY OF THE GOINGS-ON here on this corner, in this house, pass me by. I hear whistles I cannot interpret, a train whose destination I have not learned. I recoil from fumes whose toxic nature I suspect but do not know for sure. I pass neighbors with whom I've never spoken. I even sidestep my own family in my hurry to get someplace else. Meanwhile, the landscape continues to change. It's taking a long time for this place where I live to feel homey.

An easy cry and quick to lash out in anger, I'm often carried by excitement, fear, or simply restlessness. I lose the feel of the ground beneath my feet. By training on the meditation cushion, I reach for an unshakable sturdiness and balance. On the meditation cushion, I am teaching myself to be more mindful. Mindfulness is a technique I have been learning over many years through the study of Buddhism. It means paying attention moment by moment without judgment. If I pay attention—without fighting what I see—I may learn to see this home place just as it is, to keep the big view.

In many ways, I'm an unlikely candidate for the tasks I've taken on. As an explorer of the terrain, I suffer from geographic (as well as geologic) dyslexia, often mixing up lefts and rights, norths and souths, to say nothing of longitudes and latitudes. When it comes to adventures, a penchant toward worry counters the urge to explore new territory. And rather than paying attention to where I am, I tend instead to bump my shopping cart into others at the market, to step in dog poop on the street, to daydream past my stop on the subway. As to figure and ground, more days than not, I'm intently fixed on the figure caught in life's daily dramas.

Training in paying attention is more challenging than I'd expected. For twenty-five years I've gone on meditation retreats away from family and friends. But to sit myself down on a cushion in my own house, to practice paying attention on a daily basis? No! It has felt well-nigh impossible.

Despite these hindrances, through the soles of my sneakers and through a mind that like the landscape is also changing, I continue to explore. Taking on what's hard for me, I risk intimacy with the rocks and potholes of the factory zone; with commercial lots; with the soil in my own backyard; with my neighbors and family; with my own blood, bone, and turns of mind.

I am indeed looking for home. But many years into the search, I am just realizing that. This is the story I tell. In the telling, I follow the spirit of journals I've kept over many years, where everything—personal diaries, maps, shopping lists, seismic reports, and tide logs—is always kept in the same notebook. I explore the terrain where I live through myself, myself through the terrain.

PART ONE

Running

escaping what's here
and now

We run our whole life chasing after one idea of happiness
or another.
—Thich Nhat Hanh

Chapter 1

on the run

ALIENATED, OUT OF PHASE with life, I take off for my neighborhood run. Driven by longings for something other or better, I head down across the tracks toward the green of Aquatic Park, a freeway's jump to the San Francisco Bay. It's one of those restless days. I'll let the whistle of a morning train stream through my thoughts, let the colors of front-stoop gardens, the salt-tang, smoke-dank, jasmine-sweet air wash through.

As I race down toward the Bay this morning, grievances—at home, in the neighborhood, even from years past—chase me down my block. A litany of judgment, of blame. Patrick refuses to listen; Katy's challenging me for no reason; I have too many writing deadlines. . . .

Running down the block, I pass the purple fourplex that some in the neighborhood refer to as the crack house. The familiar characters are hanging around out in front leaning up against cars, smoking, talking on cell phones. Years back, when pregnant and hopeful I first hunkered down by the strip of soil in front of the ugly hedge to plant some primroses, Dee sauntered by. "Baby," she warned me, "you lives in a drugs neighborhood!" Not what I wanted to hear as I prepared the garden for starting a family in this new house. Not what I want to remember now.

3

At every turn this morning, on these streets, in my memories, I am at odds.

As I run past the Pilgrim's Rest Church on the corner, I pass our postman. "How's the kid?" he calls out, with his warm Spanish cadence. As usual, he stops to chat. While I jog in place, he puts a foot up on the church steps, leans his elbow on his knee, and cups his chin in his hand, settling in as if he came this way today particularly to check up on me and my family. "Good weather, eh? Gonna see the Giants play this weekend?" He pauses. "And how are those roses?" He reflects for a moment. "Did I ever tell you my mother has roses just like yours?" How satisfying, on a morning such as this, to pause, to be drawn for a moment into contact.

I run now toward the cottage where I first lived when I fled the East Coast for Berkeley. As I run past, I pause for a nod to the dilapidated charm of this little house—its weathered shingles and colorful (albeit unkempt) front garden, its attic window through which twenty-two years ago I could peer out onto the chaos of this very street.

To get to know this terrain, to make it my home, I feel a pull to understand how I ended up here at all. What drew me here?

"Here" is not just across the continent to this street in Berkeley. It's also a way of thinking that offers me a lens for reflecting about life and for living in this place. It's not as if California or Buddhism were mine by right of birth; I was raised in New York City and without Judaism by a Jewish artist mother. I took vacations in the Berkshire Hills with my Unitarian, fervently atheist professor dad. So when I came here to Berkeley and to Buddhism, I traveled in space (three thousand miles), in time (back twenty-five hundred years), and in culture (halfway around the world).

Slowing down my pace, I lope past what was once the First Presbyterian Church, then the Saint Procopius Latin Rite, now a Coptic church of the Ethiopian community. The priest in his robe and flat hat nods and smiles as I pass. Along the street comes my neighbor Haddie, as usual pulling along her fold-up marketing wagon filled with groceries. I appreciate Haddie, short and squat, her polka-dot bandanna setting off her cheeks like dark plums. By the parking lot of Spenger's Fish Grotto, I run by the day workers chatting in Spanish or Tagalog; they line up along the street above the builders' store waiting for someone to pick them up for digging, hauling, or painting jobs. Yes, I think, a neighborhood with folks from all over the world is where I want to be. But soon I pass someone, most likely drunk, passed-out in the bushes. I race ahead, feeling at odds once again. Some of my friends have moved out of the flats farther up toward the hills, but that's not what I want either. Nothing feels quite right.

I hurry past the new strip of cafés and upscale shops where women with designer bags and shoes stroll by to dine and spend. Again, distaste. It's not that I want more boutiques. Here, too, I feel alien.

In the distance, the train hoots—one long call and then another. I turn my eye on myself. Maybe there's some envy of those moving to the hills, and under that envy, a desire—for a safe and tended neighborhood, all homes, no shops. I certainly have had fantasies that I might step out my own door to run on a quiet, winding street lined with magnolia, past fences laced with wisteria, delicately pruned. And my on-and-off attempts to brighten up our front yard have not necessarily pleased the eye. I remember Haddie's comment when I first planted the primroses in front of the hedge. Pulling her little wagon to a halt, she stopped and shook her head. "Unh, unh. . . ." Stepping back a bit, she surveyed my handwork, right to left and back again, then decreed, "You sure aren't much of a gardener!" Glancing up, I checked for a wink or a chuckle, but she just kept on shaking her head.

Running now in great strides, I leave the new pocket of elegance and head down one more block toward the train tracks. The train is approaching. Bells clang at the tracks. Two red lights flash on and off; candy-striped sticks slide down and cross, blocking my way. While the crossing bells continue to clang, the train rattles through, ringing its own bell and giving a long whistle.

A tremor passes through me, as it always does with that call. It reverberates with a promise of I don't know what. Freight cars from across the country rumble by—Southern Pacific, Cotton Belt, Santa Fe, Burlington Northern. This morning the train call taps into my yearnings: the romance of the rails, of "hobo" adventurers hopping trains, chasing dreams, escaping the humdrum or the painful—whatever they can't pay or can't fathom or can't bear.

Heading across the tracks, I think again of my own exit, my migration from East Coast to West. At some point in my late twenties, everything seemed to go awry, to feel unbearable. Surely everything went increasingly wrong with my dad's brain tumor. Cancer. Metastasized. An image of the hospital waiting room as the surgeon walked in. The shocking news. And in the years to come, what a tantrum I threw with my young life.

I pick up speed, bolting past defunct factories and warehouses. I hold my breath against a nasty whiff of fumes from the working factories nearby and head down desolate streets toward Aquatic Park. Sense memories return to me of my graced early twenties before things went wrong: the excitement; the intimacy of friendships; couches where I slept; typewriters, winter coats, and sleeping bags borrowed or shared; weddings (and one divorce) at which I served as witness. How was it that within such a short time friendships overturned, and all that felt familiar reversed itself, leaving me with what felt like no recourse but to take off for the West? Even now, I don't completely get it; something remains opaque.

Into Aquatic Park I follow the path along the water. I do love this patch of grass and willows and, most of all, the estuary fed by a breakwater system that channels Bay water under the free-way and the underground creeks that descend from the hills. Jogging along, I widen my view. On the far side of the park, cars speed along Interstate 80, following the curve of the Bay. Closer by, in the protection of this refuge, beneath Monterey cypresses and willows, swim coot, mallards, pied-billed grebes, and buffle-heads—like those found at the original shoreline, before the changes wrought by European settlements.

The day is heating up. A honeyed aroma of ceonothus soothes my senses. Pictures of my dad come to mind. Since his abrupt departure when I was three and over years of brief visits, he certainly had become a disappearing hero. When I heard he would soon die, I rushed from Cambridge to the Berkshires to nurse him back to health. I wasn't even thirty and thought I might lose him for good. So many weekends, driving to the Berkshires and back. Straight from teaching my last class—such a long drive on that narrow mountain road, at night, through snow, the hairpin turn, and down the hill to a dreary hospital. And always the hope that, despite reports from doctors, he might survive to become the dad I'd always wanted him to be.

But now, as I double back along the estuary, I see my dad in his hospital bed, shrunken by disease and rage, having failed even in an attempt to drive into a tree to end his pain.

The Christmas when my dad was dying, my then-boyfriend drove out from Cambridge through a snowstorm to join me at the hospital, to help. Shaggy blond hair, wool hat. I see him now arriving with his saxophones, a guitar, and a camera strapped to his back. Back in Cambridge, we two had set up such a cozy home, furnished with rocking chairs inherited from my grand-mother, my dad's mom. Just as I made my first try at joining with a guy to create a home, my dad was dying.

Racing back through the park, I can't shake the memory—my dad's fifty-eight-year-old body wasted to a shrunken version of itself, skin stretched on bone. And on one of those many returns to Cambridge, when I least expected it, how a wild restlessness took me over, a rush of passion for a second man, someone I met at a political meeting. I fixed on this secret paramour, his caustic intellect; his tough-guy talk; his long, muscled body; the smell of alcohol and nicotine that seemed to run in his veins; and the tumult of his erratic comings and goings. All this offered me, in some upside-down way, a respite from the heartache over my dad, but threatened all that I thought mattered to me in my nascent home.

More memories follow. Of the burial, and how we waited until spring. The tiny college cemetery surrounded by the green of the Berkshire Hills, the few family members hiking up the grassy slope, a heap of dirt by the newly dug grave. I still don't know if we should have opened the burial urn. This keeps coming back to me. We huddled together, unscrewed the lid— shattered cartilage and burnt bone in the palm of my hand. Afterward, I was disturbed: were my dad's ashes stuck under my fingernails?

Indeed, I came back from that burial to concoct a perfect hell for myself—a cross between *A Streetcar Named Desire* and *No Exit*. In retrospect, I feel a certain jaundiced appreciation for the extravagance of the drama: the move out on my own from what was beginning to feel like home; my obsession with my crazy romance; each boyfriend in a moment of rage smashing my grandmother's furniture. It was a hard winter for rocking chairs. . . .

But the hardest part was the dissolving of so many friendships. Now, as I think on it, I can guess why. After two years of failing to make contact with me, after so many efforts to get my attention with so little offered back to them, they couldn't stand it anymore.

The train calls again; the crossing bells ring. I stop at the tracks, heat charging my limbs. Here it is, the cross-up. I had become obsessed with a self in pain that felt so large it seemed to become the whole world. It's wrenching now, the extremity of this delusion. The world had ceased to exist, and all that was left was the heat of my pain (which I confused with myself). In the end, it felt like the only way out was to flee.

"Geography," a friend insisted. We were sitting sharing a cigarette on the front step of the community school where we both worked—three thousand miles across the continent from where I live now. I picture my friend with his broad, shining face, dark brown like bittersweet chocolate. "Geography. That's your only way out of this mess." So when my life on the East Coast fell apart into what felt like an impossible tangle, I came west on the run.

The train clatters past. I picture these steel rails crisscrossing America while freight trains such as this one carry grain, fuel, and produce from Mexico to Canada and from one coast to the other. Sometimes my images of hoboes on the road and train romance can be overly sentimental. This morning I welcome the larger view—of the breadth of this country, of the world; of distance; of anonymity; of a way of thinking that includes cycles of space and time; of our wide home beyond one particular life story.

I think of my friend's comment. It was sort of a wisecrack. For all I know, he simply wanted to get rid of me. He certainly had no idea how deeply resonant his advice became, nor through how many layers I would be teaching myself to rest in precisely that: geography, inside and out.

ON THE WAY BACK toward my house, I see our postman again. He's squatting on the sidewalk, engaging a toddler in a chat. I used to think that he had a special friendship with me and my family. But truly, setting aside a twinge of jealousy, I see that this man has a like friendship with all. As I explore the neighborhood, I see him sitting on the wicker chair on Sheryl and Roy's porch, chatting with them; settled on a stoop with Dee; or bending down to scratch an old hound behind the ears. Maybe he's talking weather with one, listening to the troubles of another. All I know is that in each conversation, he looks relaxed. As I run by now, I give him a wave, postman qua Paul Revere and mendicant monk, bringing news from afar in his letter bag and kind attention to all of the neighbors.

I run back up Delaware Street, through the spruced-up historic section, on past James Kenny Park where kids are out playing baseball. I keep thinking of the postman. On every stoop and stairway, with kids and dogs, women and men, this man seems truly at ease. He seems comfortable in any context.

Unlike me. Much as my mind is set on the contrary, more often than not, I am uncomfortable. In fact, on a day like today, it seems I'm uncomfortable in any context. Everything feels wrong, and I'm looking for a way out.

Take this morning. I've been uncomfortable with Patrick, with Katy, with neighbors. Then I found myself uncomfortable with the flats and doubly uncomfortable with my own discomfort. And as I remembered the ups and downs (mostly downs) of the personal saga that brought me to this place I so long to make my home, what an extreme version of "uncomfortable" I saw—horror in the face of loss, of sickness, of death. How this sent me running from romance to romance, from friend to friend, and finally across a continent. "On the run" doesn't even name it. I came here on the lam.

It has felt impossible sometimes to take in the rude shocks of life. A softening washes through my chest. This is human, I tell myself. An ache now for Katy; for Patrick; for friends and boyfriends east and west whom I couldn't truly see for who they were; for my dad; and yes, for me, too. I've only known how to close down my mind, how to run. I haven't known another way.

Buddhism teaches about this same sad human tendency—

discomfort with life as it is. During meditation, I have sometimes seen that judging stance that separates me from others,
from my feelings, from experience itself. Now I see it in this
morning's run: I've focused on *what* I want to avoid and *what* I'd
rather have. There's another way to see it: alienation is a *how*;
it's simply a stance one might take. So the alienation itself, the
very nature of it, not its objects, bears examination.

A breeze picks up and loosens my tight thoughts. Or perhaps
it's not the breeze that loosens, but the insight. Alienation is
habitual, not tied to context.

A whistle in the distance. Soon a train will be coming. All
over the world, the bells at practice centers, at temples, at
churches call people to pray, to meditate, to pay attention. Here,
we have the hoot of the train. Throughout the day in the streets
of Ocean View, in my attic bedroom on hot nights when the
skylight is open, and now, softly in the distance, I can hear its
call. Maybe I can take this whistle as an invitation to notice, in
this moment, what's going on, to notice my stance. Am I seeing
true? To see the particular within the wide span, and from that
big view, learn how to be more comfortable, to be at home,
come what may.

Chapter 2

circling the yard

THROUGH THE FRONT DOOR, living room, and kitchen dash Katy and two friends. They throw open the back door to the yard and head down the stairs, shouting, "Let's climb the tree!"

With Cleo nipping at their heels, the whole gang clambers up into the soft needles, feathery, new, green. The dawn redwood towers thirty feet tall, high above everything else in our yard. Unlike some of its current arboreal colleagues, it preceded us here. When we moved in ten years ago, it rose with an optimistic flourish just above the fence in the northeast corner. Planted by the people who sold us our house, the dawn redwood—whose ancestors date back many millions of years—is a migrant to California from China.

Appreciating the lives of the trees, I take a turn in the yard. To truly get to know this yard, these trees, feels essential to my quest. My ruminations from yesterday's run continue, the hoot of a train a prompt to look around, to open up the view. I wonder again about my flight from Cambridge to Berkeley; I puzzle over other passages and pilgrimages, my own and those of others. I contemplate migration—the movement of life from this place to that. Wondering where they came from, how they ended up here in this yard, I scan these trees. Some, like the dawn redwood, were already here when Patrick and I arrived;

others were given to us by friends; still others were planted in memoriam. The willow volunteered.

An arroyo willow spreads new leaves over the corner of our yard by the compost bin, at the juncture of the fences separating our property from our neighbors' to the north and west. I stand beneath the light canopy of spring leaves. The willow certainly had an arduous passage. When we first moved in, the seed arrived from parts unknown and, near the fence separating our property from Carmen's on the east (not here in its present corner), it first took root.

When it sprouted up, I spotted the invading "weed" and plucked it out. My brother, ardent gardener and arborist that he is, protested, "That's a tree!" and handed the limp seedling to Patrick. "My best guess, a willow," my brother added. We wasted no time replanting it where I'd so cavalierly yanked it out. A tree, we all agreed, shouldn't be casually discarded.

Standing here now by the willow, I take a focused look at the lance-shaped leaves, dark green on top, with a pale underside. The foliage above me reaches west over the fence toward Grandma Darlene's, where Michelle is sitting on the back steps hanging out with her friends, smoking cigarettes, and laughing. The willow also reaches north, over the fence between our yard and Sheryl and Roy's. In front of Roy's three-car garage, the cats lounge alongside the perennial line of bowls. Indeed, the willow in its maturity is neighborly, with three yards in its purview.

Soon after our first wrangle with the willow, Patrick and I scanned the yard from our kitchen window, looking out toward Roy's garage, the centerpiece of this panorama. "That's it!" exclaimed Patrick. "We'll transplant it. If it's really a willow, when it shoots up, it'll hide Roy's ugly garage." With a leap uncharacteristic for his stocky, forty-four-year-old build, he bounded down the back steps to dig out the seedling and replant it here in the back corner. And here, it grew—rapidly—only to suffer yet one more assault.

Those were mad tree-climbing days; Katy and company shimmied up any available trunk. One avid climber tackled the willow sapling, only thrice his five-year-old height. The slim trunk split down the center, and Patrick, continuing his role as steward, tied it back together with twine, hoping it would mend.

A nod to this willow—graceful through transplants, flexible of limb, quick to grow, strongly anchored. Of course, willows are water lovers and thrive by marshes and streams. The long, narrow leaves—offering minimal resistance to the flow of water—are not easily torn off during floods. There are few willows in the neighborhood now. But when Strawberry Creek used to wend down toward the Bay through what was once Willow Grove Park just south of here, there must have been plenty. The name of our street, Willow Avenue, is a testament to that. A nod to our yard as well, a hospitable spot for a willow.

In a male willow like ours, buds open into upright catkins of yellow flowers brimming with pollen. The female willow has catkins of green flowers, each of them an ovary tipped with feathery stigma to catch flying pollen. The seedpods in the female split open to release hundreds of tiny seeds. With their fluff of cottony hairs, these seeds ride the wind; some find suitable habitats. When they do, they put down roots. This is their particular expertise. Willows (not only seeds, but branches as well) love to root. Fences of freshly cut willow sticks send out new tendrils, anchor themselves, and transform into trees. In fact, some gardeners soak willow bark to make a rooting solution—willow water—to help cuttings from intransigent rooters.

RESTING HERE BY THE WILLOW, I return to my own passage (it's somehow essential to bear witness to that) so I can leave it behind and truly be here now.

What led me to finally wrench myself out from the mess of my life in the East to head west? Even cleaning house, attending meetings, how I battled through a morass of obsessions, unable to see others, unable to see what I was doing. But when I did catch a momentary glimpse, it was obvious: my upset was not simply due to circumstance. To find relief, I had to address my frantic mind.

In the late sixties and the seventies, when the teachings of Asia continued to migrate to Western countries from Tibet, China, and Korea, a few of my friends had turned to Buddhist meditation to train their minds. I had learned to meditate in the mid-seventies. My first instruction had been from a friend (like me, of New York Jewish descent) who made a pit stop at my house at 5:00 A.M. and set up cushions on the floor of my bedroom. He was on his way to lead the early-bird sitting at a local center for a Korean brand of Zen Buddhism.

In a last-ditch attempt to recover mental balance, I then drove off—on my friend's say-so—to Boulder, Colorado, to study meditation with Joseph Goldstein, another New York Jewish Buddhist. How little I knew about Buddhism; yet when no other efforts had worked, I'd fixed on meditation.

Fragments from the summer in Boulder return to me: Each day I rose before sunrise to join others on their meditation cushions to practice paying attention. Not letting myself run, I sat still. And when I sat still, I cried. That's all I could do. I cried for my dad, that he was gone; I cried for the boyfriends, the one I'd left and the other one with whom I was still obsessed, even here, half a continent away; I cried for my once-friends; and I cried for my life as it had been—which, I was coming to see, would never again be as it once was.

But there were moments of respite. An earlier memory returns to me now. I was just over twenty, camping in the Berkshires. It was the first time I'd ever tried to identify a tree. There I was, an intellectual New York City girl who could concentrate on a library catalogue or a poem, maybe distinguish a Rothko from a Motherwell. But I couldn't concentrate enough on a leaf to tell an oak from a maple. It took a lot of effort to look at a particular leaf in a way I had never looked at anything before. All my faculties absorbed, body and mind slid into one. What a release—just like today with the willow. In a flash of attention, through a confusion of thoughts, the effort itself dissolved into vastness.

Some moments during meditation were like that. When the obsession was about to take over again, there was a space around it. I would see it coming. In those few graced seconds, I wasn't running toward or away; everything was there.

I can't remember much of what Joseph said in his daily talks, only the warm voice, the familiar New York accent. But the way he laid it out was so clear—the four noble truths, the noble eightfold path. Something in it rang true: the basic truth of impermanence, so resonant with my own sense of loss; the truth of suffering, resonant again with my pain in fighting those losses, in resisting life as it was handed to me.

At the end of that summer in Boulder, I knew two things. One was that I felt the pull of the meditation cushion, the pull to sit down and know that I was sitting. The other was that I needed to make a drastic change in the way I was living my life. So I continued my flight across the country, driving through Colorado, Utah, Nevada, California . . . out toward the Pacific Ocean. There were many others on this trajectory. A few friends from New England were already settled around the San Francisco Bay—writing poetry and painting, starting "free schools" and communal houses, studying meditation at the edge of the continent—only an ocean away from the Far East. This was the latest sweep across—a 1960s and 1970s "westward movement."

IN THE DISTANCE, a faint halloo of a train. A signal again to take notice. The kids are scrambling down from the dawn redwood, picking mint to make tea, dashing up the back steps;

Cleo, barking, bounds by in tandem with the kids. All disappear into the kitchen. Craning my neck back, I gaze up. The willow rises strong above me, its split is healed over with a barely visible scar. Finches and chestnut-backed chickadees flit through the boughs. More than twenty feet tall now, by summer when the leaves are dense, this willow will definitively hide Roy's garage.

I look out toward the center of the yard to the cherry tree, one of the first trees Patrick and I planted. The cherry (a lovely ornamental of Japanese descent) was for Bob, who co-owned our house and without whom we couldn't have bought it. Bob's girlfriend came from New York to help us dig the hole. It was a simple ceremony, perhaps a month after the rafting accident in which Bob was killed. Where an apple tree had died just before we moved in, we lowered the root ball of the cherry and packed the soil. That cherry looks like Bob—tall, slim, somehow intelligent, with a masculine grace. Delicate buds are forming all along the branches of what we call "Bob's tree."

High up in the dawn redwood, there's a whoosh of yellow and red. Blazing yellow chests and scarlet heads. Not finches, mourning doves, or Steller's jays; these are no local inhabitants. They're western tanagers, stopping over here in their long migration south from Canada to their wintering grounds in Mexico. In a flamboyance of red, black, and gold, they fly down the coast along with other migrants—navigating, some say, by the stars, or by the sun, or by the magnetic fields of the planet.

A train calls, loud and harmonic—two notes, a pause, then another two. Here I am in the center of this yard in company with an arroyo willow, an ornamental cherry, and a dawn redwood. I am able (at times) to sit still on a meditation cushion. I have committed to teaching jobs. How did I finally commit to a place? The answer is clear. It wouldn't have happened without Patrick. Having fled from boyfriend to boyfriend, with Patrick I finally came to rest. Patrick slowed me down, absorbed my agitation. Through his steadiness, he steadied me so I could settle with him and put down roots. Right here.

Patrick first moved into my tiny flat with his spare belongings in tow: a toothbrush; a suitcase; several well-splattered cookbooks; some murder mysteries; political tomes from professorial stints east and west; a law school diploma from a sojourn in New England; a few trinkets from a childhood in the foreign service—Sri Lanka, Bangladesh, Yugoslavia—and later years in the Peace Corps in Togo. That's Patrick. Despite world travel, he owned only what he found essential. I've always loved that about him. He traveled light. Then, with me, he knew he was ready to stay put. And through Patrick, I found a way into some basic streams of life from which I'd always felt shut out: buying a house, conceiving and raising a child, knowing neighbors, tending a yard. This yard.

THE BOUGHS OF THE DAWN redwood sway in the breeze. By fall, the needles, now a tender new green, will turn brown, and on some windy night, a cold blast will come in from the Pacific Ocean and blow them off, leaving the branches bare. Our first fall here, we winced at the stripped and mangy look, convinced this tree was dying. Come February, to our relief, new buds appeared. My brother told us, "This is a deciduous conifer. Millions of years ago, these trees learned to release their needles to survive the winter."

Even then, when he casually mentioned it, I felt stirred by this ancient heritage. As I did with the water-loving willow, I began to research this tree, to feel the evolution of the dawn redwood moving through me, through this yard, extending the sense of home through the millennia.

Bare or in full leaf, I appreciate this tree: Katy's climbing tree. Ever since she was three, she's been pulling herself into the lower branches and climbing up. In her early climbs, she would nestle in a comfortable nook that afforded a broad view of the neighborhood. She'd wave over the fence to Dee, who, sober or drinking, made friends with little children, and Dee would call back from the street, "Hi, sugar!" Or from a perch over Carmen's yard, Katy would chat with Carmen planting bulbs. Or she'd wave to Sheryl feeding the cats. "Sheryl! Up here, it's Kakey!" (For years, she couldn't pronounce her own name.)

If Patrick has grounded me in a yard, surely it has been Katy who has tied us to our neighbors and to another once-Jewish Buddhist teacher, Jack Kornfield. Jack taught me to bring kindness to my forty-two-year-old womb struggling to conceive, and later passed on to Katy his own daughter's riding-sized stuffed horse, worn nubbly with love. And Sharon Salzberg became another important teacher for me, opening up my understanding of home to its vast inner dimensions. In more recent years, my drive to bring Buddhist teaching to home life has led me to Gil Fronsdal, a teacher, a scholar, and a household man whose clear-eyed, blue jean–clad wife and exuberant toddler son radiate the vibrancy of family.

Katy and Patrick together have led me to a kind of Buddhism embedded in life, in family, in home—in nonviolent relations to neighbors and place, in the ecology of the whole. I remember a weeklong retreat especially for families that we attended with Thich Nhat Hanh. "Thai" (his nickname, which means "teacher") draws on the Buddha's insight into interdependent coarising: "This is, because that is. This is not, because that is not. This comes to be because that comes to be. This ceases to be, because that ceases to be." This is a fundamental teaching; as Thai puts it, all things "inter-are."

WANDERING THE YARD NOW, I circle around to the front to visit the princess tree. The princess, with its velvety purple flowers, shades the hills side of our front yard, reaching high past the second floor of our house. When we first moved in, my friend Marie launched us here with the young princess—a slim trunk and a puff of rich bloom. After a late frost the second year, it withered to the ground; then, surprisingly, it resprouted, elegant and robust, with five strong boughs branching out from the root.

I cross over to the Bay side of the house and think again of our friend Bob. Bob's death by drowning was the first of a quick series of deaths and cancer diagnoses among our friends and family. Patrick's father, Charlie, died of throat cancer; within months, Patrick's brother found their mother on the floor, dead from a stroke or a heart attack. We never knew. Then that same brother began treatment for colon cancer and, more recently, lung cancer. And I was diagnosed with breast cancer.

For Granddaddy Charlie, I planted a wisteria. When the ground was wet from spring rains, I dug a hole for the young wisteria by a trellis on the southwest corner of our house. For several years, its drooping lavender cascades flared open after the March rains, then it sent out new leaves and wove along the trellis. One spring, the storms of El Niño appeared to have killed it. It bloomed early in an intense burst, then the blossoms shriveled up. There were no leaves. Perhaps the roots rotted out with the rain. Just in case it might have a comeback, we left it by the corner of the house, its root clenched like a gnarled fist rising out of the earth. It's April now, and the wisterias in Carmen's and Sheryl's yards have gushed into luxuriant bloom. Only a single vine rises from the root of Granddaddy's wisteria and winds through the trellis, bare of leaf or blossom.

Before you plant the wisteria seed, you need to scarify it— shake it up in a jar lined with sandpaper or notch it with a knife. When moisture seeps through a seed coat, it provides oxygen and creates pressure in the interior of the seed. The cells of the embryo begin to divide, the embryo swells until it ruptures the softened coat, and a root erupts. But a seed such as the wisteria has armor so sturdy that it doesn't allow moisture to penetrate, thus resisting germination.

Because the seed's journey is often rough, spanning distant terrains with drastic changes in heat and cold, moisture and dryness, a coat may possess great resistance to environmental extremes. To germinate, some seeds simply require water. But some require violence: to be shattered by force (I'm told by a botanist friend that some seeds only crack open when trampled by elephants); others need intense cold, and still others fire. Seeds, with their wide range of protective coats, coevolve with their particular habitats. The seeds and their habitats inter-are.

THROUGH THE GATE, I return to the backyard. So many migrants live here. The dawn redwood is from China, as is the wisteria; the cherry is Japanese; the princess tree, Brazilian. (The arroyo willow is indigenous.) I migrated, too. I'm getting to know this place, settling in, and beginning to pass down a history. I traveled a great distance with a hard and thick seed coat until I was able to take root here.

A breeze rises from the Bay, rustling through the boughs of the dawn redwood. The clouds quicken through the blue expanse. Seeing my own flight as one in a multitude of migrations, I feel something open up beyond this one figure to the wide ground. I'm moved by the sense of vast change in time, in place. Twelve thousand years ago, early humans migrated from Asia to North America, traveling along the coast in plank canoes or following the mastodon across the ice bridge from Siberia to Alaska. Birds and trees and animals, attuned to the sun and stars and magnetic fields, crisscross the planet while evolving lands and seas—driven by plate tectonics, by the tilt of the earth circling the sun, by the chemistry of heat and cold—also continue to migrate.

Up through the new spring needles of the dawn redwood,

clouds shuttle inland from the Bay. I close my eyes. Glimmerings of thought migrate through the terrain of mind.

Dawn Redwood

From about one hundred million until about twelve million years ago, vast forests of the ancient conifer the dawn redwood grew throughout the northern latitudes of the planet. In the "greenhouse" world of the dinosaurs, when the polar regions were more temperate, and for millions of years to follow as the earth went through sometimes violent swings in climate—the dawn redwood thrived. The dawn redwood (Metasequoia glyptostroboides) grew in Eurasia and was the most abundant conifer in western and Arctic North America.

Unlike most other conifers, the dawn redwood is deciduous. In times of stress, it can shut down. It may well be that the survival of this tree has been partially due to its ability to adapt to change—not only in the face of winter, but in the wake of ecological catastrophes.

Such a catastrophe happened sixty-five million years ago, when it is thought that an asteroid, or perhaps a comet, collided with the earth in what is now the Gulf of Mexico, ending the age of the dinosaurs and ravaging the North American continent. The devastation was vast, with the exception of several locations sufficiently remote or sheltered to allow life to survive. One of these sanctuaries was the Arctic Circle, home of the dawn redwood. In the Arctic of the Eocene epoch, the earth's climate was warmer and wetter than it is today; these trees and others thrived. The dawn redwood and its fellow trees gradually colonized North America and, during the following ten million years, were crucial to the recovery of this continent's forests.

Most of the plants of the ancient North American forests are now extinct, having been driven from the continent by extreme ecological shifts. But the dawn redwood continued to survive despite the shocks of global change. With the cooling of Arctic winters, the dawn redwood and many other plant communities, dispersed to the south. But by thirteen to twelve million years ago, the dawn redwood had become extinct in North America.

Beginning in the early 1800s, paleobotanists found fossils of the ancestors of various redwood-family trees all over the Northern Hemisphere. But it was not until 1941 that a Japanese paleobotanist noted the unique features of the "redwood" fossils he was finding in Japan and first named a separate genus: Metasequoia. The analysis of the fossil record was significantly revised, and many previously discovered fossils, dating back millions of years, were earmarked as Metasequoia.

Also in 1941, a forester in the Szechuan province of China came across a deciduous conifer he did not recognize; it was later found to be identical to the fossils found in Japan. Unbeknown to paleobotanists, the dawn redwood had continued to thrive. Protected from cold winters and hot summer winds, it flourished in the valleys of the Szechuan and Hupeh provinces of China.

Through these two synchronous discoveries—of fossils in Japan and living trees in China—this ancient tree, not recognized in millions of years of the fossil record, was shown not only to have been an abundant conifer in late Mesozoic and Tertiary times, but to survive today.

In 1948, a University of California paleobotanist made a pilgrimage to the isolated valleys of the Szechuan and Hupeh provinces to honor the dawn redwood. Growing amid the rice paddies in a small village, there was the great tree—five hundred to six hundred years old; ninety-eight feet high; ten feet, ten inches in diameter. As reported in March 1948 in the San Francisco Chronicle, it was "at least as remarkable as discovering a living dinosaur."*

At the base of this venerable conifer, villagers had built a tiny temple. Believing that the tree contained a holy spirit, people from the surrounding area were said to congregate there to predict the outcome of their own crops by the great tree's spring foliage and to pray for health, fertility, and a good harvest.

---

* William Gittlen, *Discovered Alive: The Story of the Chinese Redwood* (Berkeley: Pierside Publications, 1998), p. 21.

From this pilgrimage to the revered tree and other pilgrimages to nearby forests similar to those around the world a million centuries earlier, hand-collected seeds and hand-carried seedlings were brought back to the San Francisco Bay Area. Thousands of seeds have subsequently been distributed throughout the world. The dawn redwood in Berkeley's Ocean View—known as "Katy's climbing tree," which is so often full of children—is a descendant of trees that grew in the remote valleys of China and is most likely born of the ancient tree that rises among rice paddies in the embrace of a shrine.

PART TWO

Stopping

here and now is all
we've got

Things as they are, from a human perspective, requires
an acute appreciation of loss—total loss, loss of self and loss
of world. This is what freedom means. This is the real shape
of the sacredness of the world, the union we find within
the particularity of each moment of our lives.

—Norman Fischer

Chapter 3

take more risks

THROUGH THE GATE between our yard and what was once Carmen's, our young neighbor Berto trundles a wheelbarrow of leaves and vegetable peelings in various stages of decay. It's hot today, and the air still. I breathe in a faint scent of rot as load after load is carried to our compost heap by the willow from the compost heap in the yard next door. We are hoping to protect the new owner of Carmen's house, Cathy, whose immune system has been destroyed by leukemia. Cathy has no way to fight the bacteria that feed on this decomposing life.

As Berto hauls, the pile of refuse mounts. Restless, I watch his progress as I try to make myself a comfortable place to sit on the ground. Frayed blue notebooks are spread around me. These are my cancer journals. It was five years ago—twenty-two years after I had fled to California—that I was diagnosed with breast cancer. Panicked, I descended into dread. Would I die young, be shut out from life, leave behind a motherless five-year-old?

Beneath the dawn redwood, the needles darkening now in late spring, I'm mustering stamina this morning to read through these journals, to decipher a scrawl I've never reread. I hate to think about that scary time. But I am convinced: terror of death sent me into the broad terrain. I've got to understand how that happened.

Pasted inside the cardboard cover of the first cancer journal is a photograph of Katy. In thirty years of keeping journals, this is the only picture I have pasted in. It's an Easter photo of her at five, embracing a basket of colorful eggs. All revolved around her. To take care of my babe, I had to survive.

I study this picture, quintessential Katy: shiny brown hair like Patrick's, tilted head, teasing eyes, crooked grin, blood glowing in her cheeks. On her dress of striped pastels is a polka-dot palm tree; over her heart, a yellow sun. With arms encircling the brightly painted eggs, she looks like an Easter egg herself, bursting its shell.

Reading through my thoughts on life at this scary time brings back many memories.

EXHAUSTED AND DRAINED ONE MORNING, I had descended into the backyard and thrown myself onto the grass. As my breast, pelvis, and thighs sank into the contour of the land, for the first time in many weeks, I felt as if my body might be able to relax; the toxins in my chest, in my limbs, even in my mind, might drain into the ground. In those difficult months, this became a practice to which I return sometimes even today: "lying on the earth."

After I tried it once, I did it again the next day. Each day, after a walk, I sank gratefully into a bed of clover and dandelions. Hauling my work out into the sunshine, I set up an outdoor office and did my editing right here in the yard. And belly to belly with the earth—knowing its heat, its breadth—I rested.

Driven by my imperative as Katy's mom, I was making an all-out effort to survive. I followed all recommendations, Western and Eastern: surgery, radiation, visualization, acupuncture, Chinese herbs, walking, resting, meditation. After a biopsy and diagnosis, I turned to Patrick as he drove me home from the hospital and said, "Whatever comes, I want to keep my eyes wide open." In the ensuing months, I groped to remember anything I had ever learned about how to live. And how to die.

Twenty years earlier, when I had begun to explore Buddhist meditation, it was to learn exactly this. Now, with urgency, I turned to what I had gleaned. Finding myself unable to sit on a cushion with any regularity, I began vigorous daily walking to complement the practice of lying on the earth.

Craving green, quiet, and solitude, I began to walk in the Berkeley Hills. Early each morning, I drove up, leaving behind the noisy city streets by my house, and hiked along the borders of Tilden Regional Park, our Bay Area patch of wilderness, 2,065 acres of meadows and forests in the upper valley of Wildcat Creek. But wary of wildcats and coyotes, mountain lions and rattlesnakes, and most of all, the human predators known on occasion to make their attacks on remote trails, I chose the manicured streets beyond the gates of the park. Wary as well of my own poor sense of direction, of my tendency to distrust my instincts and end up lost and disoriented, I chose familiar streets, well labeled and neatly ordered. Here I could catch glimpses of scrubby hills and wooded ravines. I could watch deer foraging in the gardens of the well-to-do and reflect in silence. And safety.

Along with this walking practice, I met with both Western and Eastern doctors. A local genius of a healer—acupuncturist and herbalist—told me, "Cancer is a chronic disease, it cannot be cured. But it can be contained." Sensing my resistance, he coolly invited me to open to this uncertainty. After several hours of questions from me, he took my pulses. He described the imbalances in the flow of energy through my body. "Here's the prescription." He paused, meeting my eye. "Take more risks!"

Oh, sure! "Do you say this to everyone?"

"No," he said. "I read your pulses. I'm saying it to you."

"What do you mean, 'risks'? Bungee jumping? Camping I can imagine; backpacking, maybe. But if you mean rock climbing or spelunking, no way!"

"More risks in your actions and in your thinking. You'll have to figure out what is appropriate for you. But," he laughed, "once you've gotten used to something, then it won't qualify as a risk anymore, and you'll have to find something else. Once you begin to call that home, you'll have to dive deeper into the unknown. At some point in camping there may be nothing left to do but to try scaling a cliff . . . or exploring a cave."

Scared, confused, even outraged by this prescription I didn't understand, I rebelled. Who did he think he was, challenging me in this way? Yet something resonated. Wasn't this the task I was taking on in Buddhist practice? The risk of meeting each moment as a surprise, without expectations, and letting it go, without holding on to it or pushing it away. I scoured my every-day activities, my relations with Katy and Patrick, for ways that I clung to the expected, to habits and safety. And I continued to remind myself of this dictum: Take more risks.

One morning, I turned off the predictable streets and, with a reckless energy, risked a wandering path into the wildness of the wood. Heart knocking, I kept right on walking through the dry grasses and sharp-toothed blackberry brambles, plunging through fears about my safety (What or who might be around the bend? Would I know how to get back?). I stepped out into the unknown.

As I struggled over my first treatment decision—whether to have the breast removed or excise the tumor—I felt stumped. Alarmed that an early death would bar me from everything I knew—as a mother, a wife, a friend—I yearned to tap into my own deepest intuition.

From inside myself, from someplace deeper than my intellect, deeper than my heritage as agnostic Jew or Unitarian, I heard the strict and bold voice of a nun: "Who needs hair? Who needs breasts?" This ascetic voice had influenced many decisions over the years—to keep my now-white hair undyed, my clothes and possessions simple. Here, the verdict was absolute. On some vast and fundamental scale, it doesn't matter whether I have two breasts or one or none, or even whether I live in this earthly form or not.

I'd planned to tell the surgeon, "Cut the damn thing off!" But all the experts, and even the acupuncturist, urged me to simply cut out the tumor and follow that with radiation. I searched my mind and heart for an internal reason to do the more limited surgery. My thoughts ricocheted back and forth over this decision: breast or no breast. I wrestled with the whole question of what it means to be embodied. What is this body? If I am not my body, can I simply let the body go and take to the mind as refuge?

As I took my morning walks, my mind contracted in fear. It was hard to pay more than cursory attention to the green and brown world I walked through. But I urged myself to keep my eyes wide open, my senses keen.

Eucalyptus pods crunched underfoot. Lupine sent out its sweet scent. Startling blue flowers burst through the spiky crowns of wild artichokes. Sticky stems of monkey flower and manzanita branches with their tiny apples brushed my bare arms. If a scary scenario took over my thoughts—of dying, of Patrick trying to care for Katy all by himself—I wrenched my attention back to flowers, trees, and nests. High in an oak hid a wood-rat nest where generations of diverse creatures had made their homes. By the creek waved frothy horsetail—ancient plants, four hundred million years old, reproduced by spores ever since plants first invaded land. With a sense of continuing life, with primeval presence so tangible here, many of my terrors dissolved.

Back at the house, when tangled thoughts closed my mind, I opened the kitchen door, as I do now, and from our second-floor landing, looked out over the garden. Carmen, weeding in her yard, waved; so did Sheryl, putting out bowls for the cats. The dawn redwood, our resident elder, rose high, proclaiming an ancient lineage, vast spans of space and time. I felt somehow more permeable, expanded.

A day before the appointed surgery, still undecided as to whether I would keep the breast or not, I spent a few feverish hours digging narcissus and anemone bulbs into the hard February soil by the cherry tree in the backyard and the princess in the front. Then I laid my body down on the ground in my favorite napping place beneath the dawn redwood. The breath of soil in my nostrils, dirt under my nails, and mud on my bare feet, the basic elements—air, water, earth—moved through me. From deep inside, a more gentle voice urged, "Through gardening you honor the body, the body of ground. Appreciate the human body too." So, cradled by earth flesh, I pledged to honor my own. The next day, I finally confronted the cancer and made my decision. I told the surgeon that unless he saw signs that the cancer was spreading, he should save the breast.

And instead of having the breast cut out—of body, sight, mind—I took another risk, to feel what I might lose. So I remembered: delicate nipples of adolescence like tender pink stars, new breasts, velvet to my touch under my nightie; erotic breasts caressed by Patrick and past lovers over these many years; milk-filled mother's breasts that suckled Katy. I felt through the history of this embodiment, always changing.

How much easier for me to be absolute and drastic ("Cut it off!" "Forget the breast!") than to look fully, to allow myself to love this changing form of flesh, bones, and blood in an open and uncertain way—not to hold on to it. Katy's plea came to mind: "Mommy, you can hug me, but don't grip." All of my habits pulled the opposite way, to clasp tight and resist change. Could I live fully in this body without insisting that it stay young and healthy and never die? The task seemed almost impossible.

ON A MORNING WALK weeks after the surgery, I took another risk. I turned off the ranger-made trail onto one beaten into the earth by hoof and paw. Braving this high trail, I wound my way up toward the crest of a hill. At a sudden twist in the path, two mule deer, a doe and her fawn, loped down past me as I climbed up. The doe was so close that I could see the quivering of her nostrils and the pink glow where the sun shone through her cocked ears. Was she heading for the gardens in the city below? What reciprocity. I hiked up from the city into the hills to be nourished, and the deer descended from the hills into the city to feast in the backyards. We crisscrossed and exchanged.

Up a steep incline and around a turn, I unexpectedly arrived at the summit. Winded, I staggered around the small circular crest of the hill. Then I lost my bearings. Which path had I followed? On all sides, narrow trails descended the downward slopes, passing through anonymous groves of trees. Below me shimmered several lakes and what looked like the Bay on both sides. From far below what sounded like a train whistled. I couldn't tell from which direction it called. Where was I? What time was it? Dizzy, I looked up to the sun high in the sky. Light-headed, unhooked for a moment from time or place, I rested in exhilaration.

Suddenly, I felt a surge of fear. Would the cancer recur? Would I die young? Concentrating all of my effort, I drew the landscape into my awareness, risked to see myself in this land. Welcoming the hills of dry summer grasses, the glimmer of the

Bay and sky, I opened the field of who or what I perceived myself to be. I saw the vast exchange.

For hundreds of years, a wood-rat nest has offered a home to frogs, salamanders, scorpions, and mice. The stems and leaves of monkey flower have offered healing poultices to generations of Ohlone people, while the manzanita apples have provided cider. With bumblebees, the lupine exchanges nectar for pollen; and with soil, nitrogen for other nutrients.

I ran my palms along my own arms and thighs. Isn't this narrow self within this particular package of mortal flesh an expression of ongoing exchange? Resting my full attention on this possibility, I felt, for a moment, more fully alive and also not so afraid to die.

Chapter 4

nocturnal mind

RISKS IN ACTION, risks in thought. Beneath the dawn red-wood, upwind from the growing compost heap, I sit quietly this afternoon, following dreamy turns of memory. I recall further risk-taking escapades from the months when I first grappled with cancer. Mostly I took risks in thought, in imagination.

As a birthday present, I'd agreed to buy Katy a tree frog, a descendant of a long lineage of frogs from the Indonesian jungle.

Katy and I walked to the Reptile Haven, only a few blocks from our house, to pick out a frog. We slipped uneasily past the iguanas and the monitors, past the Nile monitor famous for finding the nests of crocodiles and gorging itself on the eggs. Past terrarium after terrarium, tiny worlds of plants, water, and soil, we entered the section for the larger turtles and Burmese boas, their massive coils pulsating. A salesperson stepped forward, asking if he could help us. There he was with Day-Glo blue-and-pink spiked hair, a tie-dyed T-shirt, and little round glasses. A worthy compatriot, I thought, for the reptilian residents.

Holding up a small male frog, the spiky fellow initiated us. "Night," he told us, "is the active time for frogs. You can toss your frog some crickets or, if you prefer, a baby mouse. But to see him eat, you'll have to sit up and watch." He paused and then said, "A frog is most at home in the dark."

I felt a shiver down my spine. It was as if he had asked, "Are you?" For the first time in this frog-buying gambol, I began to wonder if this might be an adventure for me as well as for Katy.

Since childhood I had hated the dark; avoided caves and crawl spaces, unlit stairwells and the insides of closets; resented the coming of night; gone to bed early. But now, taking to heart my prescription for risks, I urged myself to come to grips with what scared me most. I examined this little mud-brown emissary of the realms of night.

"Don't be surprised when your frog changes color," our spiky friend chuckled. "Pets like these fuel the imagination. Think tree frog!" He showed us how to set up the terrarium—water, soil, plants, and crickets—how to adjust the heat and mist the walls, and how to hold our frog. "The store guy's nice, Mom," whispered Katy. And I agreed. Both soft-spoken and cheerful. I began to imagine that Katy and I had met, by some trick of fate, our own personal guide to the underworld.

Meanwhile, on our guide's knuckles, the frog had settled into repose, eyes lidded, legs folded in close. "That's a relaxed frog," our guide told us. Later, as he put our frog—still sitting quietly—back into the terrarium, he offered an addendum, "Of course, it's hard to distinguish between the stillness of peace and the catatonia of shock or terror."

ON THE AFTERNOON OF HER BIRTHDAY, I picked up Katy at school and we went to the Reptile Haven to claim our frog, now named Zephyr, and his crickets. When we tried to empty his carrying jar into his new home, a frightened Zephyr leapt, landing on the floor behind the toy cabinet. Amid Katy's sympathetic whoops and jumps, I finally captured him.

As he wriggled and hopped in my cupped palms, his aliveness

was palpable to me—the moist, supple body, the rhythm of breathing. His mortality was also palpable. If I opened my hands too much, mightn't I allow him to destroy himself in froggy abandon? Yet if I gripped him too tightly, mightn't I crush out his life?

Before he could make another jump, I thrust him into the terrarium and slammed the screen shut. Wildly, he leapt into the screen, then flung himself against the damp glass wall. Katy and I stared at Zephyr, our new frog friend: limbs splayed, webbed feet gripping the glass, his slippery brown body stretched splat out in panic. Pressing against the glass wall, he did battle, as if his survival hinged on shattering this terrarium that held him prisoner.

The next morning, Katy burst into my sleep. "Mom, he's gone!" I dashed downstairs and we searched high and low. Finally, in the humid depths of the terrarium, I found Zephyr settled on a leaf. A lovely jade green, he sat quietly, his limbs tucked neatly into his body. I could hear our spiky guide reminding me, "Of course, you will never know for sure what goes on in his mind." But, I let myself imagine:

During the night this frog found home, luminous and green. As he relaxed into the dark, he felt his world expressing itself through him. He felt the completeness of this world—humidity, warmth, pool, soil—all in balance supporting him. So he, too, felt complete. Why should he battle the walls of his terrarium? With the fullness and balance of his nocturnal mind, he felt those walls dissolve into mist, felt himself—as a great rain forest—extend without limit into the darkness.

Later that day, I went out to the country to spend several hours sitting among the retreatants at a meditation course. As I sat, I began to notice the bleating of sheep outside on the hill. For a time, there was nothing but bleating. When I drew my focus back to my own breath, I was startled to experience my sitting self as Zephyr, the tree frog. Limbs drawn in, chest palpitating with each breath, I sat among the bleating sheep in a field of March green.

NIGHTS THAT COLD SEASON stirred a mixture of dread and excitement. Under the roughness of my nightgown, I felt a hematoma left from the cancer surgery. Many times, I scoured this area with all of my senses, struggled to translate its dark intensity as if I were reading Braille.

During our second night with the tree frog, I awoke and could not get back to sleep; I felt trapped in insomnia. The cancer became large, seeming to encompass the whole of what I was. Worries chased through my mind. "I can't ever let this cancer recur! But then again, why shouldn't it? Have the conditions changed, the toxicity of the environment, the tendencies of my body? I refuse to die." As I fought cycling thoughts, I began to hear, as if in the back of my mind, the chirping of crickets.

I wasn't sure why I hadn't noticed the crickets on the first night that they and Zephyr had been in residence. Perhaps the air had been too cold that night to call forth their song. Or perhaps they had sung unnoticed. But now I was more attuned, having sat that morning in the rain-drenched meadow, my frog heart pumping in counterpoint with the bleating sheep.

As I listened to the crickets, I found myself resting in a forest. The walls of my room had melted into the night, and with them a narrow sense of myself, "the cancer patient." I sensed my frog brother downstairs, perhaps also listening, nestling into the dark expanse.

It was a long night of sleeplessness. Each time my thoughts locked into obsessions, I disciplined my attention on the singing. The walls would magically melt between that thought and beyond, between my bedroom and the rooms below, between our house—our big terrarium—and the yard, between our yard and other yards. Like the frog in his nocturnal fullness, I felt complete, nourished by Patrick and Katy, friends, gardens, trees, frogs, the history of the planet flooding through me. All false terrariums seemed to melt away, leaving me at one with a limitless night singing with crickets.

In the coming months, when night terrors arose, I remembered my underworld guide. From over my left shoulder, he dared me to enter the dark, to risks of imagination. "Think tree frog."

Chapter 5

mama raccoon

BRACING MYSELF AGAINST THE SMELL, I thrust my pitch-fork into dissolving bananas, liquid lettuce, molding leaves, and already-digested humus. Now that Cathy's compost is piled up in our yard, our new downstairs tenant, Suzanna, and I meet under the willow to empty our fly-infested bin, combining the two heaps to begin the compost anew. Along the fence, where for many years I have tried unsuccessfully to grow pumpkins, we sort piles in various stages of decay. I fight disgust. For a born-and-bred Manhattanite, down-and-dirty work in the garden, particularly in the compost, feels risky. Will I find some bloated rat feeding in these spoils? Or perhaps a rabid raccoon?

Woven in with memories of breast cancer, I recall my first encounters with the raccoons. Taking a break from pitchfork and shovel, I sit back down under the dawn redwood, open my cancer journals, and continue to read.

WHILE RECOVERING FROM TREATMENTS, I tried to find at least a few minutes each day to relax into the wide hug of the yard, to continue the practice of lying on the earth. One morn-ing, Sheryl called through the fence, "Barbara, come quick. You'll never believe this!" When I looked through the gate in the fence, I could see the usual line of cats at their bowls in front of the garage and then, at the far end in broad daylight, a raccoon feeding at the farthest bowl. Sheryl whispered, "It's a female."

Indeed, this mama raccoon, her teats distended and red, clearly ravenous after days of nursing her babies, had the audacity to forage side by side with the cats in view of us people. I imagined her exhausted, starving. Challenged to survive, she had felt compelled to leave her cubs in their nest in the shed of some overgrown yard and, without the protection of night, to brave this territory. Now, seemingly oblivious to the cats, she moved from bowl to bowl. Suddenly, one cat, defending his food, humped and hissed. The mama raccoon reared, bared her teeth, and flattened her ears. Darting at her, Sheryl shouted, "Git!" And the raccoon fled. Watching this exchange, I felt a kinship with this raccoon that I didn't understand.

When I submitted to the technology of radiation, I felt disowned by life. I sat in the narrow hallway in a "lineup" with other green-gowned patients avoiding each other's eyes and watching unlucky fellows roll through on gurneys. In the treatment room, technicians carried on conversations over and through me, arranging my limbs as if they belonged to a corpse or were some extension of the equipment. The door clicked shut and I was left alone with the Star Wars equipment gliding over the breast and the high-pitched yammer of the machine.

To counterbalance the touch of the radiation, the machines, and the technicians (this touch without contact), I decided to get some massage. Surprised when the masseuse introduced herself as a beginner, I commented on her strong hands, her sure sense in rooting for knots. She told me that before she worked on humans, for many years she had massaged horses. As her fingers worked the braided muscles of my back, I daydreamed of the tight flank of a mare contracted from hours of work in the ring. I felt my own back as "flank." Through the touch of the horse masseuse and her story, I took further risks of imagination, risks in the very way I saw who or what I was. I knew my animal body; I felt sister to the mare; I remembered the raccoon.

Through rounds of radiation, I continued to take naps on the earth, to peek through the slats in the fence, and to spy on that mama raccoon. As I watched her, I was shaken by opposing feelings. Sometimes I delighted in her, my heroine. How brazen she was. What courage she had in full daylight to claim her place among the cats. Other times, I disparaged her as thief. In her black mask, she stole from bowls set up for the cats. Did the ferocity of her hunger serve her? No! She scared Sheryl, who, instead of offering her food, chased her away. Distraught, I saw myself in this persona. I recognized the pain of the "intruder."

That pain felt familiar, a challenge to overturn. Old habits came to mind. After my parents were divorced, I saw myself as intruder in both my father's and my mother's homes; now in Berkeley, I often felt like a gate-crashing New Yorker, and in New York, like an infiltrating Californian. I wept into the grass for the mama raccoon, driven by her ravenousness to break in, and for myself, driven by my hunger to belong.

CALLING ME FROM MY READING under the dawn redwood, Suzanna, with her dog, Radio, at her heels, comes into the garden. I put down my cancer journals to join her, to continue our work in the composting corner. The willow is now in full leaf, and purple clematis climbs over the fence from Sheryl and Roy's. Suzanna and I are making a compost hill, drawing ingredients from our sorted piles. Suzanna plans to grow pumpkins on this hill despite my pessimistic warnings. As far as I'm concerned, in this yard pumpkins will never survive.

We lay down branches and dry sticks to let in air, then dried hay and grass clippings, then some already-composted dirt. Suzanna fluffs the layers to allow earthworms and bacteria to pass through and break down the vegetable matter into humus. For two weeks, Suzanna will water the hill to help the compost cook, thus preparing for planting. We plan to meet at the compost hill when it is thoroughly soaked to plant the pumpkin seeds together.

During these weeks, I lie on the earth each day and peruse old journals. As I listen to the sprinkler watering our compost hill, more memories from my time recovering from cancer return to me.

As treatments continued, mothers at Katy's preschool offered to provide my family with dinners. The nourishment I experienced went far beyond the meals themselves. A woman who made one of the first dinners said, "I thought about you as I was cooking this and imagined what foods would make you strong." Later that evening, as I ate the lentils and chickpeas, the tomatoes and carrots, I remembered this mother remembering me. Each evening, Katy, Patrick, and I ate lasagnas, corn soups, and chiles rellenos—grandmothers' formulas and favorite recipes passed from friend to friend—passed from these families to ours.

And I continued to be nurtured each morning by the ground itself. One morning, during an earth-nap, I heard Andy from down the street making plans with Sheryl. I listened to them talking through the back fence. Andy would be gone for a week, so could Sheryl be sure to put out extra food for the cats whose care they shared? Sheryl could be counted on to care for cats (and as they got used to the raccoons, for the raccoons, too, despite efforts of some neighbors to eliminate them). My imagination stirred. People had put out bowls for feral cats in backyards throughout this neighborhood, throughout Berkeley, Oakland, Albany, Richmond, and beyond. Who knew how far? When she fed at the cat bowls, this mama raccoon tapped into a great network that was already there. Was I tapping into such a network as well? Could I continue to rest in this vast net of connectedness, always there, needing only to be recognized?

An image of the many bowls offered me a certain romantic solace, but it didn't translate for me as a mother. During those months of treatments, I was consumed with fears for Katy—my tender five-year-old, vulnerable, dependent on me. Often, I came to my nap worrying. Is Katy sturdy? Am I passing on my upset, my fragility? If I die, what motherly soul will help Patrick protect and nurture her? Will Katy know to look for the bowls that may be out there?

In daydreams about the mama raccoon, I saw her returning to her nest. Strengthened after feeding, she nursed her cubs. As they grew older, she perhaps led them on foraging expeditions, showing them the yards of the neighborhood almsgivers. But on her rounds, she might be trapped in a broken fence, hit by a car. What if this mama didn't make it back?

At the end of one day of worry, my friend Marie said to me, "I have to believe that if I weren't there, the universe would take care of my children." This seemed inconceivable. Such a risk to trust in this. Yet just positing the thought was briefly comforting at that scary time.

OVER THESE WEEKS, as Suzanna waters the compost hill, the days are heating up. From the compost corner, I catch the whiff of decay. Eggshells, apple cores, matted hair from the brush, nail parings—all decompose, their scent heavy in the air. As a welcome breeze shakes Bob's cherry tree, tender white and pink blossoms flutter down and sift through the yard.

This morning, as I sit beneath the dawn redwood, I steel myself against a sense of loss. The ambulances came last night for Grandma Darlene, who is almost eighty and has had a stroke. Her family, including Dee—cold sober for once—is gathering.

After a period of arduous and ultimately failed treatments, Cathy has come home to die. Just my age. I palpate my breast, uneasily feeling the scar. Is there anything steady on which I can rely? I think of uncontrollable forces—sickness, epidemics, extinctions, the collision of tectonic plates or even whole galaxies. Now, years since the cancer, I feel pressed to look after myself and my family. And I'm not sure who is looking after us. I think of the raccoons. Sometimes people put out bowls for their fellow creatures, but it can't be assured. Sometimes they put out rat poison.

A sudden shout. Suzanna strides out from the compost corner. "Why didn't you tell me you were doing a planting?" she demands. When I look confused, she insists, "The pumpkins! They're sprouting! You didn't wait for me!"

"But I didn't plant anything!" I say, exasperated. "I thought we were planning to do it together." But indeed, when I follow her, I see tiny sprouts all over the compost hill, their yellow-green leaves and ovate seeds visible just below the green shoots. These seedlings certainly do look like pumpkins. I study them closely to see the new roots pushing out from the seeds as they begin to germinate.

Suzanna and I look at one another awkwardly. This seems weird. Were these seeds still intact, left over from years of failed plantings? Or did last year's market-bought Halloween pumpkin, cast out by the fence to rot, disperse seeds that found their way into the compost hill? Or what? I don't know whether this feels more unsettling or miraculous.

These mysteriously appearing pumpkins—carrying on against the odds—bring me back to visions of the mama raccoon. Even now, as I sit down in my old napping spot, the mama raccoon calls up heat in my belly. Suddenly I see it. Mammal to mammal, I feel the pull toward this impassioned mother fighting for food so she can convert it into milk. What is the key to mammalness?

Mammaries. A mammal mother is able to protect her babies in their nest. They thrive only because she can nurse.

With breast cancer, I confronted a crisis in my very mammalness, a sickness in my mammary. When I was in treatment, Katy and I continued a favorite pastime, sharing baths together. Scooping the soap dish into the water, Katy poured a cooling balm over my raw radiated breast, over the hard contour of the hematoma left from surgery. How I loved these bathtub blessings. As I recall them now, floods of other memories return to me.

So many worries of this city gal, feeling outside the cycles of life. When I was about to give birth, I did not trust my breasts. Although they were larger than I had imagined was possible, the nipples dark and swollen, I didn't believe that these breasts of mine could ever produce milk. When Katy was first born, vigorous and rosy, how amazed I was that she could so naturally root for and find my breasts. How relieved, how proud I was—a slipping into grace—when she suckled and the milk flowed.

This lack of trust is so familiar. As a teenager, I was afraid my body wouldn't know how to menstruate, that it wouldn't know how to kiss, that it wouldn't know how to make love. At forty, when for the first time I focused all my effort on having a baby, I didn't trust that I'd be able to conceive (despite Patrick's lively sperm, which, after a year of failed attempts, we witnessed in all their exuberant activity on a slide under the microscope). Once pregnant, I worried. Could I grow a baby and carry her to term? Would my body know how to give birth, how to suckle?

Distrust following distrust (it seems absurd and sad as I look back), I doubted that this woman's body would know how to live out its nature as mammal, as animal. Now, five years after I first recognized myself in the mama raccoon and wept here for my craving, I cleave to this same soil. Many times I have felt barred from the primal cycles.

Yet even now, just feeling these distrusts, I sense a shift. Lying on the earth beneath the dawn redwood, there's a welling up of precisely what I mourn. I see a lineage of mammal mothers to which the raccoon belongs, to which I too belong. Through this raccoon mama, I knew the pain of being excluded; now I glimpse a sense of belonging—to this yard, to this my home terrain where, through the millennia, life has germinated, suckled, foraged, died, and reseeded.

As THE SPRING TURNS to summer and summer to autumn, as the dawn redwood comes into its fullness then begins to shed its needles, Grandma Darlene may be dying and Cathy dies. Over these months, the pumpkin vines, thick and prickly, have curved around the compost piles. Pumpkin leaves have grown as broad as buttocks, with a profusion of velvety orange blossoms. The vines have circled over their hill, around the piles of composting grasses and straw heaped up from Cathy's garden, along the fence between our yard and Grandma Darlene's, up along the gate into Sheryl and Roy's, through the shriveling clematis with which it is entwined. Despite the loss of many fruits that molded on the vines or were eaten by raccoons, four hearty pumpkins survive. The two large ones, ripening for Halloween, grow fat and round.

I take a few moments to sit quietly here in the yard. Across the flesh of my thighs, I feel the tickle of ants; I listen to a rondo of finches and sparrows. Rustling the grass, Cleo chases along the fence following the scent of a cat (or is it a raccoon?). As Cleo settles back down to sleep by my side, my mind tunes to the rhythm of her breath. I remember Cathy's breath, so labored, when I sat in meditation by her bedside. My attention sinks now, becomes steady. All the yelps, buzzings, wriggles of this yard reverberate through me, a basal current of ongoingness.

Mother Mammal

Hidden amid the high grasses and fern forests of the Mesozoic era were the first tiny mammals. Like the dinosaur giants that dominated the planet 245 to 65 million years ago, mammals had also evolved from reptiles. But baby dinosaurs hatched from their eggs into a threatening world where they were required to forage to survive. By contrast, baby mammals—tiny warm-blooded creatures—were born from the uterus into the protection of nests where they could settle in and safely nurse from their mothers' milk-giving mammaries.

Adult mammals foraged for insects by night while their predators slept, for the jungles and swamps were fraught with dangers. Sharp-toothed reptiles could easily devour tiny mammal pups. Safer for them to remain in the nest or burrow and, when their mothers came home, to suckle.

Snug along their mothers' warm abdomens, from sweat glands in the damp fur, they suckled a miracle brew. Through the alchemy of mammal mothers, all available food was metamorphosed into milk. Insects, grass, shellfish, even toxic plants—all were transformed. This miracle milk offered necessary nutriments, protective enzymes to ward off disease. Not only that, it was easy to digest!

The Mesozoic era ended with a bang—a global catastrophe that wiped out dinosaurs and made way for mammals. A massive asteroid or comet hurtling down in the Yucatán Peninsula of Mexico caused violent changes in climate. The planet was devastated, first by heat and then by cold. The explosion incinerated crustal life-forms, then raised a dust cloud that blocked the sun. An ensuing freeze led to mass extinctions—from starvation, in particular, of the reptile and dinosaur young. But mammal young, nursing in their nests, spared the hazards of freezing weather and competition with mature animals, survived.

So, while dinosaurs were dying out, the very mammalness of mammals—the mammaries and the capacity to suckle their young—may well have offered these creatures the essential evolutionary edge that allowed them to thrive, to adapt to extremes of climate, and eventually to populate the entire planet.

Over the millennia, mammary glands evolved with special teats to transfer milk. These fit nicely into the mouths of the young—in hoofed animals near the hind legs, and in primates, on the chest (adapted to arboreal life), so the mothers could swing in trees while they nursed. (Larger mammaries have perhaps evolved as signatures of good breeders.)

Lactation has committed mammals to extended periods of parental care: building nests; excavating burrows; keeping the young warm, safe, and clean; defending the territory; and as pups grew, supplying other food and instructions in foraging, as well as comfort and emotional support.

By requiring the mother to stay near her young and form an enduring relationship, lactation may well be a key to the evolution of mammal social intelligence, leading to the gift of compassion.*

---

* Sarah Blaffer Hrdy, *Mother Nature: A History of Mothers, Infants, and Natural Selection* (New York: Pantheon Books, 1999), p. 145.

PART THREE

Looking

inhabiting
the uninhabitable

Develop a state of mind like the earth, Rahula.
For on the earth people throw clean and unclean things,
dung and urine, spittle, pus, blood, and the earth is not
troubled or repelled or disgusted. And as you grow like the
earth, no contacts with pleasant or unpleasant will lay hold
of your mind or stick to it. . . .

—from the *Majjhima Nikaya*

Chapter 6

no inner/no outer

FOLLOWING THE VISITS of the raccoon, a series of my mammal compatriots made themselves known in my life, offering occasion for risk and healing. Some of them appeared in the most unexpected places.

After months of deposits on the stove top, in the cast-iron skillet, even in the salad bowl, I finally admitted that there might be a mouse. Weeks followed of experiments with mouse-friendly deterrents—high-pitched beepers and Have-a-Heart traps—with no appearance of the culprit.

One early morning when I swooped through the kitchen preparing for my walk, I noticed that the refrigerator door was ajar. Maybe the lettuce bin had been left open the night before or a hastily shelved casserole was sticking out. Hurrying past, I clicked the door shut.

When I came back, I hurried around the house preparing for the day. I threw open the door of the fridge. There, amid the tortillas, something twitched. Crying out, I leaped back. From the shelf, a furry rodent regarded me with dark, beady eyes. Its long, spiny tail quivered. I slammed the door closed.

I ran to Patrick in the bathroom. "Patrick! The mouse is in the refrigerator!" I could see our two reflections in the bathroom mirror, Patrick's, confused behind the mask of shaving cream, and mine, pale.

Awakened by my initial shout, Katy sped out of her room. "Let's go see it!" she cried, and then flung open the door of the refrigerator to reveal our visitor.

We all crowded around. I flinched at its hard, trapped look as it seemed to challenge us from behind the yogurt. "Yup, it's the mouse all right!" said Patrick. And Katy (gloating, with the obvious relish of a ten-year-old), "It's not a mouse. I've known all along. It's a rat!"

Bounding backward in anticipation of I don't know what, I herded Katy into her room and once again hurled the door of the fridge closed. Patrick blew me a kiss as he hurried out the front door for a meeting with a panel of judges. "Just leave it there and forget about it. I'll deal with it when I get back to-night." Over my shouts of alarm, he reassured me, "Don't worry. When I come home, our mouse will be either totally frozen or fat, happy, and very slow."

Despite the generous offer (in true Patrick-style, he did manage to get me laughing), I was unwilling to carry on with this menace in my kitchen. I got on the phone. One answering machine directed me to the next, from the animal shelter to the health department. On the twenty-four-hour police hotline, I finally got an actual voice. To my plea "There's a rodent in my refrigerator!" an officer calmly directed me to vector control. Vector control turned out to be the county agency that deals with "vectors"—organisms that carry and transmit disease-causing microorganisms.

I finally reached this agency when they opened at 8:00 A.M., but the inspectors were all in the field monitoring an emergency sewer leak. By my third call, I had worked myself up to a fever pitch, all risk-averse tendencies mobilized: " 'No' is not acceptable. I have a ten-year-old and a dog, and there's a mouse in the fridge. This is an emergency!"

"Yes, ma'am," returned the bored voice of a receptionist, maybe reading a magazine or stirring her coffee. "We'll send someone out soon as they get in."

By this time, I barely cared what they did with the mouse. No matter how, just get rid of it! As I anxiously awaited vector control, I conjured up pictures of the inspectors: two cold gray men (gray uniforms, gray potbellies, doughy gray faces, with gray pistols in their holsters). I would hear their great gray boots banging up the wooden stairs, a pitiless knocking on the front door.

But at 9:00 A.M. sharp I was startled by a single pristine ring. In the doorway stood a statuesque young woman—over six feet with long, dyed-blond hair, arched brows, painted eyes, cheeks bright with blush. I was taken aback. But here she was. She was indeed in uniform: a blue shirt with a badge, navy blue pants. I noticed a few insignia of her trade: dangling from her belt, a set of keys (jailer-size); in a holster, a formidable flashlight; and swinging from one hand, a large wire cage. "I'm from vector control," she introduced herself, holding out her other hand— all rings, with long, maroon-polished nails.

"You're not who I expected," said I.

She swished her hair and lowered her eyes, surprising me now in a new way, with the girlish purity of her laugh.

"You must get calls like this all the time." I tried to make friendly conversation as I pointed the way to the refrigerator.

"Well, I wouldn't say that exactly. Most often they're behind the stove or under the sink or even in the toilet." Her bracelets jangled.

"I'm in quite a flap," I admitted.

She looked right at me (did she stroke my arm?) and said, "Of course," without any sign of judgment. I was unnerved by her empathy.

She pulled on thick vinyl gloves. From the living room, I held Katy and Cleo at bay. Through the doorway to the kitchen, I could see our inspector kneeling by the refrigerator, holding up the cage. At first she couldn't locate the mouse. She was following a trail: gnawed tortillas, crumpled Snickers' wrappers, a half-chewed apple.

"He's really scared." She seemed to know. "It's almost impossible to catch them when they're frightened." That gave me a turn. Something about the concern in her voice, the tremble for the mouse.

Suddenly I heard a coo. "Ohhhhhhhhh, there you are. Just look at you. You're sooooo cute."

Rounding the corner, I edged up to watch the chase—from the vegetable bin to the dairy shelf, down to the shelf of pancake mixes, flours, and sugars. "You can tell from the length of the tail," she commented. "It is a rat." Appalled, I watched the scaly, sparsely-haired tail disappear inside the drawer where we keep our eggs.

The thought that it was indeed a rat exacerbated my protective panic—images of the bubonic plague, of the eyeball-eating rats from Orwell's *1984*, of red-eyed rats pouncing into babies' cribs.

Our four walls, even the confines of the refrigerator, hadn't kept this rat out. I ordered Katy out of the kitchen and into her room and pushed Cleo, barking, behind her. Meanwhile, our lady inspector borrowed a bath towel and suggested that if she caught it in the towel, she would release it in our yard. "*No*, please!" I pleaded. "Nowhere near our home!"

At the same time, on some other layer of response, I kept finding myself touched by this lady from vector control as she continued a nuanced conversation with the rat. I could hear her cajoling him, a cadence in her voice that felt wholly genuine.

When the rat was (to my relief) ensconced in the cage, Katy and I joined our savior in the kitchen. I took a cautious look at the rat. Lively behind the bars, it had a hearty (and, I admitted to myself, ingenuous) look. Its whiskers and pink nose quivered;

its coat was full and soft. The cage swayed back and forth as it leapt around. "It's sweet, Mom," commented Katy. "Why were you so afraid?"

"He's a black rat," our inspector explained. "And I'm quite sure he's a he. He couldn't be more than four months old." So young. Once again, taken short, I took a keen look at the rat. I stared, mesmerized by this robust young rodent in his swinging cage. "Black rats are sometimes called roof rats," our inspector continued. "They're excellent climbers. They live in vines, like ivy or jasmine, or in the walls of a house. They like to nest in the attic or in the roof." Nervously, I eyed the stairway to our attic bedroom.

Despite the youth and apparent health of the rat, our rat lady suggested a complete cleaning of our kitchen. So after she departed with the cage (to take the rat, she said, to the mountains), I donned rubber gloves myself. Because of the health hazards, she recommended that I use strong bleach and wear a mask.

Even as she walked out the front door, in my mind, our rat aged and grew in size and virulence. The rat seemed to carry all that scared me, anything that might creep in uninvited to threaten health and peace of mind. Unlike the cancer that also took me unawares, this rat—furry and hungry—was visible and its dangers could possibly be eradicated. Propelled by protectiveness, I emptied the refrigerator; every last item—ketchup, marmalade, plastic containers of leftover soups—was hauled off to the street and into the garbage.

OVER THE FOLLOWING WEEKS, imagining the disease-causing microorganisms now inside the house and infiltrating our bodies, I ran from attic to basement, patching all cracks and holes in the walls that protected our home from the street. I bleached and scoured all crevices and corners. But, to my distress, I noticed that my mind was still permeated with rat. I found myself searching the Internet to learn about the rat's destructive powers: ravaging warehouses for grain, causing floods by tunneling through dams, starting fires by gnawing on matches, and carrying diseases such as typhus and spotted fever, and (yes) the plague.

Inside the house, I saw my continued skittishness triggered when I opened a drawer or a closet. And outside in our yard, I was wary. I hesitated as I passed the tangled potato vine, as I raised the top of the trash can or the broken lid of our compost bin. Outside on the street, I sidestepped trash-littered gutters and storm drains. As the bells for a train began to toll, I vaulted over stagnant pools between broken railway ties and ran past an open manhole releasing steam from beneath the street.

But that was not all. It started with Cleo. At dinner, I felt her nuzzling me from under the kitchen table; she looked up into my face and I back into hers. Hopefully eyeing my plate, she sniffed. There was something unnervingly familiar. Her long face, her quivering whiskers and wet nose, the dark glow of her eyes took on a disturbingly ratlike cast. I shook myself.

A few days later, it happened with a human. I was sitting in a meeting. Right in the midst of a conflict, I looked at a friend by my side, his cheeks sucked in with worry, his dark eyes scared, a hint of the trapped look I now knew. The rat.

This pattern continued with a fellow parent on the soccer field, a merchant in a store. Then, late in the night, in bed with Patrick, it happened again. We were sleeping peacefully, his buttocks resting in the curve of my belly, my knees tucked into the backs of his, my arm wrapped around his chest. With my open palm, I caressed the hair on his chest. I felt it as fur.

One evening, standing at the refrigerator, I combed the shelves, seeking the perfect snack to quell a roving hunger. Unnerved, I saw the rat in myself. The next day, I caught myself in a fit of anger about to take a ratlike pounce. As rats began to seep into my dreams, swimming through twilit sewers, I decided it was time (maybe a little past time) to reflect on the rat "image." Somewhere in the circling of rat thoughts, I remembered hearing the writer Andrew Harvey talk about a temple in India where rats are worshiped. I wondered, could this image be redeemed?

After a day on the Internet, I found the Rat Temple, north of Rajasthan, in India. Here people pray to the rats and a goddess who, according to one legend, had arranged to have children dying from a plague reincarnated as rats. To this day, barefoot supplicants enter the temple to honor the twenty thousand "rat children," to feed them grain and milk, to protect them, to bless them and receive their blessing.

THREE WEEKS AFTER HER INITIAL VISIT, the rat lady came back to help us rat-proof our house and yard. She arrived calm and cheerful. When I questioned her about it again, she assured me that she had indeed taken our rat to the mountains.

But I wanted to know more. "How do you think he got inside our house?" I asked her uneasily.

"Rats travel through the sewers, in and along the pipes, electrical cables and wires," she explained. "Someone in your neighborhood may have done a spring cleaning, neatened up a woodpile or compost heap, trimmed back the ivy. And the rat, seeking a new home, found a secret channel into yours." Chilled, I projected future invasions. At the same time, as I listened, I found her tone unexpectedly kind, even soothing—somehow attuned to the pain and needs of the rat.

Continuing her free lessons in epidemiology, our lady inspector told me about the migrations of rats all over the planet. Some black rats are known as ship rats. These stowaways came from Southeast Asia to Europe many centuries ago, then voyaged to Central and South America, while others traveled to Jamestown with the early colonists and spread across the North American continent. As she spoke, I shuddered at the specter. But there was something else: an amazement at the fertility, at the extent and creativity of these migrations, crisscrossing the planet inside and out through its most intimate channels.

On the advice of our kind inspector, we sealed the holes around our pipes and trimmed back the jasmine. But it felt impossible to erase the image of the rat on the move, stealing into our house, bringing with him the microorganisms of the street. Like his cousins who travel the sewers into toilets, our rat entered where orifices were open—into the kitchen where we eat. Just remembering this, my throat continued to tighten. On some visceral level, I now knew that the cozy enclave of the home, the sanctuary of the body, cannot be separated from the electrical cables, the water pipes, the sewer tunnels, the veins and arteries of the street. I saw that the barriers I counted on to help me feel safe, barriers between outside on the street and inside the house—or even inside the body—barely exist.

AT THE CLOSE of her second visit, the lady from vector control had left me to the task of cleaning up the nest behind the stove—urine-desecrated, molded out of scraps of trash, permeated by microorganisms of the street. Just before she went out the door, she'd turned back with her disarming smile. "I know it's really scary, but you can do it." I took it as a dare. Often, in the coming years as I have explored the streets of my neighborhood, I have remembered the rat lady, challenging me to risk: bless what seems to be the menace, all that is dark and furious, furry or uncontrollable from which I am inseparable—outside-in and inside-out.

Chapter 7

skunk practice

MY FIRST EXPLORATIONS of my street were with Cleo, my favorite nonhuman mammal. Black and white, with a soft coat and ears in the hairstyle of the Egyptian empress, our once-homeless pup first joined the family eleven years ago with her name (short, we assumed, for Cleopatra). I often walked with her down my street and around the neighborhood. Yelping and whining, she yanked me down the steps of our Victorian, into fumes of industry and traffic, past hissing cats and yapping dogs. As an inexperienced dog owner with occasionally phobic tendencies, I reined in my enthusiastic explorer and raised my defenses. I rushed through this cacophony of barks, past the Scandinavian Hall and the Church of Pilgrim's Rest, past the day workers and the fancy shopping block and barbed-wire fences marked BEWARE!

During treatment for cancer, when I took up walking as a practice, I left Cleo at home. Tired out by radiation and shaky after such a scary diagnosis, I sought escape from pollution, pavement, and barking dogs. On my risk-taking escapades in the hills, I walked alone.

But something felt amiss. Here I was, snubbing my home turf—whose streets I felt I should know and love—and, as a final insult, neglecting my best animal friend. Yet, I assured myself, such snubs were worth an hour of quiet and a patch of green. During these walks, I was, after all, training myself in basic mindfulness practice, and I couldn't afford to get too distracted. I was trying to pay attention to my breath and to my steps. "As I am breathing in, I know I am breathing in. As I am breathing out, I know I am breathing out."

Through my legs, arms, and chest, through the ache in my right breast where the cancerous tumor had been excised, I paid attention to my breath. Picking up my pace, I noticed my muscles—gastroc, quadricep, gluteus maximus—working in concert. I tracked the cycles of all my systems: lungs drawing in oxygen, circulation increasing the flow of blood, lymphatic system draining toxins. I committed my attention. I was walking, I reminded myself, to renew each cell. I was walking for my life.

Months later, having become hearty in my walking and more able to weather the clatter and demands of the world, I reassessed my protocol for solitude. I actually made myself a promise. From now on, I would include Cleo in my walks. But not here, not with the racket of dog barks and sirens. I wasn't prepared to deal with that!

So each morning now, with Cleo straining at her leash, I would wind my way up from Katy's school bus stop to follow hidden stairways and secret paths, along Strawberry and Codornices Creeks into the hills, or I would drive up to Tilden Park. At first, chaotic thoughts would pull my attention. Only gradually did I become aware of my companion; this, after repeatedly untangling her leash from around her leg or mine. At some point in our push and pull, she'd turn her head around toward me, her mouth stretched in her happiest smile. She'd roll her pupils up so she could see into my eyes and I into hers. As our gazes met, experience and consciousness would coincide. We would begin to walk together.

ONE SUNDAY AFTERNOON, a friend suggested that Katy and I join her and her two daughters for a hike in Tilden Park. In keeping with my promise, I brought Cleo. Instead of heading for the more civilized blacktop of Inspiration Point where dogs are confined to leash, I suggested that we hike at Dog Run, a wild and hilly trail where—as the name implies—dogs run free.

Tumbling out of my friend's brand-new Mazda van, we trudged up a dry slope shaded by eucalyptus and bay trees. Over-riding Katy's protests (which matched my own fears) that Cleo would get ticks, that she would roll in dead animals, that she would get lost, I let Cleo off her leash to explore.

A tingling rushed through my limbs as I watched a jubilant Cleo scrambling along the rocks to ride waves of billowing green grasses, pausing to nibble as she went. With Cleo, I breathed in the scent of wet earth, of honeysuckle, of freshly oxygenated air. In my belly, a force of life that had been somehow stymied revived.

Cleo sprang suddenly onto the trail, streaked past us off the path, then popped back into view—feet muddy, burrs in her ears, ever eager and goofy with a pine bough dragging from her tail. At some point, she disappeared into the woods. In a high-pitched staccato, Katy and I called her, "Here Cleocleocleocleo. . . . Here Puppywuppypuppywuppy. . . ."

With a surprise leap, Cleo bolted out of the brush. Squealing, she dove into the dust, rolling over and over. Raising her haunches, she rubbed her chest into the red dirt. Then I saw the vital yellow stain on her chest and face. One of the girls asked, "Is it pollen?"

Before I could answer, the putrid stink overwhelmed us. Skunk.

We couldn't possibly drive Cleo back down the hill in the new van. After some panic and much exhilaration, we came up with a plan to deal with the residue of our meeting with this least-favored mammal. Cleo, Katy, the older sister, and I would risk Wildcat Canyon Road through Tilden Park; my friend and her younger daughter would drive the Mazda down the hill to buy the much-touted tomato juice for Cleo's bath and return in my '69 Toyota, which had been through a lot over the years and could weather a little skunk stink.

Diminutive beside the redwoods rising over us, our tiny troop snaked single file along the narrow shoulder of the winding road. Cleo's leash stretched taut; she was in the lead. Drinking in whiffs of skunk musk so strong that it was at moments unrecognizable even as skunk, I held Katy's hand in mine; her friend, holding Katy's other hand, brought up the rear. I chanted silently, "Breathing in, I know I am breathing in. . . . Breathing out. . . ."

It was already getting dark. As they shot past, some cars began to turn on their lights. Leading the children along the edges of the woods, I was scared but also elated. What romance, in the deepening dusk, to hike along what I imagined might have once been an Ohlone Indian trail in the days when bobcats, wildcats, and grizzly bears roamed these hills, when bald eagles and giant condors flew overhead.

With adrenaline coursing in my veins, my senses were keen, gauging the road—the breadth of the shoulder, the angle of the curves, and the speed of the cars. I felt my own animal instinct to survive and protect my family pack. When cars skidded around the switchbacks, I found myself flattening the children against the roadside trees, protecting them with my own body.

Relieved to see help in the form of a park ranger, I flagged down her pickup. The girls squeezed in next to her in the front seat. Cleo and I scrambled into the back. Or rather, I climbed up and Cleo leaped in amid shovels, buckets, a spool of heavy rope.

As the pickup plunged along the winding road, wind sucked my hair so it flared out wild, seared through my thin shirt and chilled my flesh. Cars coming toward us flashed by and disappeared into the curves of the road. Wrapping my arms around my own torso for warmth, I strained to see through the window of the cab to the backs of the girls jostling against each other.

With a sudden jolt, the truck leaned into a curve and Cleo careened along the floor, with bricks, shovels, and pitchforks toppling. Alarmed, she jumped out of the way. Dodging the sliding shovels, she fixed me with her liquid brown gaze. She pleaded, "Do something!"

I knew what to do. Bolstering myself to endure the putrid musk, I enfolded Cleo in my arms, anchoring the two of us amid the tumbling tools and ropes. I could feel Cleo's trembling body exchanging heat with my own. Clasping her to me, breathing in that unthinkable stench, I sealed a bond with Cleo, with the skunk, with the night woods. I succumbed not so much to skunk stink as gamy life stink.

Somehow, in that hug, I felt contact with Cleo's ancestry. Shuttling back through time, I sensed in her the shepherding dog of the Australian grasslands, the wolf, the dingo with whom shepherd dogs mated where meadow met forest. Fully, I inhabited that moment. Including all that had shaped it, all that it might shape. I felt Cleo's healing flank against the scar in my breast. I absorbed her rhythm.

THIS ENCOUNTER WITH THE SKUNK sent me catapulting back to risk whatever fumes or adventures might come my way in my own home neighborhood. I am still trying to figure out precisely how and why. It's true that I was wary of trail walking and potential encounters with further skunks, that I didn't want a smelly Cleo in the car. But there's some alchemy I don't fully understand, something else I sense in this passage—from what felt like an embrace with a skunk to a return to my home street.

I fix on the word *inhabit*. It seems to name both experiences. Inhabit. The word suggests something I would like to explore.

At that time, all I knew for sure was that I was unaccountably drawn to return with Cleo to my home neighborhood, to risk the plunge back into the clamor and tumult of the city streets. After having, for a moment, inhabited Cleo's animal body as mine, I sensed I might be able to get to know my own block through Cleo's ears and nose, to sniff out life processes— squirrel tracks, dog pee, excrement, garbage, dead possums.

But not just that. Through Cleo's sniffs, I sensed I might find more ease with all that seemed quintessentially city—the lip of sidewalk rising from the asphalt street, the telephone pole, the brick walkway to some boarded-up apartments.

The morning after the encounter with the skunk, the yowl of my neighbor's cat, the yelping of the Doberman down the block seemed to call to me. Following Cleo (still redolent with skunk), I took to my own street. As Cleo sniffed ahead, I felt my attention bounding with her.

Through the morning mist, we headed down, away from the turbulence of San Pablo Avenue with its muffler shops, its video stores, its discount markets and gas stations. We headed in the direction of the Bay. On an incoming wind, I thought I caught a whiff of salt.

Raring for action, Cleo hurried past Victorian houses, past stucco bungalows, past Spenger's parking lot and artists' studios. Along the strip of grass bordering the street, she tracked the hidden smells of life—bees in the blackberries, a hummingbird nest, possum droppings. Enlivened by Cleo's excitement, I kept pace.

But when she dragged me toward concrete warehouses, toward aluminum fencing smeared with gang signatures, I recoiled. Too ugly. A risk I didn't feel like taking. Oblivious, nose to the pavement, Cleo pulled me at a fast clip around a bend. Off balance and a bit lost, I found myself looking down a long, narrow path. Halfway between D and E Streets, two ordinary blocks—wide, blacktop, already active with morning traffic. We had happened into . . . I didn't really know what. Here was a pathway—two, three, four blocks in length. It led between the concrete walls of a warehouse and a wall of corrugated aluminum, then a wall created by what looked like a rusting bus, seemingly abandoned. Cleo, smile wide, enticed by a new scent, kept pulling. On the pavement lay an old mattress and rolled up in the corner of that, a frayed sleeping bag. I felt my belly tighten. Was this route dangerous? Who might be hiding here? Would I intrude on someone homeless and hungry? Would a stranger leap out of the shadows?

"As I am breathing in, I know I am breathing in." I felt the breath moving through my body—through my locked jaw and shoulders, through my chest and belly, down to the soles of my feet on the concrete. "As I am breathing out, I know . . ." Another breath, mingled with worried thoughts. The day before I had embraced Cleo stinking with skunk. This felt similar. In its way, it was a meditation practice. Skunk practice. Ever so faintly, balancing distaste, I felt a tug of curiosity. More than that, a tug of recognition. This was my home turf. Could I inhabit it?

With some caution, I took a more focused look. The path was paved here at the opening, but down a block it seemed to change. I made out a dirt trail with moist green margins overgrown with fennel and blackberries. As far as I could see, I detected no cars, people, creatures of any kind. I drew Cleo's leash in tight.

As I walked through the mist, I looked more closely. I noted the faded graffiti, mystery glyphs without meaning for me. I stopped to study the wall, which was indeed a bus. It was painted white with baby blue trim. On the dashboard, I could see little clay statuettes (were they naked figures?); above the blue-and-white striped steering wheel, a good luck charm—

tinsel with aqua glitter. All the windows were blocked by torn pieces of material in faded floral patterns. Teetering on my toes, I craned my neck to see. Did people live in there? Even now? I thought of the 1970s and 1960s, the communes on wheels of the Hog Farm and Merry Pranksters. In the next yards, battered motorcycles conjured up vintage bike gangs, pulling my thoughts even further back into the fifties, into a vortex of time.

Nose still to the ground, Cleo followed a trail of scat, and I, senses opening, tried to keep up. The wall created by the bus gave way to a plywood fence, waist-high, so I could see through soft feathers of fennel to the houses in back. In the mist, I made out littered yards, shabby houses dissolving into the ground.

Distaste for the unkempt and decayed closed my throat. But I urged myself to stay and look. With small square windows, tall basements, and high porches, were these Victorians? Another joggle back in time. Somehow they didn't look quite like Victorians. Of course! This wasn't a formal presentation on a public street, but an insider's view. This was the back side. Intrigue outdistancing resistance, I continued farther across a street, re-entering what I now termed "the alley."

The rough dirt alley, with its center strip of tufted grass, stretched north toward a green hill in the distance. I examined this path, seemingly created over many years, the grass tamped down into tracks. I imagined wagon wheels. Blood thrumming through my veins, I leapt puddles, grazed my head against the brambles. I followed Cleo's zigzag trail from smell to smell. So the two of us, stumbling and spattering mud, muddled right into the shadow of what looked like a wooden barn. Again, I stood still and took note.

Here we were, a short walk from the Shell station and Burger King of San Pablo Avenue. But I had a sure sense that this was a remnant of a farm, left over perhaps from—was it the 1850s?—when Europeans first settled here by the Bay. Through the fog, I could almost see a wagon trundling ahead of me, its wooden wheels sending up clods of late winter mud from the worn tracks. (Had I read Katy one too many fantasy novels, the kind with cracks between worlds and doorways into the past?) I shook myself. I could not shake that uncanny intuition that Cleo had sniffed her way back into another era.

Suddenly I realized that it was late. I'd have to hurry home before I could finish exploring this alley. Like Cleo, I took in a long sniff, tart with the scent of wet fennel and a residue of skunk. "Breathing in, I know . . . Breathing out . . ." For a moment, I was in the open pickup truck, flank to flank with Cleo in a swoon of musk—fully present, yet at the same time transported back through history across woodlands and savannas. In this alley, something similar was going on.

I turned and looked behind me to where I first left the street—toward cars, factories, buildings—then down this trail, which must have been molded by horseshoes, by wagon wheels, by feet. Mud seeping into my sneakers, senses saturated with the history of the alley, I felt a wash of warmth inside.

Chapter 8

homeless

through the fence

Slamming the window shut, I prevented Katy from leaning over the sill and hearing the shouts. "Troublemaker!" "No good!" Cleo, barking shrilly, pawed at the pane. Katy challenged me, "Why can't I look out?"

The jumble of shouts in the street was now unintelligible. But through the window I saw the three women, as I had on other evenings. Past the backdrop of wisteria long since bloomed, by the late summer garden of penstemon and gaura, I watched them—three generations—outside my window in battle.

Up on the front porch, littered with splintered glass, Grandma Darlene shielded the broken window. Hastening down the steps, Donna, her reedy twenty-year-old granddaughter, screamed toward the street, "Get out! I don't need no mama the likes of you!" Dee, invariably the protagonist in these fights, hollered up from the street, "Can't I break in my own bedroom window?" Unsteady on her feet, stumbling on her bad leg, she weaved backward toward the corner. She called up at Grandma Darlene, "You take in that skinny-assed daughter of mine, but you lock me out of my home to sleep in the street!"

Katy, Cleo, and I vied for space at the window. "What's going on?" Katy persisted. I cradled her chin in my palm; tucked a strand of hair behind her ear; and with a sweep of my arm, sent her away from the window. "Too much violence outside . . ."

My nose pressed against the damp glass, opaque with dog breath and paw marks. I worried, could someone get hurt? Should I call the cops? Should I try to intervene? Stepping out on my front porch, I scanned the block for help, but the neighboring Victorians were dark, the gardens empty.

Donna suddenly descended the steps, her long slim legs leaping two at a time, her ponytail swishing. Just then I heard the sirens, and two squad cars pulled up. As the officer handcuffed Dee and escorted her to the car, she called out, "They throw me out on the street. Everybody hears it." She pointed up at me on the landing. "She hears it. Ask her!"

Choked by a conflux of feelings—fear, fascination, anger—I was unable to speak. As I watched Dee pull her bad leg into the squad car, I noticed that the hood was up on her jacket. The beat-up jacket seemed strangely familiar to me. Just noticing it, with the fake-fur lining peeking around the hood, I felt an ache of tears. Why was this?

I turned away. I double-locked my door.

This tumult in the street churned up uneasy thoughts. In my daily walks I was returning to my neighborhood, getting to know the place where I lived. But here I was, afraid of fights right outside my own door, locking the neighbors out. As a mother and a caretaker of a home, I was afraid. Since the breast cancer, I yearned particularly for a safe space for Katy and for my own healing and peace of mind. And as far back as I could remember, I'd been scared of violent conflicts, refused to watch bloody movies. I'd avoided TV coverage of riots, shoot-outs, or wars. I'd often closed my mind to violence, denied it ever erupted.

Then there had been the more benign happenings of unpleasant or uncomfortable cast: the rat I was sure must be a mouse; the mouse, who before his testimonial in the skillet and appearance in the refrigerator, I'd refused to believe had invaded our kitchen. Despite my prescription to take risks, my modus operandi was still: retreat inside, seal the difficult out.

THE MOTHER OF KYLA, Katy's best friend, called me on the phone. She said that she'd heard the kids had gotten a little wild over here that past Saturday. I said that, yes, they had been driving me crazy and that even Kyla, usually so responsible, had crossed me. But in the end, I had made it clear that I'd reached my limit.

"Actually," said Kyla's mother, "when Kyla 'crossed' you, she was upset by something you'd said and was speaking up to protect Katy."

I wrenched my mind, trying to dredge up what I had said, but I had no recall. "What did I say?" I asked.

"Kyla won't tell me," said her mother, lowering her voice. "All she would say was that you shouted and swore."

I still couldn't remember, but I sensed that what she said was true. On and off over the years, I'd been unnerved—sometimes truly shaken—by my own vitriolic outbursts at family and friends (this, from an ever-smiling persona, enthusiastic, generous).

I'd longed to offer Katy a peaceful childhood, an oasis from the cross fire of life's dangers. But in some disturbing way, the family conflicts next door seemed to mirror those within my own home. Spiraling down through the generations, both were driven by old habits of reaction and lashing out. I didn't hurl bottles at windows and fight in the street, but on occasions such as this, I shouted scary words I didn't even hear myself say. Inwardly, I attacked, defended my turf, shielded whatever was broken inside. What good did it do to close out the raging of the world when the very fury I shunned was inside me?

If I could only catch an angry impulse before it drove me. How could anyone overturn habits so entrenched? So much in me resisted settling down and noticing what seemed to be happening in the world, in my mind. So much resisted just experiencing whatever that was without immediately leaping up in reaction to fix it.

But that night I was so turned around that it felt like I had no recourse but to sit myself down on a meditation cushion. Putting aside all distractions, I did just that. First I noted the in and out of my breath and then the emotions, such a momentum. Blames competed in my chest against all the pressures of life— the escalating fights in the street, the demands of work and family—that had conspired on that Saturday to drive me to such anger. Then I turned on myself. How could I? Contemplating this, I was barely able to keep still. I didn't enjoy sitting there. Not one bit. But I stayed put. Skunk practice again, teaching myself to include the difficult.

As my chest began to soften, memories flooded. Among them came an image of my homeless neighbor Dee's jacket—the one with the hood that had made me cry when Dee was climbing into the squad car several weeks back. I remembered two incidents from years before when our family first lived on this corner.

IN THE LATE SUMMER HEAT, I watered my vegetable garden. Arcing over the lettuces and zucchini, back toward the Blue Lake beans, a fantastic whoosh fanned out against the fence between my yard and Grandma Darlene's.

Late that evening, the doorbell rang. Through the crazy chaos of Cleo's barks, I opened the front door. Dee stood there.

"Keep that dog down! That dog don't like black folks . . ." Before I could reply, she told me, "Your goddamn water ruined my clothes."

"But I didn't know . . . I'm sorry . . . Where were your clothes?"

"Where you think they were? You know my mother kicked me out! I stack my clothes the other side of the fence." Then bitterly, "Where else I keep them? They lock me out of the backyard." It was true. All she had was that little passageway.

"You see me come here every day to change my clothes!" She sniffed, her lower lip quivered. She swung away and clumped down the stairs.

There really was a lot of space between the fence and the end of my garden. If I gave it some attention, I could adjust the hose so the flow of water stopped before it reached the fence. I called after Dee, "Next time, I'll be more careful."

Several weeks later, the torpor of Indian summer settled over me and the garden. The air was fetid with factory fumes, exhaust, the stink of rotten landfill. Seeking relief, I watered the garden. As the rush of water cleansed the air and revived the wilted lettuce and burnt zucchini leaves, I also felt fresh.

Two nights later, a pounding at the door interrupted dinner. It was Dee. She braced herself against the evening wind, hugging something in her arms. "You done gone and ruined my whole wardrobe!" I forced myself to look more closely as she whipped the soaked and muddy clothes from her bundle: a sweater with rhinestone buttons, a pair of jeans, and the hooded jacket with fake-fur lining. "You owe me! Didn't I tell you where I keep my clothes?"

"I'm sorry," I spluttered. "Of course I'll pay for the . . . I . . ."

There was nothing I could say. She was right. I had forgotten about her. I had been absorbed in the world on my side of the fence, exclusively.

In the silence of sitting still, these two incidents had returned to me in explicit detail. As I revisited the memories, I kept reflecting on the fence between our yard—what I defined as my home—and the one next door, on the fence in my thinking that allowed me to pretend that my actions didn't affect whoever or whatever was on the other side. In its way, this was a kind of violence, the violence of not paying attention. When I didn't pay attention, it was easy to slip into the view that the world of my yard was the only thing that counted. It was easy to assume that my view, whether I was with Katy or Dee or anyone else, offered the only way to see.

One evening, several months after I first remembered these confrontations with Dee, I stood at the living room window overlooking the vegetable garden where, years back, I had soaked Dee's clothes. I looked out at this year's beans and peas, toward the fence. But I couldn't see down into the narrow walkway between the fence and Grandma Darlene's house, where I was hoping Dee didn't still store her things. I tried to imagine what it might have been like for Dee to head toward her once-home on those nights after I'd soaked her clothes. Just as my home was for me, this space between Dee's mother's house and the fence must have been her place for retreat. Just as when I headed back toward our corner in my walks, when Dee turned toward this same corner, she must have felt the pull toward home. During her walks, perhaps across town, Dee must have savored the thought of reaching that safe place. She must surely have expected to sort through her belongings, to find her zip-up jacket, the one with the hood, so snug for a chill summer night.

Looking out over the garden, I recommitted myself to take care. Not such an easy task. I pictured the watering hoses, the showers and sinks, even the washing machine connected to the same water source. It would take ongoing vigilance each time we took a shower or used the washing machine to adjust and readjust all those faucets. But that's what I would have to do to control the water. So many times I'd forgotten. The washing machine had gone into the spin cycle, and with sudden force, the water had surged out of the sprinkler by the vegetable garden and over the fence once again.

Redoubling my concentration, I thought this through: When I didn't pay attention to the cycles of the washing machine, that great whoosh of water suddenly spilled over the garden and into the yard next door, maybe destroying someone else's things. When I didn't pay attention to my frustrations with Katy, they escalated. I found myself bursting out in angry words I didn't hear myself say.

In my explorations of this home terrain, what I found outside led me to examine myself. What I experienced inside seemed to ripple out. I couldn't go out without going in at the same time, go in without going out. That's where meditation began to seem so crucial. When one trains oneself to pay attention to the breath, one contacts a place where inner and outer meet. In following the breath, one can become aware of inner states of mind and how they interface with the world.

Chapter 9

skunk practice

through deep time

REFUSING TO BE DAUNTED by what I encountered—outside or in—a passion took me over with unexpected urgency: I would get to know my yard, my neighbors, and neighboring blocks; I would learn their history. Hoping that I would recover a long-latent New York City chutzpah and overcome my geographic dyslexia, I risked talking to people I'd never met and going places I'd never been. I sorted north from south, east from west, and set out to truly know this neighborhood.

With Cleo's enthusiasm to urge me on, I headed into the streets. On my back, I carried a pack full of guides on neighborhood flora, fauna, geology, and history. I angled back and forth down my block, one hand pulling on Cleo's leash, the other clutching an open guide.

It intrigued me to learn that in the 1850s, following the eighty years of Spanish ranchos, Ocean View—this very neighborhood where I lived—had developed as a new European settlement, the first in the East Bay. In 1853, a Captain James Jacobs of Danish heritage returned from the goldfields in the lower slopes of the Sierra Nevada, where he'd gone to make his fortune with fellow forty-niners. He began to moor his sloop a few blocks west from what was now my corner, between the outlets of Strawberry and Schoolhouse Creeks, launching what was to become this Ocean View settlement. Ocean View. I'd never thought about it before, but now I realized that the name described the once-view. These days, it hardly felt appropriate. The city—with all of its factories and freeways, the imposing University Avenue freeway overpass, and the several miles of landfill—divided us from the Bay and from the ocean view. As I walked down from my house now, there was no ocean to be viewed.

By the time of the Ocean View settlement, the overgrazing of the cattle on the Spanish ranchos, compounded by the introduction of European grasses, had already altered the natural grasslands. Much of the native bunchgrasses had been replaced by grasses carried on boots and clothing, in the ballast of bricks, mixed in with seed of other crop plants, or in the coats and digestive tracts of livestock. To feed the fortune seekers mining gold in the foothills of the Sierra Nevada, millions of additional cattle and sheep had been introduced and continued to destroy the native grasses. Deeply rooted perennials, these native bunchgrasses had stabilized the hills year-round. But the alien grasses were annuals; they died in the summer, leaving the hills brown and, in the rainy season, due to their shallow roots, left those hills vulnerable to massive erosion.

Meanwhile, the hydraulic mining of Sierran gold seekers wreaked damage through streams and rivers all the way to the San Francisco Bay. Blasting apart hillsides with pressurized streams of water, miners sent a billion cubic yards of sediment into streams and rivers, clogging riverbeds, causing extensive flooding, and depositing the finer materials along with mercury (used to separate ore from gold) in the Bay and billowing through the Golden Gate into the Pacific Ocean.

Shifting peoples, shifting terrain. In a foray into local history, I spent a day at the Oakland Public Library, poring over early voting records. Penned in fine script, what was grandly titled the Great Register of 1894 offered detailed portraits of Ocean View pioneers (brown hair, light complexion, scab left thumb, scar right cheek) hailing from all over the world—Ireland, Prussia, Denmark, Germany, England, Norway, Nova Scotia, Prince Edward Island, Mexico. I imagined these immigrants arriving in Ocean View, people on the move. (A stray thought of Dee. Was this migration a form of homelessness? Is there another way to understand homelessness?)

But once they settled here, these immigrants became farmers, milkmen, boat builders, coopers, tanners, glassblowers, brass finishers, shoemakers, cigar makers, gold prospectors, saloon keepers. They dug, nailed, raised cattle. They crafted with dirt, wood, water, metal, hides, growing things (and a few with ale and whiskey to ease the daily grind).

A reciprocity became clear to me as I reflected on these records, and later, as I learned of the migration of thousands of refugees to Ocean View when the Great Earthquake and fires of 1906 destroyed more than half the lodging places in San Francisco. The forces of water, earth, and fire certainly drove the lives of the settlers, while the settlers, at the same time, worked the land and the sea. Indeed they were shaped by their world while they shaped it—in wrestling to make this place their home.

To further my study, I visited the Berkeley Historical Society and the Berkeley Architectural Heritage Association. No matter where I went, everyone told me to call Stephanie Manning, Ocean View activist and historian. Stephanie had spent years scouring frayed copies of the *Berkeley Gazette*; reading telephone directories, deeds, and personal wills; piecing together the history of this neighborhood. Along with her husband, Curt, she had written many of the essays in local history I was now reading.

When I reached her on the phone, Stephanie's voice was animated. Taking a wide view, she began with the Bay, emphasizing that Berkeley is directly opposite the Golden Gate, the mouth of the Bay that opens into the Pacific Ocean. Before the turn of the century, the arid city streets of the neighborhood—now paved over with creeks in culverts—were wet and marshy, organized around creeks such as Strawberry, Codornices, and Schoolhouse that flowed down from the hills into the Bay. I thought of the muddy soil a termite inspector found under our house and the damp dirt in our yard, then of the willow that seeded itself here and flourished—as willows do—on the banks of local creeks.

Along the curve of land just ten blocks below my house, where the eight-lane Interstate 80 was now choked with cars and trucks, a sandy beach once extended into sand dunes. Over many centuries, sand had flowed south from the delta, in through the Carquinez Straits, and along the shore. The tides flooding through the Golden Gate had molded the shoreline as an arc. North of Strawberry Creek, sand dunes heaped up where the alluvial fan went inland, and the sands connected as a kind of bridge between the mouth of the creek and a rocky prominence to the north called Fleming Point. To the south, the same kind of arc continued with a thinner beach that was subject to tidal action. Just listening to Stephanie, I could imagine early settlers walking the few blocks down from our house to the beach, digging for clams in the dunes, and spreading out picnic blankets while their children and dogs played in the sand.

Stephanie also mentioned neighborhood landmarks, some of which—like Sisterna Hall on University Avenue—became the focus of community life. The large barnlike Scandinavian Hall around the corner on H Street was built in 1908 by refugees from Scandinavian famines and drought. The hardwood maple floor crafted by Scandinavian carpenters was so springy it allowed dancers to do their many-figured quadrilles, polkas, and mazurkas and to circle the hall in their chain dances without tiring their legs.

The Pilgrim's Rest Church, down our block, was built in 1878 as an early church in Berkeley. With a seventy-five-foot louvered spire, its construction was completed in one month. The thousand-pound bell, donated in 1882 by the volunteer fire department, served as an alarm for the early settlement as well as a call to church services.

So close to my house—it surprised me now that I'd never taken a visit. Much as I wanted to learn about these buildings, I was shy about approaching them. But Stephanie urged me on. So the next Sunday, when the bell tolled at ten past ten (as it had as long as I'd lived on the block), I hurried over to sit on a wooden pew in the back of this little church. What felt like a particularly friendly service (children laughing and crying in the front pews or dashing into the aisles) was followed by coffee and cakes in the community hall.

On learning my interest in neighborhood history, the deacon in charge invited me to peruse the church log. For several days, I pored over a frayed leather-bound volume, a tall black ledger held together with masking tape. Dating back to 1878, line after line of spidery script recorded the history of the church, replete with the names of early settlers that were becoming familiar to me through the writings of Stephanie Manning. Here were the pioneers: Zimri Brewer Heywood, who started a lumber company with Captain Jacobs at the landing dock where Jacobs moored his boat; the most politically prominent of Zimri Brewer's thirteen children, Sam Heywood, who helped organize and raise the money to start this church. There was the proprietor of the inn and grocery store, which were connected by a foot-path to what had come to be called Jacobs Landing; the owner of the Pioneer Starch and Grist Mill; the owners of the shop that made decorative sashes, moldings, and furbelows for the increasing numbers of Victorian houses.

The journal seemed to be predominantly a record book, meticulously divided into columns of names, dates, and places of origin—once again from all over the world, from Canada to Chile to Germany. An index at the start of the ledger introduced categories: baptisms, confirmations, communicants, marriages, burials. A record of each ceremony listed particulars. I thumbed back to the burials, beginning in 1879 and numbered 1, 2, 3 . . .

Date	No.	Name	Age
1879	1	Jas Driver	41 yrs

Residence	Date of Death	Cause of Death	Place of Burial
San Pablo Ave	Jan 16	insanity	Oakland Cemetery of Canada

But beyond the particular sufferings and idiosyncrasies of each parishioner, there seemed to be something more. These rituals—baptisms, marriages, burials—signified shifts, birth into life, coming of age, communing with God, joining to create a family, passing from life into death. Each ritual, so painstakingly recorded, marked an initiation—not only into a new time, a new phase, but perhaps also into this parish, into inhabiting this place, into more deeply coming into this place as home.

ONE MORNING, I took a neighborhood walk with the renowned Stephanie. We began in front of my house. Wiry and lithe, her chestnut hair wild, Stephanie leapt off her bicycle, ready to talk. Waters from a recent rain rushed through the gutters down toward the Bay. With dramatic flair (I later learned she had been an actress), Stephanie set the scene. Pointing to the overflowing gutters, she instructed, "Imagine this as a stream full of trout and salmon. It could be Strawberry Creek right outside your front door. And peel away the asphalt. See these streets as dirt. Twenty years ago, when we interviewed Mr. Wright, he said the streets were paved with red soil that they mined up at the top of Cedar there in the hills. At ninety-seven, he still talked about walking right down the block here as a child to the Seventh Street School . . . through the red dirt. Barefoot, he said. Barefoot!"

We wound back and forth along the streets of what had once been the old settlement. Captain Jacobs's house, probably the first building, had been demolished inadvertently by the city's redevelopment project over thirty years earlier. Stephanie conjured up the early history. Captain Jacobs and Zimri Brewer Heywood had enlarged the wharf to accommodate receiving and shipping; supplied local residents with lumber for building their homes; and along with the Irish Catholics and other immigrants, sired some of the growing population, thus helping this tiny settlement to expand.

We completed our tour at the Delaware Street Historic District. As we walked, Stephanie described the clash in the 1970s between angry residents and the Berkeley Redevelopment Agency. The city had threatened to tear down dilapidated West Berkeley houses to build an industrial park. Although they succeeded in destroying forty homes, Stephanie and other neighbors stopped the bulldozers and finally convinced a new radical city council to landmark and restore this block of vintage Victorians. Some early homes were reconstructed and others slated for demolition were moved in. Some gutted Victorians on nearby streets were restored. Sixty-four units of new low-income housing were built near Delaware Street in a compromise agreement that ensured the preservation and restoration of the historic district.

On this tour, we walked briefly through the alley Cleo and I had found. "What was it for?" I asked. "Why was this the only alley in Ocean View? Had there once been others?" Stephanie urged me to take on the alley and research it myself. In the following weeks, I went to the architecture library at the university, called the Berkeley Historical Society, and searched urban geography periodicals. But to no avail.

So on my weekly 6:00 A.M. walk with my friend Loie, we

headed with determination toward the alley. In one of the guidebooks, I had found passing reference to John Brown's barn (built in the 1880s in the alleyway between D and E Streets). Loie and I stopped and paid homage to the barn that had so teased my imagination on my first outing. But this was the only alley reference I had found. Over these weeks, I had in fact become fixated on this alley, as if it might somehow provide me a back way into the history of the settlement. "I'm stumped," I told Loie.

Loie, a West Berkeley neighbor who was, like me, another New York–born Buddhist, gave me just the right nudge. Outside one of the alley houses, an elderly woman in her housecoat came out of a shabby Victorian. As she bent to pick up her morning newspaper, Loie took her (and me) by surprise. "Excuse me," Loie called out. "I was wondering if you knew about the history of this alley?" Chutzpah! And at the crack of dawn, no less.

And 6:00 A.M. or not, this lady was ready to chat. "Of course, it goes back long before my time, when Mr. Peters lived here, and before Mr. Peters, his grandmother." She hitched up her housecoat so it wouldn't drag in her flowerbed. "Course you could talk with that Stephanie Manning." (Stephanie again. With a random neighbor . . .) "That Stephanie," continued the lady, "she's the one who found out the history. We all got out there with her and stopped all those bulldozers!"

The woman looked up and down the nearby houses as if she were taking stock. "But if you want my opinion on the alley . . . they put it in because of the flooding." She pointed at the lower story of her house. "See my house, and over there at Charlie's, and back around the corner over at Mrs. Connors's. They're all built tall with high basements. That would have been because of the tides. In those days, they had their rainy months, just like we do now. But I bet their winters were mean, what with the waves from the Bay washing all the way up here." She nodded knowingly. "After all, the old shoreline was only a few blocks down, there around B Street."

The lady paused. She was getting excited. "So when D Street was flooded, I'll bet you could still have your ice and coal delivered by wagon. Right along this alley." She made a sweeping gesture with her newspaper. "Just past the tide line. Plop down by your kitchen door, along the back side."

Who knew? Sounded like a reason for an alley. I did love the thought of the tides washing up this far. The contact with the Bay. Over the centuries, the alluvial soil of West Berkeley had been eaten away by the tidal action coming through the Golden Gate. These streets must have once been marshland that stretched along the beach north of Strawberry Creek where the alluvial fan went inland up toward Fleming Point. As Stephanie kept saying, this terrain used to be wet. So maybe there was something to this lady's guess. Again the thought of the interface of lives with water, wind, shifting earth.

The next morning, I returned to the alley with Cleo. I had never followed it to the end. This time, I allowed Cleo to draw me farther down the path, crossing several ordinary blocks to a segment that felt particularly run-down. Entering between a wall of concrete and another of shattered wood, I peered into the visible yards. Amid discarded furniture and rubble, one crumbling Victorian remained. Then, before I was ready for it, smack against a chain-link fence, the alley ended.

Accosted by the odor of trash and something else burnt and foul, I felt disgust rise in my throat. Ugly. And there's nobody around. Get me out of here. I turned to leave, but Cleo held her ground. Nose to the grass, she proceeded inch by inch in a thorough inspection. Held by the power of some scent not detectable to a mere human, she wouldn't move, not one iota. I gave a fierce yank, but the handle of her leash bit into my palm. Stubborn foe, she lowered her head and countered my weight.

The taut metal leash hiked her collar up so it squeezed her ears. She was determined to stay.

Ludicrous. Chained to this alley, unable to buck the unjust authority of my dog. But here I was. In contrast to Cleo, I did not want to be here. Skunk practice once again. I cajoled myself into a superficial glance. Through the links of the fence, a small paved courtyard was cluttered with trash barrels and cartons. Then, through the grid of a second fence—this one topped with coiled barbed wire—long crisscrossed chutes reached into the gray sky. On the ground was heaped some kind of gravel or sand. All still and silent. This had to be some kind of defunct industry.

Released when Cleo had completed her sniff, I headed out. At the entrance of this segment of alley, I nearly knocked down a young woman with a baby in a backpack. She balanced her groceries as she carried them into the alley house on the corner. Taking my inspiration from Loie, I swallowed my discomfort and asked, "Excuse me, what industry is that, down at the end of the alley? Is it still in use?"

"That's the sand treatment plant," she said. "It's mostly at night that we hear them up and running. I'm not sure why, maybe for making new roads. That's when they truck out the sand."

Sand. It wasn't until later when I got back to my house that I put it together. How perversely appropriate. Right there, at the far end of what felt like a time tunnel back through the early Ocean View, a factory processing sand. I'd been learning about that beach, once only a few blocks down from the alley, along the Bay. I looked through my books. According to the oral history of an old-timer, Paul Spenger, the sand was in "unlimited supply." Zimri Brewer Heywood's son Sam, who had taken over the lumber business along with his brother Charles, sold sand for mortar at fifty cents a load—wheelbarrow or wagon—clearing the beaches. Whatever sand was left was used by the

Works Projects Administration in the 1930s as fill material for the new road paralleling the shoreline.

I SIT NOW in my backyard feeling the dirt beneath me, wondering about the dirt and sand, how they evolved in this place. In the grass, I've piled up books on soil, on the geology of coastal California. I'm up against my dyslexia, which definitely includes geology, but I persevere. Sand and dirt are both what geologists call "sediments." Weathered and transported by wind, water, and glacial ice, these loose pieces of rock and minerals are broken down from much larger rocks. From boulders to cobbles to pebbles to sand to silt to clay.

When I call my friend Wendy—gardener, ecologist, soil crusader—she tells me that as rocks break down and become more granulated, they can hold more living matter. The sediment that underlies the dirt in this yard was probably carried here by creeks descending from the hills. More fertile alluvium may well have been deposited here and throughout the inland margins of the Bay several thousand years ago by the Sacramento River—rich with the life of the Sierras. The sand that was sold from the beaches must also have been carried here by the Sacramento River and swept along the shore.

At the very site where 150 years ago sand was in "unlimited supply," new sand must now be shipped in to be processed because the beaches have been decimated.

There are crazy consequences sometimes in this struggle to transform a place into a home.

Chapter 10

homeless

in the street

SHOCKED OUT OF SLEEP, I flinched at the rattle of super-market carts down the dawn-dark streets below. A hint of jangling outside the window conjured faceless fantasies of the homeless rummaging through cans and bottles. Despite my recent intimacy with backstreets and alleyways, with those who actually lived *in* the street, I continued to remain a stranger.

Restless in my bed, I tried to fall back to sleep. Since treatments for breast cancer, my sleeping had been poor, and I hadn't truly slept well since Katy was a baby. Now, caught up in my own jangling worries, I recalled a lullaby I sang Katy for many years whenever she woke up in the night. When she was an infant, I cradled her in my arms and suckled her back to sleep while I sang:

> *"I gave my love a cherry that has no stone.*
> *I gave my love a chicken that has no bone.*
> *I gave my love a ring that has no end.*
> *I gave my love a baby, with no cryin'."*

Silently, I hummed the old tune to myself hoping to lull my agitated mind. But to no avail.

With determination, I tossed the blankets off. I'd seize this time to meditate. But before I could sit myself up, I slipped back down to the pillow, pulled the covers up over my head. For years of sleepless nights, it had been hard enough to find the energy or patience to attend to Katy. It was too hard now to muster more of the same to tend to my own mind.

Squinting through the blinds in our attic bedroom, I scanned the dimly lit street. I made out the familiar line of cars: our bashed-in '69 Toyota (Patrick's commuting car) with its peeling Stop MX/Cruise bumper sticker; our old tenants' (the ones before Suzanna) Dodge truck, littered with tools and boxes; and the two '87 Volvos, ours and our tenants'.

Down the block, parked across from Grandma Darlene's, shimmered that new gold Lexus, the talk of the block. As far as I could tell, it belonged to the hang-around boyfriend of some girl across the street. Polished each day by the boyfriend, the Lexus shone in all its glory, ready to provide rides for neighborhood admirers, many of whom were carless. No one at Grandma Darlene's had a car—neither Donna nor her grandmother, and Michelle, at ten, was too young. Certainly not Dee, so often drinking, in and out of jail, and so far as I knew, still homeless.

With the coming of daylight, I finally generated enough energy to drive across town to an early-bird yoga class. I pried open the door of the Toyota, with its busted lock. Taking in a long breath, I was hit with the unmistakable stench. Tobacco. I knew Patrick would sneak a few puffs on his cigar between the BART train station and home, but the scent of nicotine had never seemed so caustic as it did this morning. Why? Irritably, I squashed the half-smoked cigars farther down into the ashtray, slid it closed, and took a second long breath in relief, only to find another unmistakable odor. I sniffed again. Yes, alcohol. I felt queasy.

As I drove toward the yoga class, I tried to picture Patrick cruising from the station, taking a few draws on his cigar, then circling to the corner liquor store to pick up a Budweiser to drink in the car before he came home. Not likely.

Just as I turned off the engine of the car, a dark heap in the backseat caught my eye. A pile of blankets? I flashed, "A dead body!" Someone had rolled a drunk and stashed him in our Toyota. The bundle quivered, exhaled a pungent scent of beer and tobacco. An eye blinked at me from between the folds of the blankets. "It's Dee," it said, throwing back layers of material to reveal a wool cap, a familiar face. "Where the hell am I?"

Dee! From next door. Despite her fights on the steps and our exchanges years ago over her wet clothes, Dee had mostly been pleasant enough to me. Supremely relieved, I didn't miss a beat. "You're on Alcatraz, below Adeline. I'm going in to my yoga class. I'll be out in an hour if you want a ride back across town."

The car was empty when I got out of class, but I thought of Dee all day. When Katy was first born, Dee would call from her steps to mine, "How's the baby?" And when Katy was a toddler, Dee would wave. "Hi, Sugar!" Over the years I'd run into Dee all over the neighborhood. Wiry and diminutive, she'd pace up and down our street, sit with other folks on the sidewalk outside the post office, or stand on the corner by the liquor store deep in conversation with her cohorts. Most often, she'd weave down the block swearing to herself or engage Donna and Grandma Darlene in their ongoing clash of tongues. Drinking or sober, Dee seemed to be at the hub of a complex web of relationships in the neighborhood.

THE EVENING after the surprise encounter in the car, I went out front to get the mail. As usual, folks from around the block were hanging out—some in front of the purple fourplex down the block, some in front of Grandma Darlene's. Dee sat on the stairs with her younger daughter, Michelle. Dee and I had so often crossed paths without acknowledgment. This time our eyes met. She leaned toward me and whispered, "You ain't goin' to tell on me, are you, girl?"

When I'd told Patrick, it had turned out he'd known all along that she slept there. "Don't worry," I said to her now. We continued to chat on the stoop in a way we'd never talked before. After all, I knew now that she'd been sleeping in our car. She knew that I wasn't giving her a hard time for it. That I risked to share a secret with her. And she and I had been across town together.

I studied Dee more closely, her small face and pointy chin. Maybe she was cradling something in her arms. She nodded toward Michelle, so willowy and pretty of late, with her many tiny braids. "My girl's eleven today! I got her this little mongrel puppy for her birthday." Michelle gave me a shy smile, then looked gratefully at her mom. Dee opened her coat to reveal a silky ball of fur with a wet black nose.

Over the next few days, shrill yelps sounded from next door. Along with increasing yipping, fighting seemed to be picking up again between Dee, who was still locked out, and the residents of the house. Or maybe I was noticing these battles because I was more attuned to Dee. Just as she slept in the back of our car, I felt somehow as if her consciousness were sleeping in the back of mine. In a funny way, it seemed as if my consciousness might be sleeping in the back of hers too.

In the afternoons I saw Michelle strutting up and down the street with the puppy on a leash. She announced to her friends, "My mom gave me my little pup for my birthday!" As far as I could figure out, the shouting was about the rights of this untrained puppy to stay in or out of the house. Some wanted it in the house, and some wanted it tied up in the front. The boyfriend from across the street—sharp-boned and slim with his dreadlocks and goatee—joined in the uproar with vehemence. He was always affable with us when he was polishing his car, but someone said he was afraid of dogs.

In our house, too, conflicts raged. We were all on edge for the first week of third grade. Incensed by Katy's dawdling, I screeched at her, trying to get her out the door to early orchestra rehearsal. In the background, I heard a tumult of shouts next door and yelps from the puppy. I yanked Katy toward the front landing, my voice harsh. "Right now!" Warding me off with her elbows and shins, she ducked out of my reach and backed into the foyer. A shiver of anger ran through me. I had to grip my own arms to prevent myself from walloping her on the bottom. From next door, voices outshouted the yipping: "Don't you dare!"

Sick at heart about myself, about Katy, about the climate of upset on the block, I navigated the rest of the day. That night as I put Katy to bed, I caressed her on the cheek with my finger-tips, felt the tug mother-to-daughter. If only in these morning spats I could simply let her be late.

A few evenings later, Patrick and I ran into Dee and Michelle sitting on the front step. They were leaning into each other. "Hey, Dee, how's it going?" I called out. She turned a pained face toward me. "No one told you? He killed it. He murdered it, my girl's puppy. Right here. On these stairs, yesterday!" I felt a tremor. "Strangled it with his bare hands."

For a moment we were all still, waiting in the silence of dusk for some gratuitous sign that it wasn't true. The freeway rumbled, faint in the distance. No solace from the familiar high-pitched yelps. Finally I spluttered out, "Who . . . ?"

"You know who," Dee said. "That no-good boyfriend, that's who! That smart-ass, scumbag, dope-dealing punk." She paused. "You ain't goin' to see his fancy car on this block. The police took him away!"

As we drove off, I pictured the boyfriend, tall and bony, nodding to us, polishing his car. I whispered to Patrick, "Can this really have happened the way she said?" Echoes resounded in my memory of the frantic yapping the other morning, the escalating shouts next door. And mine at Katy.

For the next week, a squad car remained parked across the street, waiting. A pall clouded our corner of the block. Everyone spoke in hushed voices, moving quietly. Katy knew the puppy had somehow disappeared, but she asked few questions.

Awakened one night by bellowing in the street, I peered through the blinds. Two more squad cars and an ambulance squealed around the corner and stopped in front of our house. Dee stumbled past the princess tree, its blossoms an eerie mauve in the flashing lights. She gripped her belly. "That son-of-a-bitch boyfriend jumped me from the bushes and kicked me in the stomach. He says I ratted on him to the cops." This time it was an ambulance taking her away as she called out her lament, "What about my little girl's puppy?"

EVEN THOUGH SHE'D BEEN SLEEPING through the night for several years, Katy started waking with scary dreams, demanding that we lie down with her to help her get back to sleep. So many years at bedtime, I'd sung that lullaby until she drifted off, and in recent years Patrick had lain next to her, offering his warm calm presence to ease her restlessness. She'd always insisted he stay until she was fully asleep.

Anxious and unsettled these weeks, I too lay in bed at night unable to sleep. The puppy, the casualty of this recent violence, called to mind all that is precious and vulnerable. One night I awoke particularly agitated. I started worrying that Katy would wake up as well. Sure enough, she came running up the stairs telling us that she'd had a nightmare that wouldn't go away. I followed her downstairs and lay down with her on her bed. She kept tossing around, casting her pillow this way and that, telling me I was lying too close, then too far away. My body also jittery, my thoughts colliding and spinning in worry, I grew increasingly uncomfortable. Neither one of us would ever get to sleep at all if I kept lying there next to her.

Suddenly I knew what to do. "I've got it, Sweet Pea. I'll sing you the cherry song from when you were a baby, then I'm going into the other room to meditate." I began to sing:

> *"How can there be a cherry that has no stone?*
> *How can there be a chicken that has no bone?"*

Then, countering Katy's request that I stay with her until she fell asleep—what she had insisted on so adamantly these many years—I got up and left the room.

In the dark living room, I plumped up a cushion right on the couch, folded my legs, and straightened my spine for meditation. I began by simply listening. Katy in the next room, turning over, breathed with the uneven sighs of restlessness. The refrigerator buzzed; the night train let out a long whistle; and in response, Zephyr the tree frog let loose a full-throated mating call. The crickets whirred, rubbing their legs together, a sensuous chorus. A siren cried out. I remembered Dee nestled in her wraps in the back of the car.

Gradually, as I sat and followed my breath, I heard Katy's breathing becoming more regular until it found the soft rhythm of sleep. I went upstairs and slept also. Katy slept through the rest of the night. In the morning, for the first time in weeks, when I came downstairs Katy continued to sleep peacefully.

When I woke her for school, she said, "Mom, I slept through the night!"

"I'm so proud of you, babe," I said.

"When I woke up, I thought to myself, 'Mommy is protecting me with her meditation.' And I went back into my dreams." She met my eyes fully with hers. "Will you meditate like that every night when I go to bed?"

Driving back from school, I thought of Katy's word: *protecting*.

Perhaps she pictured the vigilant sentry sitting up straight and alert, paying attention to everything that was happening in the night, noticing any danger. Didn't the Buddha say something like that? "Protect your happiness." Indeed, as I sang and meditated, I had felt like I was attending to this most precious and vulnerable possibility—a sense of home in myself, in Katy, in all of us.

On and off at night, I continued to wake up, apprehensive that Katy would somehow sense the churning of my thoughts and awaken too. I became convinced that even when Katy did not know what I was doing, the rhythms of my mind changed the rhythms of hers. Another incentive for a regular practice of crossing my legs and stilling my mind.

One evening as I sat, the lullaby I had just sung suffused my meditation. Silently, I continued to sing to myself, to Katy, to Dee in our car.

> "*A ring when it's rollin' it has no end.*
> *A baby when it's sleepin' there's no cryin'.*"

A friend had told me that the name of this lullaby was "The Riddle Song." Indeed, each line seemed to pose a riddle pointing toward some of life's mysteries. In my mind's eye, I pictured those mysteries—blossoms, eggs—rolling through the many years, through the evolution of this place, through the early Victorian settlement, through our lives now.

One afternoon, the winds picked up from the Bay, sending garbage and dry leaves in a fluttering rush up our street. The phone rang. "This is Michelle," murmured a young voice. "You know, from next door. I was wondering if you could lend me some money so I could buy a new jacket." She paused. "I gave mine to my mom. You know she's homeless. So she needs a warm jacket."

I hesitated, then said, "Maybe I could loan you a jacket."

And she, "Okay, but it's gotta have a hood. My mom always likes a hood, and I do, too." I winced at the old memory. That soaked jacket with the fake-fur lining. Then I recalled seeing Dee earlier that day wearing a bright blue new-looking jacket with a hood fastened tight against the autumn wind.

Several months later, I was walking with Katy past the liquor store. On the pavement, leaning against the wall of the building sat a couple of neighborhood men I'd seen around but never spoken to. Dressed in layers of frayed clothing, they were un-shaven and, I surmised, homeless. Maybe they were the home-less scavengers I'd heard in the night these past years sorting through the cans. With them, passing a cigarette, sat Dee. "Hey, girl," she said. And I, "Hey, Dee!" She turned to her friends. "This here's my neighbor and her kid." One man looked up. His eye, as it met mine, had a perceptive lilt; his grief and smile lines deeply creased. He reached out his hand and shook mine.

I thought of the rolling ring. Dee took care of her daughter by getting her a puppy. Michelle took care of Dee by passing on her own jacket. And Michelle brought me into the circle to take care of her. Over the years, I'd offered Katy lullabies, and she gave me meditation—which is what I'd needed all along but couldn't give to myself. In the back of our car, we'd offered Dee an occasional shelter from the cold, and she connected us—hand to hand—to unknown neighbors.

Chapter 11

skunk practice

in the industrial zone

DUE TO THE DARK of the fog rolling in from the Bay and my continued wariness of people out in the street, I decided not to risk the long walk down to the industrial zone. I took my car. After the revelation about the sand plant—shipping sand to this shore once lined with sandy beaches—I had begun to trace the progression of industries in the early settlement. Just as I backed out of the driveway, an image of the deserted streets below the tracks gave me pause. With the motor still running, I hurried back into the house to fetch Cleo for this possibly risky outing. Despite her nature—trusting to the point of foolhardiness—I hazarded the hope that Cleo might provide me with some protection (to say nothing of spirited good company!).

Thinking about those early industries, I wondered: What did they offer? What did they take? The sand was soon sold, used up. What else changed? I noted that the starch and grist mill, the lumberyard, the planing mill, the standard soap company (as well as the many factories that followed), were all built where supplies and goods could be shipped easily—along the shore. And the early settlers who nested along that same shore set up their homes near fresh, free-flowing water (for drinking, for vegetable and dairy farming, for power) at the mouths of creeks feeding into the Bay. So my search for remnants of early industries brought me to the original shoreline.

Earlier in the day, seeking buildings of early industry, I had called Stephanie. She'd had lots of suggestions, including the Suendermann Plumbing Company (c. 1875); the Cal Ink Industrial Site (1903–1978); and the Manasse Block Tannery (1898–1970), where cow, pig, and horse hides had been treated with tannic acid and made into nice leather. She described taking a tour of the tannery with the Landmarks Commission. "There were rooms with four-, five-foot ceilings and hooks to hang the animal skins. The walls were black from chemicals. The stink was sickening." Her voice lowered. "In a preliminary environmental review report in 1986, it was found that a train tanker car storing diesel fuel was buried down by the tracks. Did someone just dump it there? Out of sight, out of mind? Imagine the aquifer!" I couldn't imagine.

Stephanie had urged me, "Go down by the dump and check out the last remaining building built along the original shore. Behind it was a tidal slough that ran north to Fleming Point. That building's a storage warehouse now. But it was designed to be the Berkeley municipal incinerator." The incinerator was constructed in 1914 to dispose of garbage when huge numbers of San Franciscans, rendered homeless by the 1906 earthquake, moved their industries and residences to Berkeley. Later, when the incinerator failed and the city began to dump garbage into the Bay, Lewis and McDermott took over the structure for meat packaging, making it into a barn and a slaughterhouse.

A garbage incinerator. A slaughterhouse. Everything in me recoiled. And at the same time, perhaps for the very same reasons that I didn't understand, this building intrigued me. It wasn't exactly what I had thought I was looking for when I phoned Stephanie, but now I felt compelled to head down to see it. And to go at once, despite the hour and the fog.

I parked on B Street, past the dump at the very end of the

dead-end street, abutting on a few trees and shabby structures. Looking out through my car window in the direction of the Bay, past a high wall and a rectangular concrete building, I could see bumper-to-bumper traffic along the freeway. Here I was in a cul-de-sac, isolated, concealed in mist. I dreaded getting out of the car. Even Cleo, usually raring to leap into any new possibility, retreated into her cozy spot in the backseat.

Finally coaxing myself out, I met a shock of chilly air. A wash of fear flooded through me and I readied myself for skunk practice, reminding myself to note my breathing. The air tingled, damp with a faint odor of garbage. My nostrils quivered. An inland breeze whipped up torn plastic bags, sending them billowing and ghostly. Around me, a dark haze blurred the outlines of the nearby buildings as I strained to distinguish one from the next. Through the chain-link fence to the east, I made out a red fire truck and a series of bins; evidently this was an extension of the dump. To the west, I again scanned the concrete structure mostly hidden behind the wall and a high, slatted gate. To the northeast, through an empty lot, I noted a shedlike factory remnant decaying into the pavement. Behind the barbed wire in the dump area was a large warehouselike building. Where was it, this incinerator? What a pointless chase. I couldn't even figure out what it was I'd rushed here to see.

Back in the car, I leaned my elbows on the steering wheel, face in my hands. In the backseat, Cleo began to whine. When I finally looked up, the fog had begun to dissolve. Once again, I ventured out onto the street. I felt drawn to study the concrete building I had noted when I first arrived. It rose perhaps three stories to an ornamental mission-style roof. The whole structure seemed sealed off, impenetrable. There was something unnerving about it, a creepiness heightened by the thick wall enclosing it, the empty courtyard, and the barbed-wire coil over the slatted gate. There were no windows. This must be what I'm looking for! An incinerator wouldn't have had windows. There must have once been a tall smokestack, perhaps removed when the concrete chamber was reincarnated as a slaughterhouse.

High on the front wall of the building, from just below the roof, hung a metal fixture—a remnant of some sort of pulley system, perhaps for hoisting garbage or cattle? Hay to feed the livestock? Or maybe carcasses? Squinting through the slats of the gate topped with barbed wire (always barbed wire), I kept studying the tomblike structure. I had to force myself to stay put in this eerily familiar terrain surely borrowed from some dark and recurring dream.

At first I barely heard it, but it continued; a twittering began to irritate my attention. Then it swelled into quite a cacophony—raucous cheeps, sucking and spitting sounds, screeching, low warbles. Birds. As I followed these calls, I began to focus on a tree above my head, then below it, searching for flittering wings. I strained to see through the mist; a glimmer of afternoon sun revealed sudden color, a corridor of green. I took a sharper look.

A line of acacia trees and willows arched over . . . I did not know what. Another damp blast of wind took me by surprise. Where did it come from? Suddenly I recognized where I was. Between two tangled banks of vines and reeds, I saw the dark crack of a creek. Descending from the hills above, it flowed past me out toward the freeway and most certainly beyond, to a bay I could not see. Another rush of icy air carried a licorice scent, and I turned to appreciate the delicate sprays of fennel festooning the banks. This must be Codornices Creek, I thought, descending from the hills where I followed it when I first took my long walks with Cleo. Like the mouths of Strawberry and Schoolhouse Creeks, this would have been a likely spot for early industries. Cautiously, I stepped forward under the cover of the willows and looked up and down through the dissolving mist. At first, all I made out was a mess of green ferns and nettles. But on closer scrutiny, the scene came into focus, took me in.

Velvety orange nasturtiums cascaded through blackberry brambles and thickets of matted green. Water hemlocks, several feet high, waved their lacy umbels of tiny white flowers. Sprays of lavender and yellow Scotch broom shivered in the breeze.

Despite the racket, I hadn't yet seen a single bird. They had to be there. Above me in the willow I saw a plastic bag caught in a branch, swelling and rippling eerily. Then, at last, I saw the birds. High up in the willow perched four or five fat shimmery black and brown birds. They had to be starlings with their fluffy brown young; then, in another branch a California towhee called. Squeak, squeak, squeak. Somewhere, what could only be a finch continued its melodic warbling. I was absorbed.

Drawn farther in along the creek, I came on a wooden bridge, fragile and decayed. Not sure it wouldn't give way completely beneath me, I took a gingerly step. The view from this bridge took my breath. What had been tame turned wild: a surging of life along the steep banks—fern and goldenrod; even more nasturtiums, masses of heart-shaped leaves with vibrant orange and yellow flowers. Vines and creepers lashed around one another in a fighting exuberance for sunshine and space. And rising from the dark of the water below waved cattails three times my height and whorls of feathery horsetail, a plant heralded for dating back four hundred million years to the time when plants first crept from sea to land. The birdcalls seemed to multiply, reaching a crescendo. Then silence flowed back from the recesses of the tangle. I noticed the white morning glories twining throughout—delicate papery flowers like the serene faces of nuns amid this vegetative violence.

Startled suddenly by the headlights of a car, I jumped back from the bridge. I found myself on a dead-end street by some deserted buildings and a few trees. I had lost sense of time and space. Looking around at broken bottles and Styrofoam cups, at the decaying buildings of old industries, I remembered what had drawn me here. I took a renewed look at the concrete structure, trying to picture it here by the shoreline with the creek rushing past into the slough. Behind the taint of garbage, could I smell fish, taste salt? In a way I had not understood earlier, I got it—why this was the last remaining building built on the original shoreline. When cremation failed to solve the city's garbage crisis, they began to "fill and cover" in the slough behind the defunct incinerator and in large areas of tidal marsh- and wetlands. Clogged with garbage fill, the shoreline bulged and spread, diminishing the Bay.

To the north wound the creek—a reminder of this home terrain before the Europeans wrought their changes on the land. Now the creeks were mostly in culverts and, like the sand that had to be imported, water was piped in from the Mokelumne River high in the Sierra Nevada. To the west, cars sped on the freeway where the slough used to flow. To the south, in the direction of what was once Jacobs Landing, the early settlement had developed. Down several blocks now, a plume of black smoke churned, darkening the already-gray air. And from that spot, I thought I detected some sort of clanging. It had to be a factory—a working factory in this late-twentieth-century world. This world is my home. A breeze now from the south carried a new smell: burnt and chemical—not salt, not garbage, not the wild perfume of skunk, but fumes.

Maybe the next day, in this plunge into my neighborhood home, I would visit a modern-day factory, one sending out smoke right now along a street that only 150 years before was the original shoreline.

THE NEXT DAY, with my little notebook and pencil in one hand, Cleo tugging at her leash in the other, I headed down toward the factory zone. I passed a factory where they made ink. A group of workmen were sitting on the stoop out front, smoking cigarettes, drinking coffee. One guy had angled back his chair so he could sun his face. Through his visor, he seemed to be watching me yanked along by Cleo. He tipped back his brim and teased, "Who's walking who?"

"Just what I sometimes ask myself," I sported back. Then, worrying that these workmen might think I was spying, I made vague gestures toward hiding my little notebook in the sleeve of my sweatshirt. But the oldest guy in the group, perhaps noticing the notebook, leapt up and reached to shake my hand. "Name's Tommy . . ." he introduced himself. With some uneasiness, I looked into his pale, loose-skinned face and realized it was friendly. He leaned toward me, shaking his head. "Management's moving to the suburbs. Laying us all off."

"This is my home neighborhood," I said to explain myself, maybe to excuse the notebook.

"Yeah, it's all very well for the neighbors. No more ink smell. I know. People complain. But what about us? We depend on this job. I've worked here fifteen years . . . and that's nothing compared to him." He indicated his companion. "He's worked here twenty. . . . You going to write up our story?"

I found it too complicated to explain that I was not from the *San Francisco Chronicle* or the *Berkeley Voice*. "Not exactly," I said.

I continued to head down toward the larger factories. After crossing over the tracks, I hit B Street, the section I'd seen in the distance the previous day. Some of this broad industrial street was unpaved, but unlike the narrow dirt alley, it was full of rubble and potholes, some with slick puddles of suspicious content. Littered with blown-out tires, old box springs, broken bottles, and rusty nails (one of which I found embedded in my sneaker when I got back to my house), B Street was difficult to navigate. Huge warehouses and factory buildings lined both sides. The smell of industry was strong and I was finding it difficult to stay in contact with my breathing. But I coached myself. "When I breathe in, I know I am breathing in . . ." The clanging and fumes overwhelmed my senses.

As I regathered my attention, I noticed a sign posted by one of the buildings: "Detectable amounts of chemicals known to the State of California to cause cancer, birth defects or other reproductive harm may be found in and around this facility."

I read the sign through again.

I remembered the research I had been doing on breast cancer. Cancer is a disease of the DNA, a master molecule that encodes the genetic script of life. Cells become cancerous, dividing uncontrollably, because their normal genetic machinery goes awry. This can be caused by viruses, defective genes inherited from parents, radiation, and environmental poisons.

What am I doing here? I asked myself. Here I go to great trouble in my diet and lifestyle to protect myself from suspect chemicals to stave off a recurrence of breast cancer. Yet perhaps I'm someplace I really shouldn't be.

Ignoring the warning, I continued down the block past other facilities to a series of great open-faced factory buildings. I stopped to take in the tumult of sound: machines whirring, grinding, yammering; the whistle of discharging steam. A guy in a hard hat walked past me. "What are you making?" I called to him. Through the din, I thought I caught a few words. ". . . here are parts for eighteen-wheel trucks."

Was this the factory alleged by neighborhood activists to emit toxic substances such as phenol and formaldehyde? Despite carbon filters the company had installed in response to neighbors' health concerns, on some days the odors from that factory (or perhaps another nearby) were still pungent. All the way up at H Street, there were times when I still smelled that burnt-pot-handle stench. But before the air quality district would "confirm" my, or anyone else's, complaints, five neighbors needed to call about it within twenty-four hours and an inspector had to come out to verify all of those reports. By the time the inspector got there, the odor had usually dissipated. Winding Cleo's leash in tight, I continued to walk, watching dark plumes swirling into the sky. The twang and clangor from a great open foundry drew my attention. I gazed across the street into the cavernous darkness that was emblazoned by what seemed to be torches. Illumined by sudden flares of fire, men in hard hats and masks were at work. A loudspeaker blared out what to me were indecipherable orders punctuated by the high-pitched beep of a vehicle backing up.

Dizzy, my temples aching and my heart pounding, I was strangely exhilarated. Noticing a burning in my lungs, I turned to retreat. But Cleo, not quite done with B Street, stopped to sniff an old rubber glove left on the ground, then to squat and leave her mark.

Heading back up toward my house, I heard myself reciting mechanically, "As I am breathing in, I know that I am breathing in. As I am breathing out, I know that I am breathing out." But what, I asked myself, am I breathing in?

I recalled that the industries of the early settlement provided basics like soap, starch, and lumber—and in a mere hundred years evolved through sheet-metal working, meatpacking, and hide tanning to steel casting, ink making, and more. I remembered that the Bay Area has a high incidence of cancer and particularly of breast cancer.

It came to me that skunk practice in the hills didn't translate gracefully to the industrial zone. Skunk fumes may be noxious, but they don't destroy cells. Was this a risk I shouldn't take on? For Katy, for Patrick—just simply to enjoy staying alive, the joy of that—didn't I need to protect myself? But didn't I also want to learn whatever could be learned, then do whatever needed to be done, no matter what the risk? I didn't know.

When I got to my door, I had a sudden yen to return to the far corner of B Street I had happened on the day before. I hoped to remember the taste and feel of the original shoreline, to bring that as well to my circling questions. Reversing my course, I hurried to the car, shuttling Cleo into the back. At the dead end between the former incinerator and the current dump, I leaped out toward the greenness. I stood there for a while, breathing in the freshly oxygenated air. Just as I was about to leave, I noted high in the willow the billowing plastic bag, like a gossamer deva amid the rubble of industry protecting this secret refuge of Codornices Creek. Smiling, I got in the car to find Cleo sitting in the driver's seat. I drew her to me, enjoying the softness of her fur; the warmth and sturdiness of her body; the pure, unadulterated dog smell (no skunk, no fumes) filling my lungs. I rubbed my nose against hers, so cold, sweet, and wet.

SITTING IN THE YARD, I dig my fingernails into dirt enriched by composting life right in this spot behind my house, dirt carried here by the creeks flowing down from the hills and over thousands of years by the Sacramento and San Joaquin Rivers feeding into the Bay. I rub a little dirt between my forefinger and thumb: coarse grains of sand, sticky silt, clay, decayed roots and leaves, cat shit, fungi, bacteria. Skunk practice gets down to the fundamentals. Slowly I begin to articulate a thought: To know my home, I want to learn to inhabit the fundamentals—the creeks, the Bay, the air, the sand, the dirt. But it is indeed a challenge to recover this intimacy here in Ocean View, where it feels like the very terrain has lost contact with itself: the Bay clogged by landfill, the creeks culverted, the air fouled, the sand sold, and the dirt paved.

Chapter 12

homeless

in the yard

BY THE WINDOW overlooking our darkening yards, we leaned toward one another over a makeshift dinner. As so often on Sunday evenings, our family joined with our backdoor neighbors, Sheryl and Roy (Passover at their house, Christmas at ours). For the most part, on ordinary Sundays, we'd pool food for feasts of leftovers. In a rush of food making and eating activity that night, I staved off the worries and loneliness that tend to creep up at times as the sun goes down.

Dinner ended with a semblance of singing. Inspired by Sheryl, a musicals aficionado, lately we'd been resuscitating old show tunes. Off-key, with improvised rhythms and stumbling lyrics, the rest of us tried to follow along with Sheryl, her sure voice establishing the basics of melody and word. Katy, usually on the move, relaxed against my shoulder with her cheek grazing mine. Even Patrick, usually busy with the tasks of chef, found the rhythm, a whimsical eyebrow raised as he whistled the tunes. Sentimental songs from times past allowed us to tap into a common culture, into childhood longings and romance, and urged us to "have heart," to "go on with the show," to appreciate the "the sun in the morning" and "the moon in the evening"—basic cycles of the cosmos.

That summer, spontaneous dinners with neighbors seemed

to express precisely how I wanted to live. Neighborhood took precedence, proximity the determinant—a serendipity of what was given. Stationed in front of our open refrigerator, I'd peruse the larder while on the phone with Sheryl or Roy, who were simultaneously perusing theirs. Together we'd assess what we already had and make a meal of that. Here's what we're given; let's have a party with it.

Over dessert that particular evening, we looked out the back window. Beneath the dawn redwood, its dense needles in full summer bloom, we watched the raccoons, sated from Sheryl's cat bowls, trooping over toward Carmen's. Poor raccoons. They were under siege, threatened with homelessness. We had taken their side when they were blamed at last week's neighborhood meeting for overturning garbage, threatening pets with rabies, and digging up new plants. The woman from over on Delaware had hinted that we should poison them. But another woman had insisted we should trap them, get them out of our yards once and for all, and send them up north to the woods. As we rallied to their cause, the raccoon family ascended Carmen's back stairs, heading for her kitchen cat bowls. Roy shook his head. "These raccoons wouldn't survive up north. Like it or not, this is their home."

Just when I was beginning to doze off (true to my reputation, even when hosting guests, of barely staying awake after 9:00 P.M.), a burst of explosions shocked my attention. Gunshots? A car backfiring? Out the back window, through the darkness, it was difficult to discern what, if anything, was going on in the yard. From the street, what we now realized were firecrackers reached a staccato finale. Shouting followed, back and forth. Was it teenagers roughhousing, a fight down at the corner? Or was Dee out there somewhere drunk and yelling? Our little group in the kitchen drew together. I felt us shoring up, seeking mutual protection, bolstering our home against all catastrophes.

I CAN'T REMEMBER who had called a meeting to rout out possible violence, drug traffic, maybe prostitution suspected a few blocks down. Andy from down the block, the couple who lived between Andy and the church, and Joaquin from across from Sheryl and Roy were going. Patrick would stay with Katy, but I made a special effort to be there. It was certainly an embarrassment when the focus shifted to our '69 Toyota, to our tacit agreement with Dee that she could sleep there.

Neighbor after neighbor admonished me and Patrick ("her lawyer husband!?!") for our compliance. How could we encourage that "homeless vagrant" to store her bags of clothes and toss her bottles on their lawns and along the fences between their homes? "You know her daughter Donna took out a restraining order against her!" "She's not allowed to come anywhere near here!" "When she sets her foot on this block, we should call the cops!"

A respected community organizer—liaison between neighbors, the police, and the mayor's office, who had been invited to our meeting as a consultant—turned to me in shock. "You let her sleep in your car? Why would you do such a thing?" With an image of myself as naive do-gooder–cum–neighborhood nuisance, I could no longer look anyone at the meeting in the eye.

The thought of telling Dee to get out upset me in ways I did not understand. But on impulse, the following Saturday morning, I just did it. Fueled by the neighbors' criticism, I approached the Toyota, parked under the lush purple of the princess tree. Through the side window of the car, I could see Dee, her bad leg and her crutches propped up over the back of the seat. When I rapped on the glass, she awoke with a start. Recognizing me, she seemed relieved. "Just a minute, baby. I overslept." I told her I'd like to help her find somewhere else she might stay. She stared up at me with bewilderment. Not wanting to beat around the bush any longer, I finally told her, "You can't sleep in our car anymore."

Gripping one crutch, she raised herself into a sitting position. Jaw set and eyes averted, she transferred her belongings one by one from the backseat onto the sidewalk. An old sleeping bag, a bulging brown paper sack, and a plastic garbage bag filled with shoes and sweatshirts spilled out amid the velvety purple petals scattered on the pavement. Meanwhile, I could hear my own voice, shrill, going on about homeless shelters and dry-out programs. Dee's head turned away from me; she swiveled out of the backseat and, with some awkwardness, gathered her things. She adjusted her crutches and swung past me down the street.

After she was gone, I saw that she'd left a grocery sack with a giant-sized package of cheese and a large package of bologna. Maybe she couldn't carry anything else. Or was it that she hadn't thought I really meant it? Flustered, I carried the sack over to Grandma Darlene's and left it on her steps. After fiddling with the broken lock of the Toyota, I jammed it closed as best I could, twisted the old key, and made sure it was secure. In the glass of the side window, I caught the image of my face, like a mug shot at the post office.

Sick to my stomach, I climbed back up the stairs of our Victorian and interrupted Patrick, reading in the bathtub. "I kicked Dee out," I said. "I had to do it, didn't I?" I kept asking him. And he, "But you have done it. So why are you asking?" And I, finally, "Where do you think she'll sleep now?"

In the following weeks, Dee kept right on showing up to visit with Michelle and Grandma Darlene. But when she saw me, she'd cross to the other side of the street. I had several meetings with an alcohol and drugs counselor in charge of two beds for Berkeley residents in a county dry-out program. He told me to have him paged if I saw Dee hanging around the block, and if Dee expressed some interest, maybe he could help. At the end of the month, I called him and asked if he'd had any contact with Dee. "Yes indeed," he said. "I tracked down the lady myself." It turned out that she'd been arrested, and he'd visited her in her holding cell. In a spew of threats, she let him know definitively that she, as he put it, "wasn't interested . . . leastwise, not now."

A VIOLENT BLAST from the street ruptured the sultry stillness of the afternoon. Through my study window, I saw a semi-truck stopped, the driver leaning out of the cab toward the teenagers on the street. The truck rumbled off as the teenagers drifted into Grandma Darlene's. Cautiously, I stepped outside and descended the steps to find out what had happened. I was greeted by a gaping hole and missing posts along the stairs—until seconds before, the site of our mailbox. Reactions burst inside me—chaotic, fearful.

Jagged pieces of metal and posts from the balustrade were cast every which way around the sidewalk. The facing of our house had been battered by flying shards. I looked down the block toward Grandma Darlene's and on down the street with cars rushing toward the freeway. Soon Katy would return from swimming and come up these stairs. I was gripped by protectiveness. I pictured the metal mailbox exploding, engraving its menacing insignia in our very shingles. What had happened to our home?

Several hours later, I knocked on Grandma Darlene's front door. "Do you kids know anything about my mailbox?" I heard the threatening timbre of my own voice. Young Michelle stood in the doorway with Daryll from across the street. Donna was off at work during the day and Grandma Darlene, since her memory had deteriorated, rarely seemed to leave the inner recesses of the house. With Donna at work, there was no supervision for these kids. Young teens, more of them than I had expected—girls with halter tops and nose piercings and boys with baggy jeans and untied hightops—were milling around inside, some passing in and out of the screen door.

Michelle, with whom I'd often exchanged hellos and favors (car washes, a loaned jacket), whispered, "It was a bomb, one of them M-80s."

Daryll added, "You know, kind of a firecracker . . . The truck driver said he saw two kids run that way." He pointed toward the hills.

Something was trying to soften inside me, recognition of our shared history. I addressed Michelle and then Daryll. "I'm not saying you did it. You wouldn't do something like that . . ."

"Who'd do that to their neighbor, anyway?" murmured Daryll.

What could I say to that? But my punitive voice broke through. "The police will be coming over here to ask you kids what you know about this. What will you tell them?"

Michelle, chin jutting out, flashed back, "We didn't do nothing!" And Daryll demanded, "Why you coming over here asking us all these questions?" Both faces flattened, expressionless, eyes suddenly hooded. They don't seem to know any more about this than I do, I thought. I'm doing this all wrong.

As I turned to leave, I thought of Dee, how just the day before she had limped past, her shoulder hunched away from me. This enmity was the opposite of what I wanted. I felt an ache of tears.

Retreating from the kids, I climbed the stairs toward our home, and they retreated into Grandma Darlene's. As the cop car rounded the corner and the last kids ducked away from me, the screen door banged out a sharp whack—punctuating our separation.

FOR DAYS OUR FAMILY WAS JITTERY, the explosion having unbalanced what felt safe and familiar. After all, the mailbox quite literally had our number on it. Through that metal box, inscribed with our address, we had received communications from (and sent them out) all over the world. The mailbox felt like an emblem of our home. The bomb left me feeling so vulnerable—in some completely irrational way, threatened with homelessness.

The following Tuesday, I attended a meditation and talk at the Berkeley Buddhist Monastery. Once a month, Ajahn Amaro, a monk trained in the Thai forest tradition, would come down from his monastery up north to this monastery in Berkeley only a short drive from us. Homework and other family demands permitting, I would attend.

This evening, my thoughts circling with images of the dismantled mailbox, of the homeless Dee, of my threatened home, I sat in meditation. After a period of chanting, Ajahn Amaro gave one of his characteristically long talks. Unlike me, Amaro seemed to wax bright from early morning long into the night. At the close of his talk, as I unwittingly slipped into a nap, he invited the assembled to ask questions of the monks—himself; his co-abbot, Ajahn Pasanno, and the novice monk, Anagarika Larry. "Anagarika," Amaro commented, "means Homeless One."

Suddenly awake, I focused on that word. Homeless. "What is the Buddhist teaching around homelessness?" I found myself asking. Then I tried to explain, "Lately, I've been getting to know my home neighborhood and thinking a lot about the meaning of home, and about a homeless woman who also lives on my block."

"Voluntary homelessness and involuntary homelessness are different, of course," said Ajahn Amaro. "A monk chooses to be a kind of gentleman of the road, open to the sun and stars."

"As a monk, one moves toward relinquishing one's identity— toward undermining the false security of a conventional sense of 'home,'" Ajahn Pasanno continued. "When a monk packs up his gear and goes out walking," he smiled, "the more he carries, the hungrier he gets. . . ."

As I left the monastery and drove toward my house, I saw no one—no walkers, nobody in the BART parking lot, no cars on the road. The streets felt desolate. The moon sent out a pale light, revealing the hills to the east. As I struggled against sleepiness, the exhaustion turned into exhilaration. My mind seemed to tip, thoughts sliding at odd angles like litter from dreams.

At my driveway, no one was in sight. The only sounds were the flow of the freeway and the spatting of some raccoons in the yard. Scared for no particular reason, I felt my fragility, subject to the dangers of a city night, to the great sweep of unknown events. A glance at the balustrade, at the gaping hole, at the remains of the mailbox, and at the metal shards still on the pavement. Down the block, I caught a glimpse of the battered Toyota, the banged-in door. Now locked.

Despite the lateness of the hour, the dark of the street, I was taken with a sense of necessity. I had to keep on sitting there, to think some things through—about the mailbox, about Dee, about raccoons, about home and homelessness. Thoughts kept turning over, reversing.

Where was Dee sleeping tonight? I pictured people holed up in sleeping bags in the alleyway between D and E, on the ramp of the community hall by the Pilgrim's Rest Church. Images reeled through my mind of folks huddled deep into thin bags, of empty liquor bottles and chicken bones, of a homeless man Katy and I had seen by the library, defecating. A shiver of recognition. Was this the threat that Dee and other homeless pose for those of us householding folk? I felt such revulsion at the suffering. Maybe because it could be any of us—cold, hungry, sick. Do the homeless remind us of our own underlying precariousness?

So many contradictory thoughts, so many questions. What did it mean to inhabit this place? To inhabit myself? What makes a home a home? What makes homelessness a path, not an eviction? Once a home feels like a home, does it come with rights for those of us who live in houses? For people on the street? For teenagers? For raccoons? How large is home?

A thought came to me of our singing fests with Sheryl and Roy, our celebrations of what is given. Those familiar gatherings of neighbors felt suddenly precious and at the same time tiny, a corner on the edge of all that is given in this neighborhood, in this mixed-up flow of life events. Sitting in the dark car, I felt another surge of fear—fear of the street, fear of my own mind, fear of so many things; and underneath all of that, fear of not knowing, of not having anything to hold on to.

Chapter 13

on inhabiting

INHABIT. I'm still trying to plumb the meaning. Once, when I was having trouble using a word, Loie (with a helpful nudge) suggested that I consult the dictionary and follow the word back to its root meaning. (This led me from the limitations of the word *perfect* to the resonance of *complete*.) So now I get out the *American Heritage*. *Inhabit* traces back to the Latin: *in* plus *habitaire*, to dwell, and further back, to the Indo-European root, *ghabh*. At the end of the dictionary, I find a brief index of Indo-European roots. *Ghabh*: to give or receive.

In hot pursuit of more on "ghabh," I thumb through other home dictionaries and word root guides; I call up reference librarians and ask friends. A friend sends out e-mails to word-lovers from Muir Beach (here in California) to Paris. At the university, I get a pass for the art history classics library, where I photocopy key pages from the seminal dictionary on Indo-European roots, Julius Pokorny's *Indogermanisches Etymologisches Wörterbuch*. I am left trying to decipher my precious copy, which, it turns out, is in German, a language I have never studied.

Struggling along, I follow clue to clue. One line of roots means "give": *given* (Middle English), *giefan* (Old English), *gefa* (Old Norse). Another means "take" or "receive": *gaibid* (Old

Irish), *gabenti* (Lithuanian). *Gabhasti*, from the Sanskrit, means "hand."

THE NEXT DAY, walking the alley with Loie, I remind her of her advice years back. I tell her about *inhabit* leading to *ghabh*. When Loie hears that the roots trace back to the Sanskrit *hand*, she says it makes her think of the koan, what is the sound of one hand? Startling me, she whips her arm along her side, slicing the air with her bare palm. Her hand, fingers straight and strong, commands my attention, poised now, absolutely still, between her face and mine. "What?" I jump back.

"A hand gives and receives at the same time," she says. "There is no other."

"Yeah," I say. "When I think about inhabit this way, about home, it feels like there's only relationship: give as receive, receive as give."

AS I PONDER the meaning of *inhabit*, Stephanie joins me for another walk. In recent years, Stephanie's taken on a new preservation effort just down the block from my house: to research and save a native Ohlone shellmound, one of the approximately 425 around the Bay. Possibly the remains of this shellmound extend several blocks down from my house, beneath the parking lot of Spenger's Fish Grotto. The archaeological dig in the 1950s was several blocks farther west, under the parking lot of Truitt and White Lumber Company. With her characteristic zeal, Stephanie has started a newsletter (*Shellmounder News*); spoken out at the Landmarks Commission; and helped plan a conference at which she will host archaeologists, geologists, and descendants of the Ohlones. Just hearing Stephanie talk about this shellmound, I feel its call. After exploring the Victorian settlement, I can't wait to follow back fifty-seven hundred years into the world of the shellmound. The shellmound world draws me into vast views of evolutionary time, stirs my imagination.

But this morning, Stephanie and I put aside the shellmound for a walk and talk about Victorian Ocean View. At the close of our talk (which I diligently tape), I invite Stephanie into my backyard office for a few final questions. As a beginning investigator of the history of my home, I find myself wanting to know more about Stephanie. What drives this local historian who, more than anyone else, has immersed herself so thoroughly in learning the history of and preserving this neighborhood where she lives? I sit across from her under the dawn redwood, the tape recorder between us in the grass. "What is it," I ask, "that carries you with such passion to learn the history of Ocean View and to landmark what you find?"

From different angles, I continue to probe, wanting her to articulate something for me that I can't quite put my finger on. Here is this person with so much passion for her work; I want to know what she is trying to accomplish, what this work satisfies in her. I continue to push for an explanation but her answers don't satisfy me. I urge her to examine each motive for the motive behind that. Stephanie becomes less animated. The conversation turns awkward, then downright stiff.

Finally, Stephanie's eyes flare. "I could never ask somebody who's totally caught up in something—birds, or history, or whatever—to explain how they reached that level of passion. I'd risk dismantling that passion, and they'd go off and do something else!"

That's when I turn off the tape recorder. We sit there quietly for a few moments. Once the tape recorder is off, it's as if something has loosened. After some awkwardness, I feel my tight posture relaxing. I sense the dampness of the ground, Stephanie sitting next to me on this ground.

We begin to exchange back and forth again. I tell her, "I just realized that I'm trying to understand my own drive to learn this history." I recount the story of the skunk and how it led me back to this neighborhood. I even tell her about the word *inhabit*, and how I have traced it back to a fundamental "giving and receiving." In a certain sense, that's what it feels like is going on between Stephanie and me as we inhabit this exchange. I've pushed Stephanie. She's balked. In the quiet time we sat side by side, maybe we were reassessing each other in a kind of silent reciprocity.

As we talk now, I think I'm a little glassy-eyed. Maybe Stephanie is too. The timbre of her voice, like mine, seems to me to have changed. "I'm beginning to remember some more stories," she tells me. "One woman we interviewed just around the corner from here talked about the 1918 influenza epidemic and how it killed everybody off. At the Niehaus house, over on Delaware, everybody in that great big house died of influenza. Every last one. And then there's the story of one of the Heywood boys who died when his buggy slipped off the edge of the wharf." She pauses. "Even those early Victorians with their ramrod posture and corsets, they lived and they died. They're human beings, just like us. I want to convey that to other people."

She leans toward me. "For the shellmound dwellers, it was really more of a necessity. You had to learn the history of your home and pass it on. So you talked, like you and I are doing. Through word of mouth over thousands of years, you passed on how your ancestors got a shellfish out of a shell, or gathered tule reeds and caught waterfowl while still preserving the marshlands, or fished without outfishing the streams. You passed it on to the new generation, or neither that home nor its inhabitants were going to survive." She stops. I think she's done.

Unexpectedly, she begins again. "Even now, it's still a necessity. But we don't do it. That's what I want to do. I want to recover the history and then pass it on, especially to teachers and children who will continue to tell the story. If generations of local families know the history of this place, maybe they will stop and think about it . . . before they allow developers to plunge into some crazy scheme like filling in the shoreline, flattening historic buildings, or destroying native cemeteries."

After Stephanie has gone, I take a few moments in the yard. In the light of our conversation, I think of home in grand dimensions—through vast space and geologic time. I wonder if a shellmound dweller whose ancestors had inhabited the land over thousands of years might, in some sense, also have looked forward thousands of years. Such a person might be seen as an inhabitant—not just of a tiny tule hut, but of a whole world (bay, marshlands, meadows); not just of an hour's meal, but of a continuum. Of course, all this theorizing may just be romantic folderol.

I BEGIN A WALK down the block. Whatever the case with the mythic shellmound dweller, I sense I may be on to something. As I'm breathing in the oxygenated air from the remaining plants and trees and the chemical fumes of industry, I am breathing in the history of a neighborhood: the forty-five hundred years of native shellmound habitation, the hundred and fifty years of the European settlement, the accumulated karma of the last century of "progress." But I am not just breathing in. I am also breathing out. As I pass the history through the forge of my cells, I breathe it out changed. As I exhale carbon dioxide for the creekside horsetail and willows, I am part of the street's future moving through the millennia. Like Cleo, I leave my mark. Breathing in, I become intimate with family and neighbors, a rat, a skunk, a creek, a hidden alleyway, and factories too. Breathing out, I distill what I learn and live by that. Through ongoing giving and receiving, I inhabit what is beginning to feel more like home.

Geology

Four hundred million years ago, what was to become California was almost entirely under water. In Paleozoic times, as pioneer plants, mollusks, and arthropods invaded the land from the oceans, the jigsaw segments of the earth's rind—which are continually moving—slid into a new geometry. The North American plate reversed its direction and advanced westward.

In Mesozoic times (one hundred to two hundred million years ago), as dinosaurs roamed an earth green with ferns, horsetails, and conifers, the floor of the Pacific Ocean began to slide under the advancing edge of the continental North American plate. Born of the heat and pressure of the ancestral Pacific plate as it pushed beneath the continent, volcanic islands were scraped off and became part of the western margin of the North American plate. As mountains heaved into existence and rivers swept eroded soil into the ocean, North America began to grow westward.

In the Cenozoic era, beginning sixty-five million years ago, as mammals, grasses, and flowering plants diversified and swept the earth, erosion and deposition continued. Moving rocks of the sea floor slid into a trench along the edge of the advancing continent, scraping off muddy sediments, volcanic rock, chert, and sandstone to become coastal mountain ranges.

It was not until about twenty-five million years ago, when the ancestors of pigs, dogs, horses, whales, and birds had already evolved, that the California of today began to take form. In a radical tectonic shift, the relative motion of the Pacific and North American plates changed, meeting sidewise instead of head-on. The deep cracks or faults in the earth's crust shifted; these included the faults underlying the San Francisco Bay Area: the San Andreas fault (which runs up the peninsula) and the Hayward fault (which runs through the East Bay). The motion along these faults began to stretch the western part of the continent. Everything west of the San Andreas fault moved north, sweeping great mountain ranges three hundred miles north.

About three and a half million years ago, when the forerunners of humanity appeared in Africa, the Pacific plate turned and made another slight shift in direction, jamming its shoulder against much of California. The compression caused by this shift resulted in thrust faults parallel and subparallel to the San Andreas fault. Compression involving a number of these faults created the Berkeley Hills, which rise in sharp escarpment over the flatlands.

California continues to be slowly wrenched apart along the San Andreas fault, which forms the boundary between the Pacific plate (moving north) and the North American plate (moving west). The parts of California to the west of the fault are moving north at the rate of one or two inches per year relative to the rest of the state. Although most of the movement takes place along the San Andreas fault, some movement also occurs along a number of closely related faults. In the San Andreas fault system, the Hayward fault is one of the most active.

The rind of the earth consists of twenty or so vast tectonic plates, which are nearly all in continual motion. Earthquakes are the incremental steps in this continual plate movement. According to the U.S. Geological Survey, there is a high chance—particularly along the Hayward fault—of a major earthquake in the San Francisco Bay Area in the next thirty years. As the great tectonic plates move—scraping, tearing, and buckling against each other—the rocks along their edges rupture, sending out shock waves that sometimes result in violent shaking. It is impossible to accurately predict the time, size, or location of future earthquakes.

PART FOUR

Seeing

letting go of hope

At one time, I had wanted to find some place where I could take shelter, but I never saw any such place. There is nothing in this world that is solid at base and not a part of it that is changeless.

—from the *Sutta-Nipāta*

Chapter 14

vital statistics

exhaustion

A SIGN OVER THE COUNTER reads Vital Statistics: Birth and Death Certificates. In the waiting area facing the counter sits a line of people of various colors and ethnicities: many young parents leaning over strollers and holding babies; two darkly dressed women, one middle-aged, her arm around her bent and wrinkled mother. On the counter, two piles of forms prominently displayed under shiny red notices balance one another. One says, Birth Certificates, $12 and the other, Death Certificates, $8.

The form for birth certificates is on blue paper, the one for death certificates on white. On the wall behind the counter, just above and precisely between the blue forms and the white, hangs a daily calendar, freshly ripped to proclaim today's date. Here we are, right now, absolutely on target, between birth and death.

I've come to request the death certificates of suspected early inhabitants of our Victorian house. I'm following what seem like clues. But clues to what? I'm not sure. I feel a pull to risk: to solve a mystery whose very nature remains cloudy to me. I only know it isn't simply statistics, dates, or names. Anyone who delves into local history, as I do, must pass through this Bureau of Vital Statistics—which seems to me, as I survey my compatriots, like a special way station for the life cycle.

"BEGIN WITH THE HOUSE," Stephanie had said. So I explored: When was it built and by whom? How many families over how many life spans had lived here and made their imprint—on the house itself, on the yard, on the neighborhood, on the land—and were in their turn shaped by this land, this house? As I undertook my study, I began to imagine generations of lives grounded in this place, cycling through.

We moved in ourselves when Katy was in utero. Taking a look at our house now, as it is beginning to show signs of decay, I remember my first view. Through the weariness of pregnancy, I'd roused all the energy I could muster for that first arduous climb up the steps. Except for the spire of the Pilgrim's Rest Church, this was the tallest Victorian on the block. While to the practiced eye Carmen's Queen Anne—with its wrought-iron fence, scallops, and fans—might well have seemed more noteworthy, to us, our house-to-be made up for the grandeur of architectural detail through sheer size.

Once we entered, the tall ceilings (at least ten feet) belied the small footage of each room, particularly the living room, which opened up into the attic along an airy stairway to bedrooms we envisioned for us and the baby. From within and without, to us this house felt both grand and safe, rooted in a sturdy foundation in addition to a sturdy history—of what we imagined, in Victorian times, must have been an eminent Ocean View household.

JUST BEFORE CARMEN MOVED away to the foothills of the Sierras, she had offered to pass on all that she had gleaned on the history of our house and the rest of our corner. With Sheryl and Roy, she joined our family for dinner one evening. After dinner, I got out my journal and pen. Despite the lateness of the hour, excitement burned away my usual evening fatigue, and instead of falling asleep on the couch, I sat up and took notes. I didn't know quite what I wanted from Carmen's stories. Only the scent of lives.

Carmen had learned what she knew from Thelma Steel, who had lived across the street for many years, on the corner of Willow and H. According to Thelma, a Finnish carpenter who built and lived in Carmen's house had built all of the houses on this corner as well as other houses in Ocean View. Carmen pronounced the carpenter's name "Oh-fee," but wasn't sure how to spell it. So here he was, Offe (as I later learned)—not simply a resident, but a builder of houses. When we bought our house, we had been told by the former owners that it was built by a sea captain who might have built Carmen's as well. Was Offe a sea captain?

Carmen didn't know, but she had pieced together three generations of family history involving the houses on this corner. Carmen guessed that Offe had built Roy and Sheryl's house in back of his own for his daughter and her husband, who had moved in as a young couple and raised a daughter, Edna. In her turn Edna had lived there with her husband, someone named Wertman. "Yup. Sometimes mail is still delivered for Edna Wertman," Roy confirmed.

As we pooled our stories about the history of this corner, Roy conjured up a picture of three old ladies from diverse climes: Thelma Steel (English); Edna Wertman (German); and Mrs. Louie (Chinese), who lived where Paul and Genevieve do now. The three got together each day to catch up on the local scoop (perhaps somewhat as we neighbors do now). A Mexican family rented the front house from Edna after Offe died (with four girls, who slept in bunk beds in the little back bedroom, and seven boys, who all slept in the basement!). And black families, including Grandma Darlene and her husband, migrated here from the South during World War II as work opened up in the shipyards.

Edna's husband had a soft drink concession at the baseball

games of the Oakland Oaks in the old Pacific Coast League. One of Thelma's sons (she had two marriages, with children from both) would hop in the back of Wertman's Model T pickup and, hidden by the cases of soda pop, steal a ride out to the ballpark.

"Cool," chimed in Katy. "Can we go to one of their games?" And Patrick, "Nope, too late for that. I bet the whole league disappeared in the 1950s." But just for that moment, we'd felt it—the scent of lives.

As our guests left through the kitchen door and passed through the backyard to their homes, I joined Cleo on the dark landing at the top of our back stairs. Cleo was posted at her favorite watching place, her paws neatly folded over the top step. With Cleo, I took in the big view.

In its corner, reaching over the three yards, rose the dawn redwood. A smile. For a brief moment, I saw our local history from the vast perspective of that tree: generations of life passing through our little patch of land from all over the world—trees from China and Brazil; people from Finland, Africa, Mexico—a sense of vitality converging and cross-fertilizing.

It took a year after Carmen had passed on her farewell tales for me to begin planning my own research. But recently, I've gotten down to business. With a friend, I sat down to brainstorm over strategies. "I plan to read old tax records, to scrounge through realtors' files." My friend told me about her research into the history of her own family through church diaries in North Carolina and her plans for a summer trip to Scotland to trace her ancestry in ancient cemeteries. She said, "In reading these records and files, you're elaborating on your identity, incorporating a bigger history than your own history. It's a healing thing to do."

I didn't think it at the time, but as I mulled it over later, I noticed that for my foray into the genealogy of home I had chosen a history of my place, not my personal family. Having been on the run for so long, in so many apartments East Coast and West, what a relief it was now to have settled down in one place, in one house.

But more than that, I was not drawn to digging up the history of my family—divided by divorce; tainted in their views of one another by blame and caricatures; and, as city people, sparing in offspring. The history on both sides, as passed to me, was laced with feuds and heartache.

Oddly enough, on a parallel track, Katy was researching this personal family history for a school assignment. She pleaded for stories of our heritage, some of which I wished I didn't even know and many of which I was loath to pass on to her. There were prurient tales of both my Protestant and Jewish grandparents (romances conducted on the sly) and accounts of my mother's grandmother's weekly Shabbat, where two hostile wings of the family dined and lit candles every Friday night but never spoke. Maybe it wasn't so much the facts that rankled me, but the tone in which they'd been reported. Enough already.

Avid to begin my investigation—a refreshingly impersonal history—one evening, as was my habit, I stepped out onto the back landing. Now that Suzanna had moved in downstairs, there was more competition for the primo viewing spot. Cleo took turns with Suzanna's dog Radio, who would mosey up the back steps and claim the spot. That night, as I took my shift, it was Radio, placid and shaggy, whom I displaced.

Standing there as dusk descended, I made my usual pan of the adjacent houses—Sheryl and Roy's and what used to be Carmen's, where Zoe and Michael had just moved in with their toddler, Olivia. As far as I knew, the maybe-Finnish, maybe–sea captain and his offspring had inhabited our house and the others on our corner for generations. I pictured our tall Victorian, prominent on this block, resplendent with family. I was swept with unexpected loneliness—a longing more articulated than ever before—for the home I'd always wanted with cousins, aunts and uncles, and grandchildren; loving dinners of the extended clan; fireplaces roaring; the smell of the hearth.

To launch my research, I took a good look at our house, yard, and block. Stained by time, two rough-cut boards nailed on the wall of our laundry room created a makeshift plaque. The hastily painted numerals were barely legible. Was this the date our house was built? I studied the numbers: 5.18 scrawled in brown paint, and beneath that on the diagonal, 1894.

Engraved in a square of the sidewalk outside the Church of Pilgrim's Rest at Willow and G, I read, Dover St. (running east to west) and, catty-corner to that, G Street (running south to north). Incised in the center of the square was 1906. This was the year of the catastrophic San Francisco earthquake that sent refugees and businesses fleeing to Berkeley. In the rush of new development at the turn of the century, when our block was paved, our street—Willow Avenue—must have been named Dover.

Off to explore the goings-on in 1894 at the corner of Dover and H Streets, I collected maps and photocopied records and old photos. I made forays to the permit office, the Alameda County Recorder's Office, the Earth Sciences and Map Library, the Berkeley Architectural Heritage Association, the Berkeley Historical Society, and the university's Bancroft Library.

Kneeling over massive leather-bound tax assessors' books, I searched the Berkeley Land and Town Improvement Association tract for our house. Founded in 1873, this association basically extorted the land from the impoverished Spanish rancheros and, after the opening of the university, promoted development and settlement. In the 1909 block drawings, I found our lot not far from the lots of several farms. Ours was owned by a certain Jose de Rosa (a new actor in this drama). In the corner lot, there was F. Offe. (So I confirmed Carmen's story and learned to spell his name.)

Having stood in long lines, made copies of countless documents, deciphered faded microfiche; having met with the roofers about to replace the roof on our house and carpenters to replace the front porch; having dipped deep into our savings to pay the bills; having driven to and from soccer, consulted on homework, made dinner, and read Katy a good-night story, I tossed Cleo off the couch and collapsed. I propped up my feet and settled into the cushions with my notes and photocopies. Every organ depleted, every limb weighted, I was worn out.

Joining me on the couch, Patrick adjusted his glasses ("I've had a long day too"). I leaned against him, following his progress as he began to look through my sheaf of folders. With his lawyer's acumen, he took note: "Passed through a lot of hands." Shuffle, shuffle. "Looks like they must have rented it out." He studied my copies of the realtors' photos, each more modest—or downright paltry—than the next. I found myself feeling discouraged.

I got out the copy of a 1910 fire insurance map and scanned the Church of Pilgrim's Rest and the Scandinavian Hall, the rectangles to scale that indicated houses. "Ours is the smallest," commented Patrick. More shuffling. Indeed, amid all of the rectangles, I found one small box, considerably smaller than the ones on either side. "No wonder they rented it out," said Patrick. I added, "So much for our grand Victorian, centerpiece of Ocean View!"

Of course, it made some sense. We knew that contractors bought the house after the fire and proceeded to rebuild it, creating an apartment below by raising the whole building up, making it tall. But it had never occurred to us that in early Ocean View, our house was the runt of the block. Despite his scoffing tone (we'd always prided ourselves on our nonmaterial values), I was guessing Patrick might have been feeling disappointed too. So now we sat around making quips about our little box, and feeling (at least for my part) increasingly crestfallen.

"Time to order up some death certificates," Stephanie had urged me when I reported in. "All you need are your first precious names!" So here I am at the Bureau of Vital Statistics. With my white form, I feel, in some ridiculous way, awkward in this room full of new parents whose blue forms signify birth.

After a day of standing on line at county offices, I sink gratefully into a vacated seat. As I drift into a semidoze, the scene takes on a mythic cast. This special Bureau of Vital Statistics, way station for the life cycle, seems to draw people from all over the world. I sit next to an Indian woman in a sari and a Mexican woman (both with babies in tow), across from a turbaned man with his wizened mother. I think of the Company office in Conrad's *Heart of Darkness*, where two women Fates knit their black wool, sending adventurers down the river into the darkness. So here I am at what I imagine to be a required stop for someone on an adventure such as mine—a quest to find home, to encompass its history.

I've come here to follow the lineage of families who once lived in my house, to make that history mine, to feel perhaps part of a continuum in my home place. But through some unexpected alchemy, by initiation in this mythic bureau, the exploration itself becomes my instruction. "Bone tired," says the woman in the sari as she rocks an infant in her arms. And the Mexican woman returns, "Three children and none of them sleep." Waiting for my death certificate, I join in this exchange with my own tales and, in the spirit of this bureau, I tap into fundamental cycles—living and dying, giving birth, tending babies, and taking care of aging mothers.

"Barbara Gates," calls the clerk. Pulse quickening, I step forward. No records on Jose de Rosa or Frederick Offe, I'm told.

"No," I hear myself protest. "At least Offe. You've got to have his record!" His story's been confirmed. I heard it. I saw it. I gesture wildly toward the inner sanctums of the office. "I know Offe's in there somewhere." Indeed, the Offe family was known to have lived on my very own corner—for generations. I lay claim to this history.

"Well," the clerk allows, "we do have a few people with that last name." She pauses. "But not him." When I look at her eagerly, she reminds me, "Eight dollars." So, as I begrudgingly write another check, she prints out a death certificate for Annie Offe.

It's an official document on stiff paper with a pale pink floral pattern, blue edging, an embossed emblem: the Great Seal of the State of California. Stamped in red over a raised health department seal is today's date. The photocopy is in reverse; framed in pink floral, the black square with white entries becomes what looks like a mandala. Running my forefinger along the raised seals, I read down the left column. Yes, this is the wife of Frederick Offe.

Date of Birth: June 7, 1857. Age: 75 yrs, 6 mo, 8 days. Occupation: Housewife. Birthplace: Hanover, Germany. Father's name: Bening. Length of residence in city, town or rural district of death: 50 yrs.

Turning to the right column, I see it's signed "(informant): F. Offe." This column focuses on the death itself. I begin to decipher the script. It is hard to make out the principal cause, "Nephritis Interstitial." Some kidney disorder, I think. "Other contributing causes of importance:" In bold cursive, there's one word: "Exhaustion."

Exhaustion. My lip quivers. For just that second, I sense this woman: Annie Offe—born in Hanover, Germany; housewife; married to a Finnish carpenter, I surmise, for more than fifty years; living in the house on the corner of Dover and H; offering all that she had, even more than that; managing marriage, children, a house, just to live. I feel it too—just to protect our own, to carry out the simple tasks of life.

THAT EVENING, while Patrick is doing the dishes, I sink down into my favorite couch, relieved by the quiet now that the roofers have gone home and the hammering has stopped. Both Cleo and Radio are lying around the living room. Lounging here by the two sleeping dogs, I reflect on exhaustion. I think of the exhaustion of bleary-eyed new parents, of wailing babies, of someone's aging mother just wanting a place where others can tend to her. . . . I appreciate Patrick (his long day) and, yes, how worn out I am from doing my tasks—keeping up with my work as an editor; tending a house, a family, a body as it ages. Underneath all apparent differences, there's what's in common. Tonight I feel the exhaustion of any living thing as it meets the challenge to survive.

From my girlhood, a memory of my own mom comes to me. Often in the late afternoon, worn out from the clashes of the day, she would take a few moments before cooking dinner to lie down on her bed. She would pull a throw blanket up to her breast and close her eyes. All the tension in her jaws and cheeks and around her forehead would soften, smooth out. I wish I could see it now—her peaceful face, free from all efforts to get things done, to insist on her way, even to smile, to please.

Beyond the exhaustion from everyday survival, I notice something extra. It's a weariness from so many battles within my own mind—to make my family, my workmates, my friends, my neighbors into something other than what they are. Even this house, once the runt of the block (I begin to smile), how fiercely I've held to my picture of its history, the grandeur, the breadth and substance. But all clues suggest I let go this absurd fight.

This is extra—the exhaustion of looking for something outside of what is here. Basic Buddhism, yes, but quite a trick.

Can I settle into this place, just as it is, as my home? I breathe in the history of this house, all the families who have lived here on our corner, all the mothers and fathers who stretched their possibilities—and more than that—who used themselves up in the daily round.

This is one of those rare times that I'm still up after Patrick has gone to bed. Am I any closer to naming the mystery I seem to be trying to solve? I don't know. But late into the night, I feel some complex knot beginning to loosen; a sadness passes through me, pure and sweet, for Annie Offe . . . and through her, for the rest of us.

Chapter 15

homeless

an interlude with dogs

WHILE CARPENTERS PRY decayed shingles off the side of our house, Cleo digs and scratches, whines and worries her nose along the bottom of the fence between our yard and Grandma Darlene's. Pushing under the fence from the other side is a little black nose. Then I remember: it has to be Dee's new puppy. This is confirmed by high-pitched yelps from the other side of the fence. Now I'm sure. It's definitely the pup, tied up in the alley between our two houses; maybe she's in the little dog hut that Dee got years ago for the other puppy, the one who was strangled.

Mostly I've kept Cleo on a tight leash, protecting her from other dogs. And I've assured myself that this is for good reason, particularly after skirmishes at dog parks and on hiking trails. (Often I've bemoaned Cleo's probable traumas prior to her rescue from homelessness, before the Animal Referral passed her on to us.) So with Dee's new mongrel pup, I picture a brawl. I order Cleo to come in the house. She refuses. After all, she's now in an alliance with Radio, who's out in the yard too, sniffing at the fence. The two of them are staying put.

When Suzanna applied to rent our downstairs flat, we'd told her that we didn't allow pets, that Cleo couldn't tolerate another dog (nor could the yard or the house). At the first meeting between the dogs, Cleo had barred her teeth, growled, and made a territorial pounce. But Suzanna and Radio definitively won our hearts, and now Cleo—aging, with filmy eyes and an arthritic gait—perks up when she hears Radio and whimpers to join her friend.

So here they are, pals: Cleo, long haired and glamorous in black and white, with a plume tail and silky ears, an Australian shepherd (maybe border collie mix); and Radio, another rescued mongrel, her own odd mix of wheaten terrier and yellow Lab with a soft coat the color of wheat that fluffs out, Hollywood-style. Now, with senses tuned to the pup, the two senior dogs flank the fence, enjoying the side yard littered with shingles from the house-in-progress.

Inside the house, the constant banging of hammers can be insufferable these days. In fact, house renovations seem to be dominating our family life with noise, dust, and general inconvenience. It can be a relief to step outside to see the dogs. Radio has a station on the grass while old lady Cleo claims a spot in the cool of the dirt by the fence, closer to the puppy. Certainly these dogs do prompt my worries with their digging, yet in the sultry September heat, they bring a spirit of lazy comfort and camaraderie to our home.

WHILE THE PUPPY has shown up often this week, I haven't seen Dee since the day last week when she suddenly appeared after a long absence. Ever since I told her she couldn't sleep in the car, Dee has been avoiding me. When she's hung out on the corner by the liquor store or come by to check in on Grandma Darlene and young Michelle, she's averted her face from mine. Come to think of it, she's rarely been in the neighborhood at all for months. After all, there have been two restraining orders out against her forbidding her from coming within a hundred yards of her former home. One was signed by Donna, who has been in charge of the house next door ever since Grandma Darlene's stroke. The second was signed by a neighbor on the far side of Grandma Darlene's, who says that Dee threatened him and his family. So Dee has known that if anyone sees her on the block and reports it to the police, she'll be arrested and sent to jail (unless she hightails it out of here before the squad car arrives).

But one morning last week, when I was backing out of the driveway to take Katy to school, I saw Dee in the rearview mirror and caught her eye. She was out in front of Grandma Darlene's talking to Michelle. Glad at last to make contact, I pulled to a stop, called out, and waved. Without a word, she bolted down the passageway between the houses and disappeared.

That afternoon, when Katy and I got out of the car and were heading up our stairs, there Dee was again, rattling down the street with a supermarket shopping cart. In the cart was a small yipping puff of fur. "I got me a new puppy," Dee shouted over to me. And as I backtracked down the stairs, "This morning I told Michelle you was going to report me to the police. She says you wasn't."

"Nope." I went over to join her at the foot of Grandma Darlene's steps where, later in the afternoon, Michelle and her friends would be hanging out. Even though I had lived next door for over ten years, I had rarely come even this far into Grandma Darlene's household.

"That wasn't it," I told Dee. "I was stopping the car to see how you were doing."

Warily, Dee assessed me. "It don't matter what they tell me. I just come here to see my mama."

I could smell the alcohol, but her mood seemed amicable. "How'd you come by the new dog?" I asked.

And she, "I got my puppy over the other side of the freeway by the racetrack; there's a dog lady. She keeps every kind of mixed-up dog. And then some."

When I approached the cart, the scroungy little pup cowered

and growled. On sudden inspiration, I sent Katy back into our house to get some of Cleo's biscuits. Dee went on, "I'm keeping her over in my friend's backyard across town. You know, my older daughter don't like dogs. But when she's at work, I'm gonna tie up my little babe there in the doghouse." A pause. "I call my pup Honey."

"Honey," I said experimentally, holding out a biscuit. The puppy snapped for the biscuit, then shrank back into the corner of the cart.

Dee told me, "This one's a cute little mongrel pup just like the last one." (The mention gave me a shiver.) Glancing affectionately at the puppy, she added, "I'm taking care of her like she was my baby."

SINCE THAT MEETING, Dee has made herself scarce, but somehow the puppy has continued to show up in the alley next door. Seemingly oblivious to the clang of hammers as work continues on the roof, Cleo and Radio camp out by the fence, riveted on the potent puppy whines and scent. A third again the heft of Cleo, Radio's as placid and slow as Cleo is spirited; she makes up for energy with sheer stubbornness. When the two of them begin to dig, I intensify my efforts to get them inside. In fearsome shouts, I command Cleo to "come here this minute!" She glances over at the stalwart Radio, then eyes me with an intractable stare: No matter what you say, I'm not going to budge.

And I continue to fret. What if Cleo digs under the fence? I refuse to go over there to retrieve her. I've never been in Grandma Darlene's yard or in that alley, and I don't want to have to go. Narrow and littered with old clothes, blocked by the little makeshift dog hut, the alley feels like a kind of no-man's-land between our two households.

One morning, Suzanna joins me in the side yard. In the

sunshine, her beige linen dress sets off her skin, dark and radiant. She laughs when I tell her, reminding me, "In the Caribbean, we don't compliment people on how they look." She's come out to attend to a more serious concern; standing on tiptoe, she checks out the puppy on the other side of the fence. Indiscriminate animal lover that she is, she's worried that the pup isn't getting enough to eat. So Suzanna and I stand in the side yard, watching the dogs and exchanging our contrasting worries. Through Suzanna's eye, this little hut in the alley is sadly inadequate for a pup who deserves a home.

As the older dogs keep digging toward the puppy, I find myself thinking again about home, about homelessness and makeshift homes. I keep remembering the Toyota, how Dee used to sleep there, how we just about invited her to do that, how I kicked her out. I remember the feel of the Toyota. That backseat was narrow, the plastic seat covers slick and stiff. The space in the back so tight, confined. I try to imagine what it might be like sleeping on such a bed, in such a space—the windows and broken door of the Toyota the only shields from the cold and other dangers of the city, of the night. How blessed I am for my comfortable and sturdy house, to share that with my family. I try to picture taking that risk myself, to sleep out in the Toyota on the street, or even in the yard—just one night—so alone, so vulnerable.

PURSUING MY THOUGHTS on homelessness, the next Tuesday evening, I attend the meditation with Ajahn Amaro. Again I bring up my interest in home, in homelessness.

Ajahn Amaro explains, "A monastic chooses to leave behind the 'household.' Think of the word *householder*—one who holds a house." He chuckles. "In the scriptures, the household life is often described as 'cramped.' Yes, a monastic moves toward homelessness—which is open. As a 'gentleman of the road,' he has a kind of raw contact with everything. The world is his home."

It's the reverse side of involuntary homelessness, of course, the homelessness of the monk, and a radical flip on the meaning of home as well, turning all other notions upside down. Only too well of late, I see the "hold" the house can have on the householder, the demands, the expense. I do sometimes feel so weighed down, so full of household concerns that I am not open to the world. But the household is also what I love, what I've chosen. There are so many angles on home, on homeless.

The next day, I come out in the yard. Amid piled-up shingles and cans of nails, there's young Honey with the two older dogs. A frayed piece of rope trails from her collar. So she's the one who finally dug through. She must have broken free from where she was tied on the other side of the fence and scrambled under to get to her friends on our side. She's finally made it, this little tramp pup—part chow, part I don't know what, her arc of a tail waving, curving forward over her stubby legs and barrel chest.

When I try to sidle up to Honey to give her a friendly scratch behind the ears, she offers a growl and shrinks away. But she romps with Radio and invites Cleo (intrigued but socially inexperienced) to play as well. Honey may be scared and skittish with people, but she's easy with dogs. Indeed, Cleo has known that all along, as she's sniffed along the fence, whining with anticipation. So now these three once-homeless mongrels claim a home together in the side yard like lost siblings.

Late in the day, Dee finally shows up, a little sheepish to have left Honey so long unattended. I haven't seen Dee since she came by with Honey in the shopping cart. And when I think back, as long as I've lived here, I can't remember Dee ever having traversed the fence between the two households, ever having come over into our yard before. We chat with some awkwardness. I ask Dee, "Have you started getting her shots?"

"You know I don't have money for something like that," she says, her speech a bit slurred.

To my own surprise, I hear myself offer, "I'll take care of Honey's shots."

I hesitate to give Dee money for the shots, afraid (perhaps unnecessarily) that she'll spend it on drugs or alcohol and Honey never will get to the vet. So I make a plan to meet Dee a few weeks hence out in front. We'll walk across town together to the Humane Society.

It feels like a good plan. Thank goodness for the dogs for their raw call—heart to heart—for bringing us together. Ordinarily, we two humans barely have contact and never cross over (and certainly not under!) the fence.

With far-flung challenges from homeless monks and once-homeless dogs, I once again examine my sense of home, and particularly my sense of house as home. Can I center my life in my "household" home without letting that household—and all that it carries—cramp me or weigh me down, without letting it separate me from neighbors, or from finding home in the broad world?

Chapter 16

vital statistics

safety

THE LAST-DITCH, but irrefutable, way to verify the year your house was built is to check the value of your property in old tax assessor's ledgers, looking for an "improvement." As Stephanie puts it, "*improvement* is a euphemism for *house*." As I prepare for a trip to the university library to study these old ledgers, Patrick and I riff on the concept of "improvement." We consider our house from this angle: an "improvement" over the raw land.

We recall our own first "improvements" on the house in the wake of our hard-won pregnancy, how we set to work, driven by an imperative: at all cost, protect the baby. Drawing on money we didn't have, wherever we could, we fortified. For protection against earthquakes (the most ominous of threats to all Bay Area households), we bolstered the foundation. We strengthened the heating, insulation, and roof. We installed cabinet closers and plug covers in every room and protective slats and lattices on every deck and stairway. With visions of tumbling disasters, we carpeted the attic stairs (which Katy—at age one— did indeed somersault down, coming to a rude finale on her derriere on the softly carpeted landing, startled but unharmed). Even as we reminisce, this work is ongoing, with carpenters following the roofers in new efforts to fortify: replacing decayed windows, all from the original house; and replacing rotten boards in the trim, the facing, and the front porch before the rot begins to eat into the very frame of our shelter. Laughing now, we ask ourselves about the purpose of this "improvement," better known as a house. For one thing, protection from cold, heat, wet, earthquake, and other sundry dangers. Safety.

We remember the first challenge to the safety of our household, the 1989 Loma Prieta earthquake caused by rupture of the rocks along the San Andreas fault. The Bay Bridge, which spans from San Francisco to the East Bay, partially collapsed, leaving Patrick in San Francisco, separated from me and Katy (not yet a year old) in our house in Berkeley. This was scary for a risk-averse beginning mother. For protection against fire, I turned off the gas; for protection against continued shaking, I took down heavy glass-cased paintings (the ones that hadn't already shattered on the floor). When Patrick did get home, our family drew together. For several days, as the house shivered on and off from the aftershocks, we all slept in one bed. It might not have been true, but it felt like this bed in this, our own house, was the safest possible place to take refuge as a family.

DRIVEN BY A PASSION I still don't fully understand, I urge myself onward in my quest to study this corner, to learn the history of the houses—the hopefully safe harbors—and the families as they passed through. I continue on what feels like an odd type of adventure—not up a creek or an alleyway, but reading down columns.

Rolled out to me one at a time on a dolly, wrapped in butcher paper and tied with twine, the tax assessor's ledgers of the 1890s are massive gold-edged leather volumes, meticulously calligraphed in elegant script. In the silent space of the library—having abdicated my briefcase, purse, and pen—I peruse down column after column with ceremonial attention, study the "improvements" on what was still mostly open meadows and pastures. Finally, in the 1895 ledger, I find Jose de Rosa. "Value of city and town lot: $250. Value of improvement thereon: $600." (A silent hooray as I find a match for the plaque in the laundry room.) As I rewrap this ledger in its butcher paper, I appreciate these careful records honoring one version of home: the relation of family to house, house to land.

On my return to the Bureau of Vital Statistics, I'm in the ceremonial mode, now following the records not of the houses but of the families who lived in them. The clerk brings out the death certificate for Edna Wertman, who I learn was the daughter of Elizabeth Offe and William Francis Cleary and worked for the Pullman Railroad Company (I think of the train tracks a few blocks below our house). Edna Wertman died at seventy-five of "surgical complications due to an accidental fall in her residence," which was indeed 1820 H Street. When I read her mother's (Elizabeth Offe's) certificate, I learn that she was the daughter of Frederick Offe and Annie Bening, "birthplace of mother, Germany, birthplace of father, Germany." (So Offe wasn't Finnish at all, but German.) Like her daughter, Elizabeth Cleary worked for the Pullman Company and died at seventy-one of "a perforated gastric ulcer and a carcinoma in the rt. breast." (A tender pull toward these people—my carcinoma was also in the right breast—who lived and married and bore children, who worked and suffered illness and died.)

IN THE EVENING, I collapse once again into the softness of our living room couch. I read over my death certificates. Katy joins me on the couch, and when I think she may kick me a soccer ball, she offers to paint my toenails, then showcases a panoply of colors. Surprised and touched, I extend a foot, soon adorned in Ardent Umber. When Katy's done with my toes, without comment she paints her own fingernails Icelandic Blue.

For the past several years, Katy has cut her hair in a boyish bob and worn shorts and soccer shirts exclusively (except for Christmas and at an older friend's bas mitzvah, when she begrudgingly offered to wear long pants instead of shorts). She's found plenty of passions from sports to bird-watching far more compelling than looking at herself or combing her hair. After the crescendo of cake and juice at the final fifth-grade bash, it felt to me as if Katy suddenly noticed herself in the mirror. At any rate, she began to take time to part her hair on the side or to draw it back with a band or kerchief. And she took to wearing earrings shaped like miniature turtles.

Tonight, she tries on an outfit she might wear for our trip back East for my mother's eightieth birthday party, a silky red skirt and a black tank top with skimpy straps. Later, stretched on the couch opposite mine, she leaves on the tank top with her soccer shorts. I look over at her, amazed at the shift from the sprite she seemed just weeks before. Settling more comfortably into my couch, I extend my tired limbs, spent from a long day and poor sleep I've never been able to improve since the medications for cancer and inevitable changes in my own cycles. Half-dozing, I lie there admiring my daughter—amazingly, just eleven and a half years ago she was in the protection of my womb. Now, with her hair pulled back, high color in her cheeks, turtle earrings, bare arms, and legs strong from soccer, she looks so vibrant and pretty, with hints of the young woman she will someday become. She glances my way. "Mom," she protests. "Stop staring at me!"

I remember once when I was Katy's age, I had spent the weekend at my grandparents' apartment on Manhattan's Park Avenue. My grandmother enjoyed her special lady's boudoir outfitted with a dressing table and chaise longue. I loved to stay with her. Once, after a leisurely soak in the bathtub, a dousing of Jean Naté cologne, I ran out naked to get my pajamas. My grandmother exclaimed in appreciation, "Young bodies are so beautiful!"

Since my initiation at the Bureau of Vital Statistics, I've found myself consumed with thoughts of babies, of growing old, of dying, and (somewhere in between all that) of growing up—memories of coming into womanhood able to carry on the life cycle. Casting a brief look back now at Katy, I have a mix of feelings: of pleasure in her loveliness, and then a shiver. In this new phase, I sense a new kind of vulnerability. I am overcome with protectiveness.

And I am confused. It's my job as her mother to protect her. But another part of my job, as she grows, is to let her find her way. Then there are the Buddhist teachings reminding me that ultimately I cannot protect her from the inevitability of change—of growing up, of aging and dying, of the dangers of our warring planet, as well as the great heavings of the earth and the ongoing collisions and burnings of the cosmos. I feel an impulse to keep Katy safe in the house with me, to shield her from all dangers. I think of the Buddha's father, King Suddhodana, known in teaching tales for his obsessive protectiveness, who locked up the young Prince Siddhartha to try to keep him safe in the palace, protecting him from even the knowledge of sickness, old age, and death. I love this tale which teaches through opposition, dramatizing the very obverse of the Buddhist path—a path of inclusion, of opening to whatever is true, of risking to encompass what a friend calls "the full catastrophe."

AT THE END OF THE WEEK, strong winds whip in from the Bay, shaking our house. Now encased in scaffolding and wrapped in netting as painters burn off the old paint, the house rattles and billows. Late in the afternoon as the winds pick up, sending trash along the gutters, I can't resist one more try at the Bureau of Vital Statistics.

Already the lights are dimmed; this bureau of the life cycle is closing down for the weekend. But I'm determined to find Frederick Offe. He's the one I feel I've got to track down: the builder, a progenitor of this family who inhabited our corner through generations. I waylay the clerk. "Do you think you could do one last search for Frederick Offe? You found his wife and that was so helpful."

She gives me a sniff. "Well, there was just one more Offe listed: William." Maybe his brother. I write out another eight-dollar check.

It's almost closing time when she returns to the counter. She begins to organize the checks in the cash register, turning off some lights. "Been a hard day?" I ask, trying to soothe her, knowing full well that my demands have contributed to the difficulty. Another sniff.

Finally she hands me the death certificate for William Hans Offe. "Father: Fred Offe. Mother: Anna Bening." (Indeed it is family.) "Address: Willow Avenue." (He lived with his parents.) "Occupation: Carpenter." (Like his dad.) "Informant: Fred Offe." (Died before his dad. Rattled, I review what I've read.) "Male. White. Single. Date of Birth: Mar. 18, 1880. Date of Death: Mar. 16, 1913. Age: 32 years, 11 months, 28 days."

The clerks are turning off more lights, straightening up their desks. Hurriedly, I read down the second column. "Cause of death: Bullet wound in the brain." Then, several lines down, in parentheses: "Suicide."

A shudder of responses—nausea, excitement, shame. Now I've got the real dirt, I think, the stuff of fiction, and in the next breath I am afraid. I shouldn't know this. I've gone too far.

All evening while I drive home, make dinner, and try to get to sleep, I am preoccupied by this young man. I can't stop wondering, even worrying, about him. He shot himself, I note, two days before his thirty-third birthday. What sequence of events could have turned so dark that he felt compelled to end his young life? I keep reading over his death certificate searching for further clues.

As the painters continue to wash and sand, winds from the Bay pick up and the dark netting draped around our house flaps like a giant sail. Cleo, Radio, and little Honey next door pace and howl. I am taken by old fears, a sense of precariousness, of the extent to which life can prove itself unsafe. The stories of the early inhabitants of our house—jumbled in my mind—get mixed up with my own stories. There's no assurance that a parent can protect a beloved child. Frederick and Annie Offe were parents too.

Each investigation at the Bureau of Vital Statistics offers an occasion to learn something about my own family and myself as well and most of all, to see beneath the individual story to the ways of human beings—fallible, sometimes poignant, with our fears and our yearnings. As I mull over the yearning for safety, the drive to protect, I think of the Buddhist teachings on refuge. In Buddhism, taking refuge is said to offer another kind of safety. A student takes refuge as an initiation to the path of practice. This is refuge in the awakened mind (the Buddha), in the truth of the way things are (the dharma), in one's community (the sangha).

But as I try to understand refuge as safety, I balk. Safety from what? Certainly not from exhaustion, accident, or carcinoma in the right breast.

Talk about taking refuge as safety feels to me like a trick— along the lines of that other trick, the one that I began to unmask as a child, that I continue to unmask. It's the promise that those older and wiser than myself would take care of me, that everything would be all right, that there would be a happy ending. So in taking refuge as a student of Buddhism, sometimes I feel as if I'm going along with a false promise in which I can't put my trust.

Continuing to reflect on William Hans and his family, on all the uncertainties of life, I call a favorite meditation teacher, Gil, and ask, "Isn't it said in Buddhism that taking refuge offers a kind of safe home? I don't see how anything could possibly offer safety." He says, "Of course it's not the conventional safety; it's not that all kinds of painful things won't happen in the world, in your life." After a pause, "But if you live your life in such a way that it is an expression of refuge—of your innate good-ness—you know that you're not going to add any suffering on top of that. In a sense, the safety is from yourself." I think of the habits of my own mind, of the anger, denial, reaction, projection. Serious mind training would indeed be required to protect me from myself!

THAT NIGHT, the winds rush in from the northwest, reaching a ferocious pitch, shaking the house, and waking up me and Patrick. It's hot in the attic despite the wind, and we can't get back to sleep. The rattling scaffolding crashes against the exter-nal walls of the house. Bolting from her mat on the floor, Cleo scrambles up onto the bed; she nudges our faces with her wet nose, burrowing in between us, her tail between her legs. I peer out the tiny attic window at the head of our bed to see the shroudlike netting swelling like the sail of a death ship.

As the hot night wind shakes our house, I remember how nine years ago, in just such weather, firestorms set off by a brushfire raged through the dry grasses and trees of the Berkeley and Oakland Hills, burning down homes, including that of some of my close friends. Tonight, it feels like fire weather, earthquake weather. I remember the Loma Prieta earthquake when Katy was a baby, which happened on a hot autumn day like this one.

Opening up my mind to the wide view, the view of the dawn redwood, of geologic time as it unfolds, I take the risk of seeing the vast and continuous changing of things. I think of the on-going movement of tectonic plates through which earthquakes, mostly too subtle to be noticed by human touch or ear, are moment-by-moment occurrences. I think of the Great Earthquake in 1906, with fires in its wake devastating the homes of San Franciscans and sending many fleeing to Berkeley. I remember the predictions of an earthquake of perhaps greater magnitude along the San Andreas, Hayward, and other faults, possibly slated to decimate many homes, even here in Ocean View. Encompass this, I tell myself, the full catastrophe.

A shelter of wood or bricks or metal is a refuge, but not to be counted on. Who knows what great wind, what shifting of tectonic plates, could shake the frail refuge of a house? No matter how carefully we replace the roof, the windows, the rotting boards—no matter how elegantly we seal and prime and paint—a house cannot offer the safety I long for. When I take the vast view, all the work we do on our house makes me laugh. It's not that we shouldn't do our best to protect against possible dangers, but ultimately, boards and nails and shingles and bolts are unreliable. A house is not a home.

Even now, when this house is seemingly stable, with solid walls and a roof, I yearn for some sure version of safety, of home, that I can count on to endure. Gil described a safety from oneself, a safety that can only be accessed through training the mind. That safety seems to come from learning to be truly *at home* in any context. But it's easy to get the two kinds of safety confused, to keep trying to win an enduring safety, a feeling of being at home, through a house or something else that you can buy or build.

Outside in the darkness, the racket becomes more intense; the black netting billows. With the house rocking in the wind, Cleo squirms her body along mine, cries, and makes guttural barks. She worries her nose along my cheeks and ears, finds my eyes with her own.

Right here on my bed, I sit up to think things through. Patrick's warm thigh rests against my knee, and Cleo soothes her trembling between us. With ebbs and rises of wind song, my fragmented thoughts come into alignment.

I don't know what led young William Hans to suicide, but I can only imagine that what was happening in his heart was so dark, so painful or frightening, that he felt he could not encompass it, that he was driven to escape. Turning to myself, this much I know: When I am driven by house upset, by day-to-day ups and downs, by fears of shifting winds and earth—all that I do not want to include—I do not feel at home; I do not feel safe. As I've tossed this way and that in the bed trying to get comfortable, I have not felt at home. Even now, I struggle with dislikes and discomforts. Sitting here, I know how not at home I am.

But just knowing that, I see the reverse. I may not be able to control whether my house is stable, but I can train my own mind to be stable, to include. When I just stay put, upright and still, and teach myself to include whatever doubts or fears, whatever ups and downs come my way—without escaping from them or being driven by them—I begin to know that other version of safety. I am more at home.

Chapter 17

homeless

a second interlude with dogs

AS THE DAY APPROACHES for my walk to the vet with Dee, I begin to doubt that Dee will actually show up. Now, heading home from taking Katy to the school bus, I'm half-hoping Dee won't be there. I'm uneasy about spending so much time with her. But when I drive up to our house—still encased in scaffolding—there Dee is. She seems sober. At least her speech is not slurred, and her gait, except for the limp, is balanced. Ducking around the corner, she comes back with the scruffy little pup on a leash. Leaving behind Cleo and Radio as they poke their noses through the front gate and plead to come, we take off across town.

These are soiled streets between our block and the Humane Society. We pass the squat purple fourplex. It's too early now for any of the usual suspects to be hanging around out front. We cross University Avenue with its fast food restaurants and gas stations, with its line of cars backed up on the approach to Interstate 80. Turning onto a side street, we walk against one more mean wind on this fogged-in autumn morning.

At first I feel clumsy as I try to make conversation with Dee. I'm wondering if we look an odd pair, a middle-class white woman—with a mass of silver hair, a lavender scarf trailing behind her—walking with a frail black street person bundled in a ragged ski jacket, a wool cap pulled down low over her ears.

Dee tells me that she feeds Honey the best puppy chow. "I take Honey to that fancy supermarket up the block. When we stand outside long enough, some white lady'll come out from doing her shopping with a big bag of dog food for Honey." She laughs disparagingly. "They treat her like they never do me." I feel a pang since I'm here paying for the puppy's shots, not Dee's medical care.

We talk about the kids hanging out on our block. And I ask if any of the guys is Michelle's boyfriend. She says she thinks they're all just friends. I tell her my own worries about Katy as she grows into a young woman. Mothers worry, we agree. As we talk, I give Honey a biscuit. What a surly little pup, I think, distrustful and maybe rightfully so. But after a few biscuits, she is sniffing sweetly at my heels, begging for more. I'm beginning to relax a bit as well.

At the Humane Society, I pay for the full round of shots, while at the same time wondering if Dee will ever bring the puppy back. We both go in while the vet administers the shot. Dee learns how to calm the trembling puppy by stroking her gently, chin to ears.

As we're walking home, Dee says to me (as she had weeks before), "I take care of this puppy like she's my baby."

I say, "What worries me is how you don't take care of yourself." (Maybe it sounds a bit stilted or preachy, but I'm bumbling toward a conversation I've wanted to have for a long time.)

Dee says, "I know you worry yourself about that."

I tell her that it's upsetting to me, and probably other people on the block, when she gets into fights and drinks. Then I just ask her directly, "Do you ever think about giving it up?"

"No way," she says. "I like my vodka. I take it with a beer chaser." Then she laughs.

I say that I've known plenty of people who drink. I find myself being a lot more honest than I would ever have expected. "The great escape," I say. "I've seen it in my own family. And there was a time when I drank a bit too much myself, and I had a series of boyfriends who were real drinkers. Most nights they drank themselves into a stupor and passed out."

She says, "You know about drinking then."

I ask her how it is for her in jail when she has to dry out. She says they give her something to knock her out so she gets through the hard part. That's when I remind her about the counselor at the county dry-out program who has a few beds at his discretion. I don't tell her that this is the guy who she chased out of her holding cell.

She says, "Don't know. Maybe I'll call him sometime."

And I remind her, "You'd have to be sober."

"Yeah," she says. "You know I can do it, baby. Like today, I didn't drink 'cause I knew I'd be talking to that vet."

We talk back and forth about drinking and quitting. I'm imagining that even as we talk, her mind is fixed on her morning vodka (chased with beer). But I'm touched to be talking so intimately after years of on-and-off clashes, misunderstandings, resentments, and fears.

In many ways, Dee and I are alike. Over the years, I too have suffered over feelings of exclusion, have been driven by angers, by cravings. I too have a child I love and for whom, at times, I ache with worry. And each of us is an easy cry. But mostly what Dee and I share is camouflaged by all the seeming contrasts. A nod again to the dogs who take no stock in fences—either wooden ones or those in thought based on race or class. Thanks to them for this conversation, so resonant, at least for me. In tending to Dee, to Honey, somehow I feel cared for myself. It's that circle I felt before when Dee used to sleep in the car.

NEITHER DEE NOR HONEY shows up for several weeks. The wind is still, and a stale heat descends. Cleo and Radio flop down in the cool dirt by the fence and, it seems to me, dream their dreams.

Then one morning when I'm driving down the block I hear Dee. Her husky voice is unmistakable. I back up my car. On the far side of the street, I see her with the pup on the frayed leash. Tail curved forward in a happy arc, Honey is pulling ahead, stepping perky. But Dee's walk is weighted, her limp pronounced.

Out the car window I call, "What's happening, Dee?"

She mumbles down into the sidewalk. "I just can't leave her tied up at my friend's when I'm gone. I've gotta find that dog lady down by the track." I pull on the emergency brake and Dee leans heavily against the car. "I'm due back at Highland Hospital. I'm sick, baby. I got cirrhosis of the liver. If I didn't quit drinking, the doctor said I was going to die for sure."

I say, "I'm sorry."

And she goes on, "I haven't been able to eat anything for five days and I'm running green bile at both ends." A pause. "I'm on the wagon. Had to do it." Then she gestures toward Honey. "I hate to give her back. But when I'm in the hospital, I can't take care of her like I should." As she talks, she wipes some tears from her eyes.

In the coming week, Dee is nowhere to be seen. But not to be deterred, Honey keeps trotting across town to her little alley, to that home place where she's been fed, where she's felt a tender hand. She arrives with enthusiastic yips, sniffs around the little hut and continues to dig under the fence to the older dogs. I remember how, when we first adopted Cleo from the Animal Referral—after a month of keeping her close, of tending her with hearty food and hugs—we left her at our friend Peter's for a weekend while we went to the beach. Cleo leapt Peter's fence, circled through backstreets, crossed University Avenue, and somehow found our gate, where she barked until neighbors kindly let her into our yard. Despite the distance and unfamiliar route, she'd found her way home. I've heard many such stories.

For another week, Honey finds her way here, sometimes digging her way under the fence. But Dee's nowhere to be seen. Just when I'm sure she's in the hospital, or has maybe ended up back in jail, Dee returns to check in. She's on crutches. Making her way around the scaffolding, the piled-up cans of paint, she scouts our yard for Honey. Dee says that she's been in the hospital all week with water in her knees. She tells me that she's in bad shape. Even though she's hobbling and slow on her crutches, to me she seems more steady than usual and her speech is clear. I tell her that she may be hurting, but she looks good. "I've seen you look a lot worse," I say. And she agrees, "I know what you mean, baby."

After Dee leaves our yard, I can hear her with Honey by the doghouse on the other side of the fence. She's muttering, "You come here 'cause it be the one place you think you can find me. You come like it's yours. You don't know it's not your home."

It gives me a shiver to hear her say that. Of course, it's true of Dee herself. Then I think, who's to say it's not Honey's home—or Dee's, for that matter? How much does the ethos of home have to do with belonging to something from which, by definition, no one can be separated? No matter to what lengths Dee goes, tying Honey up or locking her into someone's apartment across town, Honey makes her way back to the spot that feels like home. Likewise, despite two court orders, despite the risk of going to jail, Dee is defying all external punishment, writs, orders, and common sense and holding to something fundamental, an allegiance to home that no one articulates but, on some level, maybe everyone understands.

As Patrick and I refurbish this house, as I continue my exploration of its history and the history of this terrain, I feel a like pull to Dee's; I know the draw of a place. But there's something more going on here as well—for Dee and Honey as there is for me. It has to do with caring and being cared for. Once I tend to this house, once I tend to Katy and Patrick and they to me; once Dee tends to Honey, or I to Dee, there's an alchemy of give-and-receive, of inhabiting an exchange. For both the one who cares and the one who's cared for, there's a more powerful draw—of home.

From the alley next door, I listen to Dee tying Honey up, saying good-bye. She may be crying. "I'll come back when I can, little babe. First I takes care of myself. Then I takes care of you."

Chapter 18

vital statistics

turning to the fathers

DISTURBING DEATH CERTIFICATES and momentary insights aside, I pursue my house research with excitement. My own ancestors worked in business and real estate; they wrestled with their minds. The Ocean View pioneers were farmers, boat builders and tanners, milkmen and sailors; they lived by creeks and bay, and wrestled with earth, water, and fire. I picture them, these Ocean View ancestors, bringing to their homes a vibrancy not available to my intellectual city-bred forebears. Surely, through the vital statistics I'm gathering, I will catch a glimpse of that primal hearth I'm longing for.

Keeping the Offes in reserve, I'm hoping I'll have some luck with Jose de Rosa, who first owned and maybe built our house. In old Berkeley city directories, I find "De Rosa, Jos, mariner, r. Dover St." At last the rumored "sea captain"! It wasn't Offe after all, but de Rosa. He's listed again in 1915, then, as far as I can make out, he disappears. Was he a mariner during World War I? Where did he sail off to? Did he die in the war?

At the Family History Center of the Mormon Temple, I continue my sleuthing. What an array of genealogical files—census records, voting and property records, passenger-ship lists, military lists. With the assistance of a kindly lady volunteer, I find my mariner only once, in the census of 1900. It's Jose Da Rosa

(Da instead of de). In tiny cursive writing, the vital statistics are laid out. Born in 1859 in Portugal, he immigrated here in 1874; he became naturalized, married Rita E., a U.S.-born citizen of Portuguese heritage; he had two children, a boy and a girl; he was a watchman on a steamer (not quite a captain, but to me a romantic calling).

As I'm leaving, I waylay the kind volunteer. "Why do the Mormons set up these libraries for studying genealogy?" Leaning over the card catalogue, she gives me a quizzical look, lowers her voice. "Why, my dear, this has been decreed by the Lord in the last chapter of the last book in the Old Testament." The volunteer pats my arm and gives me another look, then her card. "Call me dear, please, if you have any other questions . . . Anything at all."

When I get back to my house, I find the falling-apart Bible I think I remember my mother gave me when I went away to college. On the first page, my name is scribbled in pencil in my mother's hen scratch. I've always assumed someone in my mother's religionless family had stolen (or perhaps permanently borrowed?) this Bible from New York City's Weylin Hotel. (On the cover, the telltale source is written in gold: "The Weylin.") This feels appropriate. Like all the religion I've ever had, it's not quite mine, but on loan. I open to Malachi, chapter 4. "Behold, I will send you Elijah. . . . And he shall turn the heart of the fathers to the children, and the heart of the children to their fathers. . . ." As I read this, tears well up. I keep rereading the words. Turn the heart of the fathers to the children. The children to their fathers. Thoughts of my own father, his father before that. Not what I was looking for at all . . . a turning toward my own forebears as home, generations of fathers, of children.

RETURNING NOW to my neighborhood family, today I'm ready to skim old *Berkeley Gazettes* to find some obituaries. Not my research of choice. A bit morbid or dark, like back alleys and death certificates—maybe bad luck. Once again, I've had to overcome some initial resistance. But as I reel through the faded microfilm, I find myself drawn more intimately into these Ocean View lives. Frederick Offe, whose date of death I found in the California Death Index, died at ninety-three. Offe "built some of the city's first houses, many of which still stand in West Berkeley. A German immigrant boy, he came to America at the age of seventeen, he made his way around the horn to San Francisco and lived with relatives who owned some of Oakland's finest hotels. . . . His wife was the former Annie Bening, whose parents were early-day settlers in West Berkeley." Continuing to cross-check the death certificates for dates, I scroll through March 1913 *Gazettes* but fail to find an obituary for William Hans Offe. Frustrated, as I scroll backward, I catch the word *suicide* in a front-page headline. There it is:

SUCCEEDS IN HIS SECOND ATTEMPT TO COMMIT SUICIDE

Following an unsuccessful attempt to take his life, William Offe fired a shot into his right temple with a .38 caliber revolver at 5:22 o'clock in the afternoon and died at the Roosevelt Hospital a few minutes later. The act was committed in a vacant barn . . . near his home.

Apparently in the best of spirits, Offe left home at 5 o'clock. He went directly to the barn and holding a mirror before him, he fired a bullet into his head. The bullet entered just over the right ear. His father heard the shot and went to the barn where he found his son lying on a pile of straw. A small hand mirror which he had used in taking aim, and the revolver, were lying at his side.

The horror of it takes me over, how this violent act must have devastated his father, mother, and sister—leaving the community of those who knew him in Ocean View shaken by confusion, maybe anger for some, and grief. The article goes on to describe an earlier attempt by asphyxiation. I can barely read the seamy details involving a gas jet turned on in a University Avenue barbershop. Just as I'm about to copy the article, to see if I can stomach the rest at a later time, I can't help skimming the next paragraph.

> It has been rumored among close friends of Offe that he was despondent over disappointment in a love affair. It is said that he was jilted a short time ago by a young woman who he expected to marry.

There in the library, in the company of fellow Berkeley residents sitting at long tables hunched over books, I hurt inside for this young man, jilted in love. I imagine a feeling of being cut off and alone, and how that may well have seemed unbearable. Images come to me of the barnlike building behind Sheryl and Roy's. Was this the vacant barn? For a moment, I picture William Hans heading out his back door, apparently in the best of spirits, with his mirror and his gun. Somewhere in some hidden cellar of my own story—of family catastrophes, of botched love affairs and broken friendships, of moments of stark disconnection from myself and my world—I recognize his pain.

It scares me to tap into this. There are disasters I fear that seem unbearable. In the evening, I again call Gil, my generous consultant on the Buddhist way. "Isn't this what dharma practice might offer, a sense that no matter what comes one's way, nothing, even tremendous loss, is unbearable?"

And Gil replies, "It's not so much a matter of how we can manage to bear whatever it is. It's a matter of learning which burdens we can put down. What's extra?" This reminds me of his previous thought on taking refuge as "safety from yourself."

Of course it's oneself who keeps hold of the extra burdens. I think of all of my own stories about the families in Ocean View, about my house, and about my own family—all of my expectations, reactions, and disappointments. I carry so many extras. Who knows what extras this young man may have carried. Longing? Shame? Perhaps some Victorian notions of failed status in the eyes of his family or friends—leading him to feel totally alone. I remember Ajahn Pasanno's comment on the homeless monk who has taken to the road. "The more he carries, the hungrier he gets."

I reflect on the Ocean View settlers. The more I've searched through census records and city directories, death certificates and obituaries, the more I've felt the weight of lives—marriages and children, rising and waning careers, separations and losses. Jose Da Rosa (husband of Rita, father of a boy and a girl) seems to have sailed off who knows where, perhaps was killed in the war. William Hans put a bullet in his brain. In my chest now, I sense a softening. I had them wrong, the pioneer families.

Just now, it occurs to me how hard all of these lives may have been and, at the same time, how hard all these people may have tried to live their lives as best they knew how—carrying their extra burdens as humans so often do. Again, memories come to me of my own family; I feel them moving through my heart with their mixed-up love affairs, separations and manipulations, boycotts and refusals to forgive. Now, for the first time, I see them each in their own way, stretching, drawing on all they knew how to muster—imagination, self-discipline, love—and never getting it quite right. As if anyone could.

This quest leads me to unforeseen turns. Perhaps it's not such an either/or exploration as I sometimes think. *Either* I'll learn the history of this home place, *or* I'll learn the history of my own forefathers. *Either* I'll explore the household home, *or* I'll explore the homeless home. Again and again, I tap into something that feels quintessentially human. The categories are not so fixed. Learning about each seems to slide into its converse in some gradual settling—outside of all expectations.

homeless and home

with the grandmothers

AFTER THE TAXI DRIVER drops her off from the seniors' day care, Grandma Darlene wanders the streets of the neighborhood looking for her way home. Twice of late, since she began to recover from her stroke and joined this program, Grandma Darlene's taxi driver has come knocking on our door. "Can Mrs. Jackson stay with you until her granddaughter, Donna, gets back from work?" He has had strict instructions never to leave off any of the patients unattended, particularly not on the street. This third time, I invite Grandma Darlene to join me upstairs or to sit in my back garden amid the ladders and old shingles as she has on the previous occasions. "No." This time she's immovable; she's staying where she is.

Trying to be gracious, I haul one of our garden chairs up onto her porch for Grandma Darlene to sit on. But she shakes her head and settles on the top step. I should have known it wasn't her way. While my family chooses our fenced-in backyard, the folks at Grandma Darlene's have always gathered right here in the front. So I sink onto one of the steps below.

The smell of paint drifts from our newly painted house. A train warbles in the distance. With their boom box blaring, some young men amble past our ugly hedge, past me and Grandma Darlene, and over toward the tumbledown purple fourplex. I watch a tall woman dressed in a halter top, hot pants, and heeled sandals smoke a cigarette outside. Unaccustomed to sitting out in the street, I become increasingly uncomfortable. At the same time, I notice Grandma Darlene relax. Clear in her memories, she tells me about having come to Berkeley from South Carolina during World War II so her husband could work in the ship-yards. "Since we moved to this house here, Dee and Donna have fought so much—you know, Dee's drinking—that we had to ask Dee to move out."

"I know," I say. Only too well. I look around warily. Dee hasn't been around at all lately. Maybe she's been in the hospital, staying in some other part of town, or in jail again. I'd heard she might have been arrested. And Honey's gone. Before Dee disappeared this time, she found a home for Honey with some "white folks" she'd met "up at the barbecue on San Pablo Avenue."

Grandma Darlene continues, "You know Dee is Donna's daughter."

I interrupt, "Don't you mean Donna is Dee's daughter?"

Grandma Darlene chuckles, a generous ripple of a laugh. "Yeah. That's it. I get so mixed up these days. I can't keep straight who is who." She includes me in this laugh and allows me my comfort in noticing her confusion. In one long peal she seems to forgive me, herself, and her unreliable faculties as they dissolve.

We sit for a while in silence. Cars rumble up and down. Parking his Buick across the street, a balding pasty-faced man in a business suit sits there staring at the woman in the halter top.

"Do you ever get a yearning to go back to South Carolina, to see your family and friends from long ago?" I ask.

"No," she says. Settling more comfortably, she rests against the frayed shingles of her house, truly her home these many years. "No, I'm not going anywhere," continues Grandma

Darlene. "There's nowhere in the world I'd rather be than right here."

FROM ITS GUTTED CUSHIONS, my own grandmother's chaise longue exhales billows of goose down, turning the attic playroom into a mess of feathers and dust. In pursuit of I don't know what, Cleo has burrowed into the feather belly of the chaise. Through the attic skylight, the shouts of Michelle and some of her friends over at Grandma Darlene's grate my ears. I haul the heavy vacuum cleaner up the attic stairs, protesting this onslaught of chaos. I'm not up to dealing with another mess, inside or out. As I yank the vacuum this way and that, I am consumed with resentment. One day life feels so full, open to the vast spans of evolving time; the next day it feels overfull, beyond control. It's certainly one of those hard days! Such demands the world makes on me! Everything seeming to go wrong just when I have the least time and energy to cope. If I could only rest.

Squatting on the floor, I scoop up handfuls of feathers and tattered bits of horsehair and silk. A memory comes of this chaise—its silk brocade intact—in my grandmother Helene's bedroom. Intended for repose in the boudoir, the chaise longue has, since the era of Louis XIV, invited the lady to abandon herself to dreams. When I was a girl in Manhattan, Mama Helene's chaise, tucked between her dressing table and her poetry shelves, always touched my imagination. Five years ago, after having been shipped west from friend to friend, the chaise arrived—scuffed and beginning to unravel—at our house here in Berkeley. But over the years that the chaise has resided in our attic, I've barely spread my limbs in its worn cushions, barely given it any attention. It's felt haunted somehow by the imprint of Mama Helene, who, twelve years earlier, died on it.

I steel myself now to take a look. Stuffing oozes out of the holes in the upholstery; the box springs are laid bare. Once luxurious and particular, Mama Helene's daybed is now decomposing into anonymity. I am filled with grief.

After vacuuming the tattered remains, scouring it back to its skeleton, I feel an unexpected pull—a turn to the grandmothers, to my own grandmother. Mightn't I just lay my body down in the neglected cavity of this chaise? Tentatively, I lower myself onto the prickly seat and sink back into the arms. I run my fingers through the homespun ingredients: goose down, cotton, burlap, horsehair, walnut frame. In the lining, I find one of Mama's hairpins. I see her reclining on the chaise, two hairpins in her mouth as she coiled her bun.

Caressing the rusty hairpin between my fingers, I remember the story of her final afternoon on the chaise. Reclining, just as I am now, she read aloud a poem by Edna St. Vincent Millay: "O World, I cannot hold thee close enough . . ."*

I love the thought that at eighty-six, after several broken hips and two cataract operations, Mama Helene still yearned to embrace the world. Or was it that? It hurts me to remember, but she said it during those last years. She wanted to die. Some say she willed her own death. Did she long rather for the beauty of a world of which she felt she couldn't get "enough"? Or maybe, like me sometimes, she'd fallen into resentment—of family, of the world, for not attending to her "enough"?

As I turn over these questions, I try to find a comfortable stretch in the sharp-boned skeleton of the chaise. How I long for rest. Thoughts on this longing, on the grandmothers—Grandma Darlene and Mama Helene—revolve in my mind. I reach back to all of the grandmothers, Grandmother Offe too, her exhaustion.

On her front step, Grandma Darlene appears to rest amid the clatter and confusion of the street and the confusion of her mind

*Excerpt from "God's World" by Edna St. Vincent Millay © 1913, 1941 by Edna St. Vincent Millay, used with permission.

(am I romanticizing?). On her chaise longue, Mama Helene extended her tired limbs and read poetry, reciting a farewell poem. But I wonder, over the many years, as my grandmother lay here in the brocade cushions, did she ever truly learn how to find rest?

IT'S SEVERAL MONTHS after my visit with Grandma Darlene on the steps that Michelle comes over and rings our bell to ask if she can borrow some cash. "I've got to get some food for my mom." I'm somewhat skeptical, suspicious of the pleas for money with which Michelle has approached me on and off. But Michelle continues with some poignancy. "My mom's living at a special treatment program. You know, for the drinking and all." I'm listening now, scrutinizing Michelle's face. This is amazing (if it's true). "She's been in for a week already, and she says there's nothing there for her to eat."

After days of back-and-forth, Michelle gives me a list of her mom's needs: soda, chips, cookies (sounds to me suspiciously like a list of teenage snacking foods). Michelle finally brings her portable phone up our front steps to put me on the phone with Dee, who does, in fact, seem to be in a residential treatment program.

So Dee comes up with another list: saltine crackers, instant chicken noodle soup, Sprite, powdered coffee, and creamer. After my trip to the supermarket, the bags of groceries sit in the back of our car for weeks while Michelle's getting the address of the program. On a sudden guess, and maybe wanting some credit for Dee's great reversal, I check to see if it's the dry-out program I found with the county, but the counselor says he never heard from Dee. When I ask around, I find that rumors are circulating among the neighbors that with Dee's recent arrest the judge gave her a choice: she either had to go to jail or commit to a dry-out program. Finally, Michelle gets the address and I drive down for a delivery, way down San Pablo Avenue. I don't see Dee, but a man who seems to be the director takes the groceries.

A few months go by, and Dee shows up in front of Grandma Darlene's. She's on release time to go to a clinic to take care of her bum knee. On the days she goes to the clinic, she starts to come around to see Grandma Darlene. When I see her on the street, Dee never does mention the care package, but she says she's sober and doing well. "See, I put back on a little weight." She stands up straight, primps a little, sets her head at a stylish angle. She describes the classes she's taking, "computer training and a Bible class every day." She tells me Michelle will be graduating and how proud she is of Michelle, and Donna too (she says she and Donna get on now), who at twenty-five finally learned to drive. Dee reports that she herself is graduating from her dry-out program. She's staying at a friend's and will soon be moving back into her own house. She says, "I'll be coming home."

After several weeks have passed, sirens wake up the neighborhood late one night. An ambulance has come again for Grandma Darlene. The next day, Dee rings our bell. She's crying. "My mama died last night." She says she's taking care of the burial and the funeral arrangements. "I'm the only one in the family who knows how to take care of something like that." I sense the strength in the lineage—grandmother to mother, mother to daughter. Dee comes in and out of Grandma Darlene's, carrying groceries, getting things done. Meanwhile, Michelle sits out in her backyard, her head in her arms. She seems too sad to speak with neighbors coming by with flowers and food.

IT'S SEVERAL WEEKS LATER that I run into Dee staggering drunk. Pacing the street, muttering cusses, she passes without meeting my eye.

"What's happening, Dee?" I ask.

"I'm heartsick to lose my mama."

"But you started drinking again," I hear myself protest.

And she assures me, "None of that hard stuff, baby. Don't you worry yourself. Just a little wine." She swings her paper bag shaped around a wine bottle.

"But . . ."

"Why you looking at me like that?" Her voice turns angry. "How'd you all expect I lose my mama without getting me a drink?" Taking a final swig, she tosses the bottle into the ugly hedge and stalks off.

Conflicts are raging again now in front of Grandma Darlene's—folks are telling Dee to keep her distance. When I see Dee in the following weeks, she crosses to the other side of the street, just as she did after I kicked her out of the car. One day when I waylay her, Dee tells me off. "Don't you know how to mind your own goddamn business? You nosy."

In the early mornings, when I take my walk, I see Dee (or I'm pretty sure it's her) in her sleeping bag on the ramp of the community hall by the Pilgrim's Rest Church, once again locked out from the place she so longs to call home.

UNEASY WITH THE UPS and downs of my own life, with what's happening on the block with Dee and Donna and Michelle, I've been trying to relax, to find a calm moment. It's been a long time since I've gotten myself on a meditation cushion to train my mind to settle into what's going on right now, to rest.

This hot September afternoon, when I go up to the attic, I notice Mama Helene's chaise neglected once again. It draws my attention as it did after Cleo's rampage. A crazy thought comes to me. The more I consider the possibility, the more it appeals. Gathering my meditation cushion, I place it in the skeletal remains of the chaise. With some awkwardness, I climb up and sit on that cushion. I make a commitment. I will sit here and be still for a period of meditation.

Through the attic skylight I hear the sounds of the street—children's laughter and traffic; drug whistles and arguments; and from below, the faint hoots of a train. The afternoon is hot. Despite the open skylight, the air in the attic is stuffy. A mist of cotton dust and goose down rises from the upholstery, sticks to my skin, and teases my nostrils. Beneath my sitting bones, I sense the chaise. A shiver of distaste—it feels like a carcass, subject to decay. Images flood, of Mama Helene (did she have to turn away from life?), of Grandma Darlene, of all the grand-mothers, of all the fathers, the mothers who have died, are dying. I have an impulse to get up and go somewhere else.

The longer I sit, the hotter and stuffier the attic becomes. Insufferably hot. An itching under my chin, a burning in my lungs, take me over. A wave of heat rushes through my limbs, and my whole fifty-four-year-old woman's body is soaked with sweat. My shoulders ache and my head is constricted. I can't tolerate this. I've got to get up and do something else, anything else. Abruptly, I see it. That's the way out: to stop meditating, to cut off my awareness.

Just as I'm considering breaking off the meditation, I think of Mama Helene on this same chaise. I imagine her distress, with a crooked back, a twice-fractured hip, and eyes recovering from surgery. It is only natural that she might have felt that the only way out of the suffering in her life was to stop living, the only way to find rest was to die. If I can't sit here in this hot attic, if I can't allow myself to experience the discomforts of body and mind, how could I expect Mama Helene to keep living despite the discomforts of old age?

To face her losses, Mama Helene must have summoned all of her energy and discipline. Grandma Darlene, over her many years, must have drawn on like qualities, a commitment and courage to ground herself amid the cross fire of life and the loss of her faculties. To stay put right here and now on this cushion, to pay attention to what's going on, I search within myself to find such commitment, courage, and discipline.

I bring my attention back to the chaise, this chaise dissolving around me—fibers made by insect larvae; fibers of cotton, of jute, of hemp; horsehair; walnut wood; the first plumage of young birds. I feel beneath the skin of my face to Katy's face—fresh and tender, the rosy skin taut on the bones. This is the face I often imagine myself to have—like the newly made chaise, with plump cushions and snug upholstery. And I recognize my own aging face, the face of my elders, grandmothers Helene and Darlene, and Annie Offe.

How hard it is to hold one's losses, to hold one's pain—to know it and somehow live through it and with it. If I can't take the risk of staying here on this cushion, can I expect Dee to stay sober in the wake of her loss? Can I expect William Hans to have endured his broken heart? If I can't rest in myself, in this dissolving world in its full heat, how can I expect anyone to find home in such a world—with its jilted loves and broken hips, its gutted cushions and chaos in the street?

IN THE EVENING, I stand on the landing at the top of our back stairs; I breathe in the savory scent of barbecues, the odor of new paint, the heat of Indian summer. In a full sweep, I survey this corner we inhabit together, each yard: ours (still littered with sawdust and paint chips); Sheryl and Roy's; and what I still think of as Carmen's—where, I remember, Cathy lived briefly and died—where Zoe and Michael are having a picnic dinner with tender-cheeked Olivia, who just turned two.

Over on H Street, I catch a glimpse of Patrick on his way home from the BART train, striding along in his lawyer's suit, his step steady, his briefcase in a jaunty swing. In our yard, I see

Suzanna holing up in a corner of our many-tiered deck, Radio by her side, her computer on her lap. Putting one finger to her lips, Suzanna points up to the top tier of the deck toward Katy (for whom Suzanna has become a special friend). High up in the corner, almost hidden by the overhanging willow, Katy writes in her journal, hugging her long legs, her hair back in a green bandanna. Absorbed, independent (growing up).

Behind the back fence, Sheryl fills the bowls for the cats. Over the fence to the west, in Grandma Darlene's yard, Michelle is sitting alone. Over the side fence to the east, at the newly painted red picnic table, Olivia points up with a shout, "Cleo!" who I now note is climbing the stairs, her limp pronounced, to join me on the landing for the big view. I have a crazy thought. This could be the happiest moment of a life. A random moment, but there are no extras; it is enough.

In the fullness of this moment, worlds revolve: family, neighbors, the Offe clan, the mariner. But it's not just that. I look south toward the dawn redwood, which is turning brown and beginning to lose its needles. I look west down past Grandma Darlene's, beyond the Pilgrim's Rest Church, the factories and freeways; I picture the Bay. I turn east toward the Scandinavian Hall, and behind that, barely visible in the distance, I see the Berkeley Hills, where I picture creeks meandering down toward the alluvial plain of the flatlands. I remember my thought about Ocean View—the terrain so clogged and paved over in culverts that it has lost contact with itself. Standing here, in the briefest of glimpses, I sense an intimacy, self to self, a rawness open to the history of this corner, the fathers and mothers, the grandfathers and grandmothers; to the history of this terrain; and now, harsh and fresh, even to my own family—that blood lineage with its feuds and heartaches, a family making do like any other.

Bay and Creeks

During the ice ages of the Pleistocene Epoch, when water accumulated in the great continental glaciers, what is now the San Francisco Bay was dry land. The Sacramento River flowed out across the broad valleys of the coastal lowlands—a broad structural depression in the Coast Mountain Range where the Sacramento and San Joaquin Rivers met. Passing through the last mountain ridge in a deep canyon (what is now called the Golden Gate), the river flowed out into the Pacific Ocean. Eighteen thousand years ago the glaciers of the last ice age began to melt. By ten thousand years ago, the sea level rose so high it flooded the coastal lowland, drowning the mouth of the river. Our current San Francisco Bay began to fill with water, reaching close to its present level by about five thousand years ago.

Over the past six hundred thousand years, the San Francisco Bay has only existed for brief periods. From four to perhaps seven times, water has flooded the coastal lowlands, creating a bay. Past bays have lasted five to ten thousand years. In its present size, the current Bay may well be slated to last another thousand more—and to end with the coming of another ice age. Every hundred thousand years, the earth's orbit shifts through dust and debris left over from the forming of the solar system. Thus sunlight is occluded, diminishing the thermal energy distributed by our planet's oceans, leading once again to glaciation and the draining of the Bay.

The Bay continues to be shaped and reshaped by ongoing geologic forces. Due to the shifting of tectonic plates, on both the San Andreas and Hayward faults, mountains are rising. As the Santa Cruz Mountains and the Berkeley Hills ascend, they squeeze what is known as the Bay Block between them, defining the limits of the Bay. Meanwhile, the Sacramento and San Joaquin Rivers continue to carry sediment down from the mountains and hills to the estuary below. The current San Francisco Bay would be twice its depth if it weren't partly filled with sediment. During the last interglacial period (one hundred and twenty thousand years ago), the sea level rose to about twenty feet higher than it is today. The Bay was larger in surface—probably covering the area now called Ocean View.

The interplay of all of these geologic processes creates an estuary constantly in flux that disappears for tens of thousands of years at a time.

Descending from the hills surrounding the San Francisco Bay, shaping the landscape, flow the creeks. Among them is Strawberry Creek, which feeds into the Bay directly across from the Golden Gate, the entryway to the Pacific Ocean. Over millions of years, rainwater has washed soil from the surfaces of the hills into the creeks, which carried it down toward the Bay. During floods, the creeks have shifted course, leaving lobes of sediment fanning out where the creeks emerged from the hills and widening where the land flattened out toward the Bay. Over the millennia, the entire flatlands of the East Bay have built up as alluvial fans have coalesced, becoming an alluvial plain on top of the bedrock.

Where creeks meet bay, the tidal marshes can be essential breeding grounds, nurseries, and escape habitats—as well as settling places for all that the creeks transport. Such mixing grounds, subject to the rise and fall of the tides, offer varying levels of salinity, providing diverse habitats crucial to the food web. Nutrient-rich detritus of dead vegetation is abundant; it feeds various life-forms. Phytoplankton, found in both marine waters and freshwater lakes, are plentiful in brackish waters. These tiny plants feed tiny creatures called zooplankton, which feed young salmon, steelhead, and striped bass, along with bottom-dwelling invertebrates such as oysters and clams. These, in their turn, feed waterfowl and shorebirds as well as creekside mammals.

At the beginning of the Holocene (our current) epoch, ten thousand years ago, when the continental ice sheets melted and flooded, the sea level continued to rise for several thousand years. Six thousand years ago, when the rise in seawater decreased, mud flats and tidal marshes— rich in mussels, oysters, clams, crab, and shrimp—expanded. Six thousand to five thousand years ago, in the fertile new ecosystems where creeks fed into the Bay, humans made their settlements.

PART FIVE

Settling

before and beneath

One hut built on the whole universe.
From there I can see mountains, rivers and good earth
As my own garden.
Once I was annoyed with human language
Of good and bad, liking and disliking.
I can hear those voices from here, like music of Paradise.

—Soyen Shaku

Chapter 20

beneath the pavement

IN THE PRESCRIPTION FOR RISK that sent me onto the deer trails of Tilden Park, then into the alleyways of my neighborhood, there was a warning. "Once you begin to call that home, you'll have to dive further into the unknown." When camping became too comfortable, I might have to meet my terrors on the edge of a cliff or in the darkness of a cave. This caveat both beckoned me and called up my most vehement resistance.

Having passed through the Bureau of Vital Statistics, having studied the families cycling through my home corner, I find myself more comfortable now in exploring house as home. I sense that I need to dive deeper, to descend through great spans of darkness and distance beyond quotidian time and space to a vast hidden realm—before and beneath. Drawn by this powerful calling, I confront an old resistance, a kind of blockade. This is something I must address because it doesn't feel like I can go around it.

Indeed, if I want to go any further, it feels like it is with the pavement itself—both in the mind and on the street—that I must become intimate. With a numb clump, my boots strike the pavement. Taking Cleo as my guide this early morning, I walk through parking lots and courtyards, concrete and asphalt. I experiment, first a few paces on the street, then on the strip of grass between the street and the sidewalk. I sense a difference, even here where the ground is packed. Ground forgives; as foot meets soil, there's the movement of relationship. But pavement is implacable.

Today I'm looking for the asphalt plant. In the United States, we use twenty-seven million tons of asphalt each year; pavement now covers sixty thousand square miles, 10 percent of the arable land. With pavement on the brain, I can't ignore this plant, located within ten blocks of my house.

It takes all the discipline I can muster this morning to head down below the fancy shops—past the bank and its paved lot where, just a few years ago, there was a specialty lettuce farm—below the railroad tracks, down into the industrial zone. Since my early neighborhood-roaming on B Street, I've so rarely ventured here. I pass a large storm drain clogged with plastic six-pack holders and cigarette butts. I shrink back from the glimmering water below, polluted by household cleaners, pesticides, motor oil, and maybe even sewer leakage. And I recoil from the streets themselves, still heaped with debris and broken glass; how neglected they are.

The asphalt plant is unmistakable with its giant vats and rusty chutes stretching from vat to vat. These huge burners heat tons of aggregate and asphalt each day. Beyond a chain-link fence topped with barbed wire, a plume of steam rises from the stack, and diesel trucks clatter in and out. Dust, exhaust, and combustion emissions thicken the air.

A memory comes back to me now. At a neighborhood meeting several years ago, a community activist came to alert residents about plans to increase the capacity of the plant. Although the plant's original permit had allowed operation twenty-four hours a day, seven days a week, the plant had limited nighttime hours. With the increased capacity and new equipment—including a higher stack—neighbors were concerned about increased noise and pollution.

Our speaker told us that, with the planned expansion, many pounds of toxic emissions a year might well be carried by prevailing winds directly into our residential community. At the time of that meeting, I was engaged with my own healing from breast cancer. I was alarmed. The threat of carcinogenic emissions whose names even sounded scary—formaldehyde, benzene, acetaldehyde—spurred me to sign up to join in a protest. Come to think of it now, I never did go to any meetings. Why not? How did I push this out of my mind?

This feels gritty, something I've continued to sidestep.

Back when I was first diagnosed seven years ago, frequent doctor visits provided reminders that I might die young. Every day I tried to teach myself to see and live with this. Each year as I've gone through blood tests, mammograms, and biopsies, the old fears have come up. But now, as surgery and radiation seem far behind me, maybe I put myself in a different category from other people with cancer. This year my whole person locks up in refusal. I will not allow even a hint of possibility that the cancer might recur. It's a stand against impermanence. I insist on a fixed me, not only free from cancer, but who—truth be told—can never die.

This plant and its emissions are unwelcome reminders of mortality—of exactly what I haven't wanted to study in the neighborhood, in myself. Walking here now, I feel shaky then, with a streak of insight, wryly appreciative. Here's another thought about pavement. Buddhism has it down. It sounds pat, and at the same time, it's true. Everything is changing, but we resist knowing it. We pave it over.

This afternoon when I sit down at my desk preparing to work, I have an unexpected yen to strip off my clothes and study my body in the mirror, to run exploratory fingers over my breasts. When first confronted with cancer, I learned how to do a long, detailed, truly careful exam; to consider my breasts from different views; then to meticulously palpate, using three different pressures. I promised myself to do this detailed exam each month.

A memory returns to me of the venerated Buddhist nun Ayya Khema. Some years ago at a retreat center, I thought I overheard her request a large mirror for her room. This was puzzling indeed, as Ayya Khema was the last person I'd expected to look at herself in a mirror. Knowing that she had breast cancer, I wondered at that time, could she be using this mirror for her own meditations on impermanence, on mortality?

At the mirror now, I force myself to study my nakedness. How neglected this body has been. Since that training years ago, I have never done the thorough exam. Not once. Remembering my young body, sweet and firm as a plum, I don't like seeing the looseness of age. But I keep looking. Seeing through the translucency of the skin to the blue veins, I appreciate these breasts. They are, after all—alive, one tender globe fuller than the other, both nipples rosy.

Lying down on the bath mat, I take a breath. Just do it. With the pads of my fingers, I circle at each step—shallow, deeper, deep—discovering the texture of terrain beneath the skin. Every tiny glide is scary, scouting the unknown. At each grain and pebble, my touch retracts. This can't be a lump. My fingers climb along the outer flesh. There's the cavity, where the surgeon removed the tissue. A shock at a sudden ridge. I have felt this hardness many times, but once again I'm taken by surprise. It demands such balance of mind to follow this changing landscape, with its rocks and ridges, its sand and gravel, its hollows and its scar.

IN OUR WALK down toward the Bay the next day, Cleo pulls me along the street toward that foul storm drain. I stare down into the slick glimmer below. If my guess is correct, this is a glimpse of Strawberry Creek, which until a century ago meandered free from the Berkeley Hills. Now—with all of the oil, lead, and zinc, herbicides and pesticides—it travels out to the Bay through two miles of concrete culvert.

Through Cleo's wet black nose, might I learn to sense beyond culverts and pollutants to the original streams? Through Cleo's paws, might I feel beneath the pavement through layers of history, through the forty-five hundred years of the shellmound and beyond?

As in our early walks when we first explored the neighborhood together, today I follow Cleo's lead. Slower now with her limp and likely to insist on lying down for frequent rests, Cleo still perks up at the prospect of an excursion into parts unknown.

Cleo flirts cautiously at the manhole cover where steam rises from some hidden world underneath. She paws at squares of concrete camouflaged in the sidewalk, at the disks of metal bearing signatures of secret domains—gas, electricity, water, sewers. If Cleo could only pry off these lids—like great coins on the open eyes of the dead—allowing me to spy through those vacant holes into an underworld below.

What is beneath the pavement here? What is hidden deep in time? Drawing on my study, I try to imagine this area as it must have been before it was developed. I see broad tidal marshes, pickleweed, and cordgrass swamps where sandpipers and bitterns feed and breed. Strawberry Creek rushes over rocks, under fallen branches, carrying soil from the hills to create the alluvial plain of the flatlands where I now live. Through the riffles of the creek, steelhead and salmon swim upstream to find clean gravels where they can spawn. Linnets and canaries, marsh wrens and yellow-rumped warblers, flit through the creekside manzanita and wild plum, while coyotes rest in the shade. In the rainy winter months, as a nearby pond becomes a lake, the creek overflows its banks. The whole landscape is lush.

Heading up toward my house now after my reverie, I hike

toward the parking lot of the once-booming Spenger's Fish Grotto, famed for its Captain's Platter of fish fry and tartar sauce and the partying at its several bars. Now, with Spenger's out of business, the parking lot is slated for new development. I stand here by the paved lot, try to encompass its history.

Beneath this pavement, on what were once the banks of the creek where it fed into the bay, was the Ohlone Indian shell-mound. Shellmound life seemed to center around the creeks for drinking and cooking, for fishing or waiting for game, for leaching acorns gathered from the hills, and as sites for wells and sweat lodges.

It's this shellmound and its world I plan soon to study. Since I was a teenager, I have had a passion to delve beneath the surfaces of the earth to learn about the evolving landscape, to study ancient worlds. I remember the dig in New Mexico where, when I was just out of high school, I joined a team of archaeologists to unearth buried skeletons, cooking ware, and underground kivas (temples of the Pueblo Indians). Ever since I first heard about our local shellmound from Stephanie, I have been fascinated by the thought of this mound dating back to 3700 B.C.E. so close to our house.

The Ohlones (or Costanoans to some historians) who lived in this lush terrain heaped their fish bones and refuse from mollusks and clams here at the mouth of the creek by the Bay and interred their dead right in the resulting heap. Stephanie showed me photos of primitive tools and burials found in an excavation in the 1950s conducted just down the block from my house. I love the sound of these simple flaked tools: pecked stone chisels, mussel shell scrapers, bird bone awls. According to this study, in their thousands of years here along the banks of the creek, the generations of Ohlone families made very gradual changes in their cultural activities. Likewise, they did minimal damage to land, creeks, or bay.

Picturing the terrain as it has gone through the many years, I drift again into reverie. During the past two hundred years, the change has been rapid. In the beginnings of the Ocean View settlement, the land beneath this parking lot was manicured as a "pleasure park," with the creek winding past a dance pavilion; later it was plowed and turned into a vegetable farm by a retired opera singer; then it was divided into parcels, which included the fishing shack of Johann Spenger. In the years that Frederick Offe and Jose Da Rosa were building houses at H and Dover, Mr. Spenger set his fishing boat into the Bay just below and sold his catch of the day from a store beneath his home.

Over the next forty years, the marshes extending west below this lot were dried out, filled with garbage, and paved over. As more city streets and lots were paved, miles of impermeable surfaces disturbed the balance between groundwater and run-off—so crucial to the life of the terrain. During winter rains, the ground couldn't absorb enough water, and flooding creeks eroded the land. In dry summer months, when the supply of groundwater hadn't been renewed, a diminished flow of water trickled through the parched creeks.

I appreciate the choices residents have made over the years for efficiency and speed in travel, for comfort and safety. But, at an increasing pace, the people who have lived here have been driven by such preferences and by corresponding fears—of mud and water and disease. The land was paved, the remains of the shellmound leveled, the railroad laid out and widened (the Pullman Railroad Company offering jobs for folks like Lizzie Cleary and Edna Wertman). The road along the Bay was turned into a major freeway, the pond on the west side of University Avenue stuffed with trash by construction companies, the University Avenue freeway overpass—a monolithic totem of concrete—constructed at the entrance to the city. The marshlands and beach were turned to landfill. Strawberry and other creeks were soiled and diverted into culverts, and the Bay—repository for oil spills, for industrial waste, for pesticides from agricultural runoff, and for pollutants leached from landfills—fouled.

Separated from the salmon and halibut, from the clam-rich dunes, from the saltwater and sea winds, Spenger's original fishing shack lost contact with its source and evolved into a bar and restaurant—which depended on this parking lot. In recent years, developers have increased their pace, digging up this land, building and repaving. They have ignored the remains of the shellmound that may well extend below. So many changes segmenting our home, paving over the relationship to life around us, inside us.

Of course, everything is always changing. It's crucial to sort out the change that happens no matter what from the change that comes from human choice or carelessness—the carelessness of not doing a breast exam, of expanding the hours of an asphalt plant, of filling the Bay with pesticides and garbage, or of paving over the life of streams.

A LANDSCAPER FRIEND OF MINE is working with a crew, taking turns using a jackhammer to shatter pavement, to open up the original soil and grow a garden. I ask my friend if I can take a detour on my walk to join him at the site, a way station of sorts for an adventurer such as myself—up against the pavement. Standing in the center of a courtyard beneath a Chinese maple tree, my friend grips the triggers of the jackhammer and bears down into the concrete. His arms and torso vibrate, but his legs remain stable. I notice his feet, vulnerable in cloth sneakers.

He offers me the jackhammer to give it a try. Since the jackhammer is heavy, awkward to maneuver, and potentially dangerous, I take this on with some trepidation. From the fat yellow body of the machine extends a pointed bit that hammers in and out with a piston action. The power of the movement shudders through my body. With my friend's help, I locate the beginning fracture and then make holes along that crack. While I work the jackhammer, one of the workers breaks out pieces of pavement with a crowbar and a pick, levering up the slabs so that the sheer weight—the force of gravity—helps with the cracking. As the crew pries up broken concrete, the massive roots of the maple, extending in all directions, are uncovered. A tiny crack, hair-thin, seems to open inside me. A shiver of home.

Imagination moist with wild mint and cattails, with the surge of Strawberry Creek, and with my awareness open, I continue to walk. I notice the street around me, notice my arms swinging free. As I pass the asphalt plant, the chemical smell seems like an assault. I notice my back seizing up. How much it hurts. For years I've tightened my shoulders against their own hurt; I've walked the streets of this neighborhood without feeling through to the rawness underneath. When something is neglected long enough, it doesn't even seem to hurt. That's paved over. We need to know our hurts. They confront us with carelessness, teach us to take care.

Getting under pavement, beneath the pretense of permanence, can be scary—it can hurt—but it can also open up possibilities. Beneath pavement is mind process, earth process, fire process, creek process. As creek water nourishes vegetation, the roots of creekside willows and cottonwoods stabilize the banks against erosion. Sparked by energy from the sun, fed by water and minerals from the earth, streamside plants provide food for water striders and caddis flies, which in turn provide food for the stickleback and squawfish. These feed streamside predators, from egrets and herons to wildcats. In the life that comes up from underneath the pavement, everything continuously feeds and re-creates everything else.

Under my jacket now, I run my fingers over my ribs and then my collarbone, feel through to my own skeleton. I think of the archaeological dig in New Mexico that I so enjoyed when I was seventeen years old; most vividly now, I remember the three ancient Pueblo Indian skeletons I unearthed. How, with a toothbrush, I delicately cleaned off each bone, the vertebrae of the spine, the ribcage. Now here in Ocean View, perhaps in Spenger's lot, there are skeletons of Ohlone families still underneath the pavement. I am convinced. With the same care with which I brushed off the Pueblo Indian bones so many years ago, with which I recently traced the contour of my own breasts, I feel through to the skeletons of the Ohlone people. I am drawn now to dark worlds under the pavement, to what is before and beneath, back through the millennia.

Chapter 21

shellmound

original use: home

FROM UNDER THE PAVEMENT, the train tracks, the factories and lumberyard; from before the Ocean View settlement and the ranchos of the Spanish—I feel the pull of the shellmound. Stephanie has engaged me in a crusade to protect the remains of this mound, only several blocks to the west of our house. Rising above the north bank of Strawberry Creek where the waters running down from the hills emptied into the Bay, this mound was one of the approximately 425 ancient shellmounds that rimmed the Bay. Archaeologists are finding that people lived on the various mounds for thousands of years as far back as 3700 B.C.E. To encompass this shellmound, my mind opens to the vast spans of geologic time.

Mainly composed of charcoal, ash, and shell, these mounds have often been called kitchen middens, a term that comes from the Danish *koekkenmoedding* meaning "kitchen refuse." At first I thought of a shellmound as a pile of ancient garbage, having no idea of the alchemy of this heap of refuse nor of the importance it would have for me in exploding my earlier understandings of home.

While common in the protected lagoons and bays of California, shellmounds are found on both coasts of North America and have been uncovered from Denmark to Australia and New

Zealand. As I delve into the history of our West Berkeley mound, my sense of life in these ancient times widens to sites around the world.

This shellmound underworld taps into my own darkness, into old fears and fascinations. It's the human burials that draw me most of all. In contrast to many other mounds worldwide, Bay mounds include this extra dimension. Amid the remains of shellfish, sea otter, and salmon; amid awls, mortars, and fish-hooks—archaeologists have uncovered whole cemeteries. In the 1950s excavation at the West Berkeley mound, almost one hundred skeletons were exhumed. To explore the world of the shell-mound, I risk a blind descent into a dim and unpredictable landscape in ancient history and in my own mind.

On the invitation of Stephanie, I have helped plan a confer-ence on what I've come to think of as "our" shellmound as well as a nearby mound also threatened by commercial expansion. At the conference, I sit in the front row as Kent Lightfoot, archae-ologist at the University of California, introduces the mounds.

"After the melting of the glaciers in the Pleistocene epoch, the rising sea level created the Bay. Four or five thousand years ago, the sea level rise began to flatten out and the Bay to take a more stable form. Wherever freshwater streams entered the Bay, great shellmounds developed, usually with smaller ones clustered around them. Most of the large mounds appear to have been abandoned, although the reasons for this abandonment are not fully known; it was possibly in the wake of some drastic environ-mental change, perhaps a great drought.

"On top of these mounds, whose cores held many generations of ancestors, the native peoples made their villages . . ."

They lived on top? Did I mishear what he said? A sense of shock and interest. People can't literally have lived over their garbage and their dead! But, indeed, evidence suggests that shell-mounds were intentionally elevated mounded villages—with storage pits, earth ovens, hearths—on top of ancestral remains; this was where people made their home.

As I listen to this ancient history, images of the landscape traverse the millennia. I picture the mounds, rising like islands over the Bay, circles of tule huts safely above the tidal action as the sea level continues to rise. From these raised villages, silver salmon, steelhead, and seals are easily viewed in the Bay below. And at night, fishermen crisscrossing the Bay recall that Orion's belt will return at midnight on the winter solstice as it has every year through the millennia. They look up at the glittering cooking fires, emblems of their precious homesite.

To preserve whatever is left of the shellmound—before encroachment of a proposed parking garage and high-end mall—Stephanie and other "shellmounders" are working to get the mound approved as a City of Berkeley landmark. This involves a long process, including approval by the Landmarks Commission, review of the completed landmark application at a public hearing, and if there are appeals contesting the landmark status, battles over appeals at the Berkeley City Council.

Designed to "landmark" buildings, the official application requires adherence to a strict form. Many local buildings in Ocean View have been landmarked. In its official application, the Pilgrim's Rest Church lists the date of construction (1878) and original use (worship). When Stephanie sends me the formal application for the shellmound, I am struck by the incongruity. It's impossible to straitjacket this mound to fit late-twentieth-century terms.

The Site and Remnants of the West Berkeley Native Shellmound (CA-Ala-307)
. . .

6. Dates of Construction:
Shellmound ca. 3700 B.C.–800 A.D.
7. Builder: The shellmound had developed over a period of
4,500 years by the use of the earliest known inhabitants.
Architect: (This line is left blank.)

. . .

9. Original owner: No known owner
Original use: Home

Meanwhile, talk of this mound circulates in the Ocean View
neighborhood. On a walk with Cleo, I notice a mounted drilling
rig in the center of Spenger's parking lot. A group of folks wearing floppy hats and leaning on shovels are standing around the
drilling rig. This is an archaeological firm hired by the owners
of the lot to do test drilling, checking for the remains of the
mound. Remembering my earlier adventure with the jackhammer, I watch the broad auger cut through the asphalt and
plunge down, spinning into the dirt to reveal the stratigraphy—
wet mud, wet sand, clay, silt, and pebbles. Cleo gives me a filmy-
eyed look, then takes a sniff as the team of what seem to be
student archaeologists clean out the findings from the drill
curves. Some use shovels and some their bare hands. I feel the
pull to dig my own hands into this mud and sand, to feel down
through thousands of years into this ancient home.

At the shellmound conference, Kent Lightfoot had talked
about a way to sense what's below the surface of the ground
without digging, removing what's found, or destroying it.
Through what he termed "geophysical methods," one might
study ancient worlds while leaving them intact. What a beautiful
idea, I had thought when I first heard it—to observe through
the senses with acoustic reflection, thermal sensing, and ground-
penetrating radar. It sounded to me like mindfulness—a way to
look without interfering. I love these methods for honoring the
history so in keeping with the way I would like to honor it.

Without damaging the meaning of this ancient heritage, can I learn from it, allow it to permeate my own explorations of home?

When I'd first interviewed Stephanie on her passion to preserve the neighborhood, I had told her about my recent interest in the meaning of the word *inhabit*, with its Indo-European root *ghabh*, tracing back to "give" and to "receive."

Several days later, Stephanie had delivered a large manila envelope to my front door. Inside was a scholarly article on San Francisco Bay shellmounds by Ed Luby, a researcher and professor at the University of California at Berkeley; he'd been a speaker at the shellmound conference. Clipped onto the article was a card with a neatly inscribed entry from the *Oxford English Dictionary* on the word *inhabit,* followed by a note: "Alas, no mention of give or receive. But check out Ed Luby's article. I think it's relevant to that give-and-receive idea you're getting at. (Reading this article has revolutionized my life!!!) Steph."

As I begin to study the shellmound, I give this article a serious read. For me too, it is riveting. As I study it, I begin to sense a kind of alchemy when food remains and burials are layered to create home. So many of my assumptions are turned upside down. First to be overturned is my sense of the composition of the mound—what seemed to be refuse. The shells, bones, teeth, beaks—the nonedible parts of what people ate—may not have been seen as garbage but as symbols of the species that provided the community with food, that offered them life. Not trash at all but sacred emblems.

If the composition of the mound was sacred, daily life on this mound may have had a sacred cast. Here on this hill, mortuary festivities—dance, music, and feasting—may have been orchestrated regularly by the community above their dead. Ceremonial relations with the sacred emblems of shell and bone may have allowed villagers ongoing communion, a kind of sacrament, with the species that fed them.

It's hard for me to see this seeming garbage dump in a new way—to overturn my habitual understandings. But when Luby calls up the image of the shaman—arrayed in bones, feathers, and teeth—I begin to get an inkling of his meaning. I recall from my youth watching dancers in the Pueblo Indian ceremonies and seeing photographs of shamans. I'd never given any thought to why a shaman might be outfitted in the feathers, fur, or antlers of the animals eaten by the community, why these totems might be seen as sacred. Now it makes intuitive sense. Somehow this opens up the shellmound world for me. The whole shellmound, after all, was made out of that sacred stuff. Bones and shells imbued with this special significance created the matrix of the mound. I picture a kind of compost heap, at the same time practical and symbolic.

So burying the dead in this sacred matrix may not have been indifferent disposal but rather the burial of one part of the community in the matrix from which the community took its life. In feasting above the buried remains of the dead, the villagers perhaps saw themselves as "feeding" their ancestors. Luby put it this way: "The dead must be fed." In exchange for this ritual offering, villagers presumably asked for help from their ancestors—to sustain the species that offered them life. When I think this through, I see why Stephanie sent me Luby's article, why she linked this theory of the shellmound to giving-and-receiving. I begin to imagine the shellmound dwellers as they gathered together for their ceremonial exchanges, that sacred giving-and-receiving—among the living, the ancestors, and the species that offered life. Truly this is a beautiful understanding of what it means to inhabit a home.

ON OUR CORNER, five neighbors are beginning to gather on Sunday evenings to meditate together in one of our homes. This gathering feels like something people have been doing here through the millennia. Our neighborhood sitting is something I envisioned one hot afternoon when I meditated in the attic in my grandmother's chaise. But it has taken a while to make it happen. When Michael and Zoe moved in next door and I learned that Michael was a meditator, I was determined to find other meditators on the block.

On a hunch, I called up a couple, friends of Sheryl and Roy's on the other side of their house on H Street. I thought I'd once seen Paul at a local Zen center, and I knew that Genevieve taught aikido. (Didn't martial artists sometimes meditate?) I found myself suggesting that we meet in Michael and Zoe's newly vacated basement. Rented out by former owners as a work space, this basement felt like exactly the right place to join with others who make their home here on our corner. I'd just go down our back steps, past the dawn redwood, through the gate, along the brick path in Michael and Zoe's side garden, and there I'd be.

On our first Sunday evening, we take off our shoes; we step down into the low-ceilinged basement, feel the cold concrete under our bare feet, breathe in a faint whiff of dank basement smell. This too has the feel of a way station, a place to join in silence and attention—to open to the unknown.

Uncertain how to begin, we find our way through Michael's music stands and amplifiers (in his free time, he plays the guitar). We're an irregular and awkward group trained in different traditions of meditation. We're not even quite sure how to arrange ourselves on the floor. After some experimentation, Genevieve and I sit across from each other. We alternate with Michael and Paul, both trained in Zen Buddhism (Soto style), who face the wall. So while Genevieve and I face in, eyes closed, the "wall watchers" face out, eyes open toward opposing walls. Zoe, who is pregnant, stretches her full length on her shawl, completing a circle.

As we continue to gather in our basement meditation group,

we develop a kind of routine. We line up our shoes at the door. We set out our meditation cushions. To begin and end our time of silence together, we ring a bell and then we bow. Ours is a ragged but satisfying circle where—as I'm imagining it did in shellmound days—home also means temple, means church.

Often I reflect on the shellmound, on its many layers of meaning. In conjuring up a vision of this corner where I live, I explode the conventional categories. Instead of separating out the house where we sleep and eat, the dump down the road, the cemetery across town, the church on the corner, I take a vision-ary leap and superimpose these domains. I call it home and take refuge in that.

Chapter 22

shellmound mind

dump and cemetery

I'VE TAKEN ON what I call "shellmound mind." This is an experiment in imagination. Can I risk that ancient experience of home where categories such as household and church, garbage dump and cemetery—so separate in our current world—converge?

On my peculiar quest, the cemetery feels like the next essential stopping place at the entrance of the regions of the dark. Months ago, when I was tracing the lives of the Offe family, I made a plan to visit some of their graves. Now I have a wild idea—to combine this visit with my shellmound experiment. As far as I can tell from the death certificates and obituaries, these graves are at Sunset View Cemetery, in a town neighboring ours. The distance between the Offe residence and the Offe graves is several miles. That's the usual way in recent centuries—to separate home from grave. So as I head off for the cemetery this morning, I have a double mission: not only to visit the graves of these ancestors of our corner, but to try to imagine this burial place as in the days of the shellmound, as if it were under my residence—to see this ancestral burial ground as home.

THE SMELL OF PERFUME overwhelms my senses. I'm in the lobby of the Danish modern chapel building of Sunset View.

I take in the ambience: orderly, pleasant, clean—stained glass windows, comfortable couches, private nooks, a small fountain, carnations.

As I enter the lobby, a receptionist nods toward me sympathetically. A group of people dressed in black is checking in, then they're ushered off by dark-suited cemetery staff, presumably for a funeral or a "viewing" down a corridor to the right. The office where I have been sent is down another corridor to the left.

I had imagined that the perfume emanated from some viewing room, perhaps to camouflage the smell of death. But as I follow the signs for the office, the scent becomes more cloying. On the telephone, the receptionist had assured me that if I came in and wrote down the names and dates, someone would direct me to the site of anyone here interred. So I fill in the form at the counter: Frederick Offe (1853–1946), Annie Offe (1857–1932), William Hans Offe (1880–1913), Elizabeth Offe Cleary (1881–1952). From the inner recesses behind the counter, a young woman clerk appears, lashes lowered, and takes my list. In her wake follows an intoxicating waft of said scent (so she's the one).

So far this expedition has the aura of a charade. Ever since I've come onto these manicured grounds, the cemetery staff has looked at me with veiled eyes of muted sympathy. But only I know that these graves I am visiting aren't even remotely those of my own relatives, even friends of friends. And despite the fact that the obituaries point this way, I'm finding it hard to believe that I'll actually locate my faux kin. It's as if I've cooked up a hoax that is soon to be unmasked.

The girl at the counter disappears and returns with a map. "They're in Adult A," she says.

It gives me a start. "All four graves?"

"They're all in one grave." (Do I detect distaste?)

I feel a bit awkward. "Is that the usual way?"

"Not at all!" she says. She looks back at her notes and adds, "It's an unmarked grave."

"How will I know then . . . which one is . . ." I pause. ". . . theirs?"

Again the girl disappears into the back, this time returning with the darkly dressed man who had ushered along the funeral guests. I think of the spiky guide with Day-Glo hair at Reptile Haven who years ago had introduced me to the realms of night. By contrast, this escort into the terrain of the dead is a tad disappointing, attired in his conventional black suit that looks shiny over his wide girth. He draws me a rough sketch, diagramming the route from the chapel past the various plots. "This here's Adult B. You'll find Adult A next to the lot for storage vaults." Drawing an X on his map, he hands it to me. "Go up to the eighth row. Count in five. You'll find an unmarked grave. One grave," he affirms. "Three cremated, and the one fellow, William Hans, in a coffin."

After the dark guide recedes to the back, the girl rolls her eyes. She leans toward me, her tone confidential. "I never could have figured out how to get you to that grave." She glances over her shoulder, gesturing back, including the whole cemetery grounds in one sweep. "I don't ever go . . . up there." I'm assaulted once again by her perfume—not strong enough, I see, to overcome the fear.

So I set off for "up there" (which, if the graves of the ancestors were below me in my shellmound home, would be "down here"). In my fifty-four years, I haven't spent time in many cemeteries, only the tiny New England cemetery for my dad, and the big Jewish cemetery outside of New York City where my great-uncle Reg was buried in a family vault.

Up the winding road, I get a glimpse of the extensive grounds, the crematory, and the urn garden. This is hardly the small country cemetery with its horse-drawn wagons first laid out in 1908 on the outskirts of town. Adult A is on a little hill with a live oak tree overhanging a stone wall in the back. Many of the graves are from 1913, the same year the Offe family buried William Hans. As I follow the curve to the crest of the hillock, I'm surprised by how many at the top are newborns with little sculpted lambs in the headstones.

A heavyset man in a work suit, gloves, boots, and a pair of goggles says he'll help me. This new guide ushers me along the path. Pointing to a grassy rectangle—blank between two marked graves—he shows me the presumed Offe grave. He hikes his foot up on a neighboring headstone that's askew on its base, leans his elbow on his knee, and puts his chin in his cupped hand. "I'm the one who digs them," he says with a heavy accent I can't quite place. "For fifteen years. At first I felt a little . . ." He shrugs, scrunches up his face. "But now, it's regular." He pauses. "I don't know what you do every day. But it's just like that."

A truck passes by filled with freshly dug dirt, some turf. A tractor beeps as it backs up into the lot of storage vaults; a booted, goggled worker raises the forklift to hook a vault and carry it off. As we speak, my gravedigger friend gives the headstone a few gentle kicks, swivels it, and sets it solidly—nicely aligned now—on its stone base. "I still do feel bad when I bury babies," he says. "I have three children. Fourteen, eighteen, and twenty."

When the gravedigger leaves, I get ready to sit on the grave. I detect a slight, almost indistinguishable parting in the grass between this unmarked plot and the plots on either side with the headstones.

Along the road, a hearse winds slowly by followed by three or four cars with their lights on bright. The tractor returns to the lot, the chains swinging free, and picks up another vault.

I sit down on the damp grass on what must be the Offe grave. Why are they all in this one grave? Couldn't the Offes afford graves for each person? Couldn't they afford a headstone? I get a chilling image of the headstone on my dad's grave where we buried his ashes.

Best to get to the task at hand. I've come here to bear witness to the forebears of my home place. And to risk truly knowing the cemetery as home. I'll start with some moments of silence. Straightening my posture, I settle into my spot overlooking the winding cemetery road, the expansive grounds. Even as I close my eyes, I am unnerved—drawn into the dark underworld of the cemetery. There's an elemental odor of newly dug dirt, a sudden rustling. Off balance, I crane my neck, open my eyes to glimpse a squirrel skittering up the live oak. Something is about to happen behind me, I'm convinced. Increasingly agitated, I turn this way, then that. In a last-ditch turn-around, I try facing uphill, buttocks unbalanced on the slope, eyes wide open. Not quite the meditation I'd planned.

On the tombstones, I see names and dates; up the rise in the hill, the graves of the children. In college, there was a little country cemetery on the campus where some of my friends used to go with their boyfriends to have sex. I never did choose to do that. I've always dreaded cemeteries.

In the following weeks, I am drawn to make further pilgrimages, taking the winding path of Sunset View to this unmarked grave. It feels like what I need to do if I truly want to find more ease in this cemetery home. For centuries, Buddhist monks (the Homeless Ones) have trained themselves to let go of their conventional identities, have trained their minds to be steady— through whatever pain or loss—by doing meditations in charnel grounds. This feels similar, on a path toward what is beginning to feel like a kind of homeless home.

THE MORNING AFTER one of my cemetery excursions, my whole family ends up in the bathroom at one time. Actually, this happens more often than I would like. We do have another toilet and sink upstairs in the attic. But the bathroom downstairs with the shower and tub—on the same level as the living room and kitchen—has the draw. So in the morning, here we often are, all of us at once.

Patrick is sitting on the toilet and Katy is in the shower. I am at the sink brushing my teeth. Sometimes it's Patrick in the shower or Katy at the sink. Whatever the configuration, Cleo—old lady that she is—still barks and paws, insisting on being where the action is. No matter how many times we put her out, she noses open the door, comes in, and either lies down on the bath rug by the tub, or—if she can maneuver it, as she has today—curls up just between your legs while you're on the toilet.

I wouldn't say this is happy harmony and that we're all enjoying each others' company. In fact, we're bumping into each other and tripping over each others' feet. And whenever we flush or turn on the water to brush our teeth or shave, that makes the shower water turn too hot or too cold.

But as I contemplate the scene this morning, I also wouldn't say there's any enmity. Rather there's a sense of allowing, of appreciation, of reassurance that, yes, we are a family, and to accomplish the essential tasks of getting ready for our day, we can—with minimal conflict and some good humor—do so all together in a very small space.

Somehow it makes me think of Frederick and Annie Offe, William Hans and Lizzie, all buried in that one grave together.

Like the Bureau of Vital Statistics, this family grave seems like a true way station, offering occasion to tap into what feels like both homelessness and home. When I sit myself down on this grave, there's a shift in perception. Beneath the conflicts and bruises of every day, I see something shared—a continuum of families dying, families living. In that precious time of living—amid all the demands, disappointments, and blames—there's a possibility to find home, to allow for one another just as we are in moments of appreciation, of love.

As I've descended through all that is before and beneath, through all layers of the mound and layers of the mind, I've felt sudden flashes of such intimacy, of almost unbearable preciousness. But underneath that, a hint of terror at the mortality of my little family. In a descent into the muck of the terrain, something seems to be cracking and shifting within my psyche. I've tapped into hidden places inside, wild and unkempt. In my everyday exchanges, feral rages and hungers have burst through me; I've been shaken by the intensity of what's been disinterred. Can I hold all this?

I've come to count on the basement meditation group. Finally, with the support of those who live on shared ground, I'm able to keep to a regular practice of sitting down and embracing whatever comes to mind. We're meeting now in the early mornings in addition to our Sunday gathering. For the early-bird sittings, Michael and Zoe have given me the key. I have to be prompt to open the door. We continue to follow a simple ritual. We take off our shoes and arrange our cushions (by now we know where each one goes). We set out a statuette of Kuan Yin, the goddess of compassion, who is said to hear the cries of the world. We ring the bell. Just having this quiet time with neighbors gives me a chance to stay put and take notice of what's flaring through, outside and in—at once ordinary and sacred—to include all that as home.

IN A VAST, open warehouse, a great mound of garbage heaves, collapses, and spreads. The air sickens with the fetid odor. Shoved around by little tractors, the mound oozes out wheels and broken machinery. All manner of mattresses, old chairs, and ironing boards mix in with decaying foods and kitty litter, paint thinner, and insecticide. Seagulls scuttle in and out, scavenging.

Over this rank and gelatinous mountain, something that looks like steam rises.

After the cemetery, the next way station is the dump. In shellmound days, of course, what we now see as refuse and mess may well have been seen as mystery, as miracle. I try to remember that as I spend a few hours here at the garbage transfer station, exploring whether I might acclimate myself to this "garbage" to risk this too as home.

Ever since we've lived in this house, all of the garbage from our household, from the Ocean View neighborhood, and (as far as I know) from the entire city of Berkeley has passed through this transfer station on Gilman Street. The transfer station is at B Street, just a little west of where we live. As I drove down for this garbage experiment, I headed through the industrial zone familiar from my walks; I passed the sand treatment plant and other factories I'd walked past; I entered a dead-end road. Familiar too. Down at the far end, across from today's transfer station, was that storage facility—once slaughterhouse, originally municipal incinerator—constructed early in the century to burn mounting garbage.

Parked here now, watching today's mound of refuse churn, I remember descriptions of garbage in the early days of the European settlement. Kitchen scraps were fed to the chickens and pigs, thrown in the nearest empty lot or creek bed. Most garbage was simply buried with the do-it-yourself approach. When the population got too dense, this do-it-yourself method was forbidden so householders hired a man with a wagon to dispose of their waste; they didn't concern themselves about where he hauled it.

EARLY IN THE TWENTIETH CENTURY, plans were made by the cities of Berkeley and Oakland (next door) to collect garbage and to send it out on barges to be dumped in the Pacific Ocean.

With this goal, private companies with horse-drawn wagons ("honey wagons") were hired to collect the trash. To reduce the bulk, Berkeley decided to burn down the trash before sending it out to sea. So that's when the incinerator was built at the shoreline. But public protest flared up because the cost of the new incinerator was exorbitant and the honey wagons were rutting the pavement and dribbling their contents in the streets. The incinerator was subsequently closed down, and in the following year the Signal Steam Ship Company hauled the wettest and smelliest garbage out to sea.

When the garbage boat was wrecked, the incinerator was started up again only to be abandoned once more after a new wave of public protest over the cost and the smell. Then a fill-and-cover method was instituted. This began with five blocks of marshy land to the west of the shore and finally filled 175 acres of bay. And following that, Berkeley set up this transfer station. Whatever is not recycled here is now carted off to Altamont Pass outside Livermore, a nearby town, to be buried.

Now, at the transfer station, I drive from spot to spot trying to escape incoming garbage trucks. Whenever I can, I park, lean my journal on the steering wheel, and scribble down impressions. The little tractors zoom back and forth attacking the heaps of refuse, clapping their crablike pincers. Those crab-tractors are pulling out large metal objects from the mound and depositing them in other bins. First comes a bicycle, then a metal bathtub, a toaster oven, an old record player, and what looks like some kind of motor.

Just as I'm about to get out of the car to take a closer look, a tractor speeds by followed by a city garbage truck, which swings in and backs up to regurgitate its load into the heap. In front of the mound of garbage, a sign reads "Children and pets must remain in vehicle." The guys directing the traffic are all in protective gear—bright orange vests, hard hats, goggles, nose and mouth masks. Better stay put.

So I settle in behind the wheel and try a few minutes of dump meditation. The whirring and beeping of the trucks takes over my consciousness—that and the aroma of the garbage. A sharp rap on the car startles me. A guy in a hard hat motions for me to roll down the window. " 'Scuse me ma'am, but would you mind, just for your own safety that is, moving your car?" It comes out that this guy's a supervisor, but that someone higher in rank has just radioed him and told him to get rid of me. " 'Go find out what that woman's doing.' " He mimics his boss's tough tone. " 'She's taking notes!' "

"You guys ought to be well paid," I comment. "This is nasty work."

He replies, "Not likely." Then, "Hey, why don't you write that down?!" Then he points at my journal and he shakes his head. "Like I said before, my job's to take care of things around here." Gesturing toward the whole panorama of this dump—tractors, bins of aluminum, the garbage heap—he says, "We here take care of the stuff that you all don't want."

I'm taken by a feeling I can't name, disgust maybe or simply sadness, for all of this waste. I'm looking out at unwanted appliances, furniture, clothes, foodstuffs that people in this neighborhood—perhaps even our family—wanted, bought, gave each other as gifts, to which we once claimed ownership, and now are throwing out. Unwanted because it's too old or not quite the right color or beginning to decay. Somehow it failed to offer the satisfaction that it first seemed to promise.

This sets me questioning. Did we actually own those things? If we did, could we just throw them away? Supposing we trick ourselves into believing that we "owned" them in the first place; when we thought we "owned" them, didn't we think we had responsibility to them? For them? Given the fact that, on some level, maybe they never truly belonged to us, do we still have responsibility for them after we've thrown them away and decided they're no longer "ours"?

AFTER MY VISITS TO THE GARBAGE HEAP, as with those to the cemetery, the imagery stays with me—landscaping my dreams, becoming indistinguishable from my own inner process. The oozing mountain of refuse churns with cast-out memories, tantrums, terrors—all that my neighborhood quest has exhumed. I'm grateful for what we're coming to call the "basement zendo" where I must show up each morning. This is a vow I cannot break because I'm the one with the key; my fellows are counting on me and I cannot let them down. So I sit myself on my cushion, countering urges to either rebury or resuscitate. I try to take a look at this as well—this garbage of griefs and rages—to tend to it as it comes into view, allowing that maybe I never exactly "owned" it either. But I can do my best to take care of it, to see it as sacred, to include it as home.

IN THE GATHERING DUSK one evening, I take a walk with Cleo. As summer bougainvillea and woodbine bloom, families harvest their tomatoes and zucchini, hang out in the street watering their front gardens. Here in someone's yard, the compost heaps are covered with canvas but unmistakable. The air is saturated with odor: manure and straw, rotting foods—all heating up, beginning to cook. A possum slinks by, eyes Cleo, and disappears from view. A swarm of shiny black ravens descends on the heaps. Scavengers. Textured by breath of compost, of ravens, of possums, of the honeyed woodbine, the evening air wakes my senses. In my belly, I feel the eros of exchange.

A breeze picks up, carries a sour after-scent. What felt sensuous now turns rank, disturbing. Did the shellmound dwellers make their piles of refuse and bury their dead downwind from their huts? Or did they simply become inured to these smells? Was their experience of smells quite different from what we modern Westerners find noxious? What was the effect of all this rot on Strawberry Creek? Ed Luby says that the lime in the shell may have acted as a disinfectant. Did this prevent disease from decomposing food and corpses? I watch the ravens attack the compost, voracious now in their pillaging. Animals and birds in shellmound days must have scavenged the shells and bones and picked them clean.

Heady from the mix of scents and the shifting hues of dusk, I wend my way toward my house. It's hard to imagine living so intimately with the cycles of decay. Images from my recent forays spin through my thoughts, coincide. Both burial ground and dump are separated from where we in our community eat and sleep, where children play. In both settings, workmen protect themselves with goggles and masks; with boots, gloves, and hats. Little trucks with chains and hooks carry coffins, while similar trucks with clawlike pincers disentangle and carry trash.

Of course, the dump appears foul; the cemetery, at least on the surface, antiseptically clean. But the two work on the same principle. Both are stations in an immense recycling plant. In one, it's animal, vegetable, and inorganic refuse that is decomposing; in the other, it's human bodies, the refuse left after we humans die. I see the two juxtaposed in the vast shellmound home of our world—where life breaks down, feeds the gulls, the worms, the bacteria and feeds into new life.

For safety and comfort, it does seem to make sense to separate our twenty-first-century houses from the garbage dump and the cemetery. To ensure a sweet, pleasant ambience, to protect ourselves from the dangers of disease, we humans have evolved toward separating out these venues. But there's another danger. Dividing our home up in this way—like dividing thought into safe and unsafe, sacred and ordinary, home and homeless—can buffer and blind us; it prevents us from seeing the fundamental relationship, the all-encompassing give-and-receive.

Chapter 23

owner? guardian?

ON RAINY WEEKENDS in the dark autumn months, I sometimes take a break from family and neighbors to stay at a rural
Zen center on the Pacific coast. In the mornings, I hike a high
hill in mist so thick I can barely recognize the path. In the
evenings, I hole up by a woodstove, tending the fire, reading
flames and the glow of embers long into the night. These so-
journs feel somehow in keeping with my quest for home—now
descending further down into the darkness, through the millennia of the shellmound, into the bowels of the earth and unlit
regions of the mind.

Before the sun rises and late in the day as the sun goes down,
I join the black-robed Zen priests in the dark of the zendo to
meditate, bow, and chant. I'm not used to chanting; in fact, with
my secular turn of mind, the rote recitation of these words
(often in Japanese or Pali) makes me uneasy. Yet, in spite of my
skepticism, there's a charge to the chants, intoned in deep hyp-
notic cadences that resonate through my body.

. . . all dharmas are marked by emptiness; they neither arise
nor cease, are neither defiled nor pure, neither increase nor
decrease . . . Therefore given emptiness, there is no form . . .
no eyes, no ears, no nose, no tongue, no body, no mind; no
sight, no sound, no smell, no taste, no touch. . .

At the close of a service, after a series of bows, I join in one more chant, which I am beginning to remember by heart.

> All my ancient twisted karma
> From beginningless greed, hate, and delusion
> Born through body, speech, and mind
> I now fully avow.

The chanting leaves me with stray thoughts, vague questions about emptiness, about the nature of experience, about the evolution of a home place. Can I control it? Is it mine?

WHEN I RETURN TO OCEAN VIEW, the rains continue. Cold city storms match my winter doldrums, moods sweeping through, dark and weepy. Over the back fence, in Roy and Sheryl's yard, the cats run for shelter, Velvet, Patches, Simba, streaking into the garage. Out front, turbid waters rush past our house.

As the water overflows the storm drains, I think of Strawberry Creek before it was culverted—descending from the hills, zigzagging through many yards. How vivid this is from my recent research into the underground worlds of creeks and sewers diverted to culverts. In the rainy season of early Ocean View, runoff from dirt roads mixed with horse droppings and urine emptied into the creek. Contaminated water flooded everywhere, in the streets, under houses, into wells, into underground water supplies. Later, with widespread use of the automobile, petroleum by-products flowed in, as did increasing amounts of raw human sewage that seeped into the creeks where the sewer and storm drain systems were interconnected. Over the years, movement along the Hayward earthquake fault cracked the culvert and sewer lines under the university's Memorial Football Stadium. Until campus engineering staff finally eliminated cross connections, large volumes of raw sewage found their way into the storm drain line, with particularly high levels of fecal coliform in the creek during the half-time of Saturday football games.

Now, according to some newsletters I've read, discharges continue from sources more toxic. Since the 1940s, certain laboratories have allegedly discharged thousands of curies of radiation into the upper watershed of the creek, and this pollution has been compounded by emissions from the 2,500 university science laboratories and releases of radioactive hydrogen from another facility.

The creek becomes an ongoing repository for the refuse of our lives. Does this creek belong to us? Is anyone responsible for it?

LATE IN THE WEEK, on one more dark winter morning, I take a cheer-me-up walk with Stephanie, talking current happenings and ancient history as we meander the streets of the neighborhood. Stephanie tells me about a meeting she's going to. It's a private, "invitation-only" meeting of people who are interested in "daylighting" Strawberry Creek—opening up the culvert, so it can run free, just as in the days of the shellmound and the early European settlement. Still not completely cheered, I say, "I should have been invited to that meeting." Several years earlier, hadn't I had the idea of engaging the local developers and merchants in our neighborhood to bring Strawberry Creek out of the culvert? In fact, I tell her, it very well may have been I who suggested this to the very fellow who is now organizing the invitation-only meeting. It feels as if it was my idea.

"Do you think you own your ideas?" asks Stephanie, maybe a bit sharply. I feel it like a slap.

I'm dismayed to see how much I have at stake in being known for my wonderful ideas. I imagine Strawberry Creek liberated from its culvert, wending its way through Ocean View, and indeed I do want to take credit. Yes, I want somehow to own it—the idea and maybe, tangentially, as its patron, the creek too!

Meanwhile, Stephanie, who doesn't seem to have seen how accurately her reprimand has found its mark, chats on about the relief she experiences in passing on ideas to so many people. "Often," she says, "people think the ideas are their own; they work hard, carrying out projects that I would never have the time and energy to do by myself." As she talks, I consider all of the ideas I get from Stephanie that feel like my own (many of which propel my explorations of this home place).

The very notion of claiming ownership—of an idea, of a creek (what about a shellmound?)—is beginning to seem absurd. As my mind moves back and forth through layers of experience, I see this tendency to claim ownership. Not just of ideas or places, but of moods as well. Later in the day, I catch a dreary mood before it takes me over. I can see it moving through beneath the surface. I stop and take a good look. This mood just may not be connected to any of the particular situations to which I might attach it. In fact, that dark flood feels downright independent and impersonal. I didn't ask it to come and I don't seem to be able to get it to go away, but even though I am in a sense carrying it, I am beginning to get the feeling that it does not belong to me.

ON SUNDAY EVENING, I wrench myself away from more research on sewers, and my mind saturated with fecal imagery, I go next door to sit in our basement zendo. I fold my legs and begin to listen to my breath. Instead I hear in basso profundo: "All my ancient twisted karma . . ." Try as I might, I cannot shake this chant nor the images, dark and rank, coiling through.

What a grim chant. I don't even like chanting. But here it is, having worked its way into my consciousness. After failed attempts to fight it, I give in and start repeating it silently to myself. I'm intrigued, although I don't want to make too much of this. It's about karma after all, and I'm not even completely comfortable using the term. Still, I do have a sense of how it is used: Karma is the law of cause and effect. This happens because that happens, which can be endlessly complicated, involving countless causes and conditions.

Just to see where the words will take me, I begin to play with the meaning of the chant. First off, the karma is not only twisted, it's ancient. For me these days, "ancient" reaches back through the Ocean View settlement, through the Spanish ranchos, through the devastation of the lives and culture of natives who tended their land through many thousands of years in broader California. It goes back through the forty-five hundred years of our local shellmound, even before the migrations of protohumans onto our continent, through the history of the dawn redwood, through the evolution of living things.

So this karma goes back a long way. Given that it carries the influences of all of history, I surely don't "own" the karma exclusively. But it does move through me. (I keep picturing my angst and grievances twisting along in the shifting stream of all things.) And here's the rub. It's born "through body, speech, and mind"—what I do, what I say, and what I think. All of which have countless consequences.

I consider the words *fully avow*, which close the chant. As I repeat them, I feel I'm saying, "I acknowledge it openly; I am aware of it (fully)." In fact, when I chant these words, it feels like I'm taking a vow. To always notice what I'm doing and even what I'm thinking.

This Zen chant brings me back to questions that have come up as I've explored my home terrain. As the movement of cause and effect twists into view, I take account: Do we dump waste, either fecal or otherwise, into the creeks? Do we bury insecticide and paint thinners in a neighboring town? Do we think toxic thoughts toward others, toward ourselves? Do we spew out toxic words? For my own part, if I can fully avow what's going on, perhaps I'll be less driven by the momentum.

All messages seem to point toward the same conclusion: I may not own this great flood of life events—this continually shifting, arising, and dissolving homeless home—but how I act and think feeds into it and, yes, I do have a responsibility to it. For it.

AT SUNSET ONE EVENING, the rains stop, offering us temporary respite. Neighborhood families step out into their yards. While Katy is baby-sitting little Olivia next door, I look out the kitchen window into the adjoining yards where jasmine and potato vine cascade over the fences. Just beyond Sheryl's fence, beneath the dawn redwood, I'm surprised to see Katy carrying Olivia. Zoe, with her now-visible belly, is there too, loping up and down Sheryl's driveway. And Sheryl, doubled up, gripping her arms around her own shoulders, is running up and down also. At first I think she's laughing—or maybe she's crying.

When I come out on the back landing, Sheryl shouts up to me, "Call animal rescue. We need an ambulance!" As I dash down to see what's going on, she insists, "For Patches. When I was coming in the driveway, I ran him over."

But Patches flees in panic and cannot be found. Sheryl catches sight of him hidden in a pile of bricks across from the garage. All of us now lean over the bricks to see traces of blood on the pavement.

"Cats do that," says Sheryl. "If they're in a state of shock, they run away and hide. They go off alone to recover in solitude—or to die." She can't stop shaking. "Ran over my own cat," she keeps berating herself, no matter how many times we remind her how slowly she drives through the gate, how careful she always is, how many causes and conditions could have led to this sad event.

Night is coming on as we begin to look for Patches, as we plan a search through all of the backyards. Zoe and Sheryl carry cardboard kitty carriers; Suzanna, who's made a flier to post, searches with Radio on leash. We're joined by Andy, who shares the care of several cats. Finally Roy, who's rushed home from work in San Francisco, joins in with a big lantern and an open can of tuna fish.

With some trepidation, I join in this nighttime posse. After scouring our yard, littered with broken lawn mowers and our once-again neglected and festering compost heap, I circle around to explore other yards. This is the first time I've ever risked entering most of these yards, the backside of what is familiar to me. I have an uncanny sense I've had before during these dark winter months—that I am stepping into the under-world of the block.

First I brave the patio of the Pilgrim's Rest Church, past an old sleeping bag rolled up under the ramp, through the tangled weeds behind the community hall. I check the court of the apartment complex, the gardens of the man who feeds the par-rots and the artist who's "an item" with the woman of the flow-ing scarves.

In the twelve years I've lived here, I've never been over in the yard at Grandma Darlene's. In fact, the last time I even knocked at the front door was over a year ago, to bring by a casserole after Grandma Darlene died. When Donna opens the door, I explain about Patches. Donna tells me that the side entrance to the backyard is chained; I can only get there by walking through the house. I'm not sure what I assumed this house might look like, but it turns out to be neat and cozy, the floor scrubbed so clean that I hesitate to enter. I take off my shoes, muddy from yard incursions, and carry them in my hand to the back door. I walk through the pristine kitchen to the yard.

Out back, the shed is a mess of broken plates, decaying chairs, and tin cans, as jumbled and dirty as the house is neat and clean. No matter where I look, no Patches. I hurry back to the house, again taking off my shoes. As I pass through, I catch a glimpse of the parlor, a photo gallery of family pictures featuring Grandma Darlene; they're arranged in the front window as a kind of shrine.

It's getting increasingly dark on the street now as some families turn out their lights to go to bed. Through the dimness, I see the glimmer of flashlights, hear other searchers. Mostly it's Sheryl calling, "Paaa-ches," with a lilt on the first syllable. This, followed by a haunting whistle, three notes—low, then high, then one in between—a long, warbling plea.

Neighbors I don't know by name come out on their porches. They hunch over Suzanna's flier in the dim light and try to recall when they last saw Patches. "I see that cat all the time; he crosses through just there." They point toward hidden pathways between fences, a fissure in a deck, a tunnel under a broken-down shack. When I concentrate my attention, picture this route, something rotates in my mind, flips open. A new map takes form, a cat landscape—startlingly unfamiliar—superimposed on the one I thought I knew.

Several nights after Patches has been found (hidden under Andy's house, bleeding and dirty, but alive!), I wake up at 2:00 A.M. I can't sleep. During these dark rainy months, night seems to be the time that my quest for home becomes most intense. Tonight my mind is chaotic with excitement. The search inside the neighboring yards has shifted my sense of the block, but I can't pinpoint how. After years of getting to know this neighborhood, I feel unexpectedly unbalanced, as if I need to begin all over again because I have it wrong. I've got to put the whole thing together, to remember how each yard fits with the next. I sit up in bed wrestling with ideas.

Of course. I will go back to those yards—Grandma Darlene's,

the apartment complex's, the church's. I'll do it first thing to-morrow morning and give them all a closer look, take stock of what abuts on what, see how they connect. This idea is so satis-fying to me that finally I feel ready to slide under the covers again. I mold my body to Patrick's and prepare to sleep.

Just before I doze off, I am jolted by a new thought. I don't have the right to go back. There's no way I can get up tomorrow morning and blithely step into any of those properties. In each case, I would be trespassing—intruding on what is privately owned.

When Patches was still missing, the ordinary boundaries, the rules for dividing up the land, were momentarily suspended. No one had said that, but we all knew. And now, even though there hasn't been any overt announcement, I know that those rules have snapped back into place.

Suddenly I see it—the whole block as one expanse. Awake in the dark, I'm exhilarated. What I'm seeing is beyond "owned." Nobody can own the fundamental ground.

Yes, we've agreed to divisions, categories by which this space is separated into our house, Andy's house, Roy and Sheryl's house, and is ostensibly owned. We assume (me too) that there's one map for dividing up this home space into owned properties. My heartbeat quickens. I'm on to something. It's the other map, the cat map. And who would say that the cats "own" the block? Not even Sheryl. I think of all the forms of life passing between the houses, inhabiting this land. Each has a map: the snails, the ants, the bacteria. Do the bacteria own the block?

Tiptoeing out of bed without waking Cleo curled up on her cushion, I cross the attic playroom, step to the back window, and look out over the shadowy yards—"ours," "Sheryl's," "Zoe's," "Grandma Darlene's." I can dimly make out the fences. I stood in the middle of those many yards, looking through the cat map for Patches. A sense of "owning" this expanse of land depends on context (humans, cats, snails, ad infinitum).

The hills rise on the horizon; the dawn redwood is stark and bare-limbed in its corner. In the various yards, white deck chairs and tables gleam by the light of a wan moon. Truly, ownership is a convention by which I might (and usually do!) describe these yards. And ownership is not the only convention. All the other ways we use to describe them are also conventions. In itself, the land doesn't have an enduring essence of any kind—good or bad, small or large, neither defiled nor pure, neither increasing nor decreasing. It's empty of all that.

A train calls from somewhere out in the darkness. In my state of mind—part sleep, part dream—it seems like a keening for rawness, for the vast mutability of things, life moving through, vanishing. I imagine Dee or some other homeless wanderer out on the ramp of the Pilgrim's Rest Church, perhaps sleeping under the night sky. Taking me by surprise, my usual thinking flips over. A yearning comes to me, a kind of envy for the monk's homelessness. For a moment, I tap into this vast homelessness in raw contact with everything. It feels like a fullness, an underbelly to emptiness.

Poor Patrick. Right there at 2:30 A.M. when he's happily asleep, I get back in bed and wake him up to tell him my ideas. "Mm," he says quite sweetly.

In the morning when he wakes up in the acceptable way, I'm hoping he's forgotten that I so rudely woke him during the night. But he rolls over and gives me a jaunty look. He queries, "Do you know what's been happening in the city of Berkeley during the time Patches has been lost and you've been spinning out your theories on emptiness and ownership?"

"No, I don't," say I, disappointed now that he's going to go off on some political diatribe about something in the city council that I may not understand and surely won't find interesting.

"The council voted that in City of Berkeley ordinances, people who own pets can no longer be called 'pet owners.'"

I begin to smile.

He continues, "One faction wanted to call them 'pet guardians' (as they do, after all, in Boulder, Colorado and North Hollywood!)." He raises one eyebrow, and I see his lawyer's mind at work: if you didn't "own" her, couldn't anyone just poach Cleo? "But a compromise was finally reached," Patrick pauses. "In Berkeley, we'll call them 'owner/guardians.'" He makes a sad, droopy-in-the-eyes-and-mouth sort of face, his lower lip curled into a pout. "So according to you, we aren't owners of our property anymore. Are we its guardians?"

"Guardians," I repeat. "I like that." But I think of "our" yard, with its broken machinery and neglected compost heap. And then other venues where we might be guardians, but so often are not. Starting with our own body, speech, and mind, and on to the factories I've walked past—and all the other places where folks in our neighborhood may well have been careless with air and water and soil.

I think of a conversation I had with Gil about the culvert running beneath many yards. When the creek is buried under our backyard, how easy it is to assume that "our" yard—inside the bounds of its fence—is owned independently from all the other yards, is independent of any relationship to the rest of the world. If Strawberry Creek were exposed, passing through all the other properties, "ours" might not seem so independent anymore, but connected to a whole ecosystem. As it ran through our yard, that creek might call to us, "Take note of what flows in, of what flows out; be guardian to the broad terrain."

IT'S RAINING AGAIN, and our early-bird meditation group is meeting in the basement. Zoe and Michael have just put down a wood floor over the cement and redesigned the space for houseguests, setting up a bed and dresser where we used to lay out our meditation cushions. So this morning we've moved our cushions to the far end. Now there's only a hint of the basement feeling here, just the low ceiling, the dampness of the air. But when I close my eyes, the dark flows back in, floods my mind with a sense of vast, ownerless space and time.

At some point, I begin to pay attention to my breath, and with that tuning of attention, I notice voices and foot shufflings above. With a start, I recognize this spot, this posture. Of course. I have meditated exactly here before. Two years ago before we ever started our group.

It surprises me that I suggested this basement for our meditation, that for months I have been sitting just a few yards away from where I am now without any recollection of my previous meditation in this very space. But as I try to follow my breath this morning, I can focus on only this. It was two years ago when, in the bedroom above, Cathy struggled in the last stages of leukemia; she lay just over us in her big bed, dying.

When Cathy's twin brother bought the house for her, it remained vacant for many months while Cathy, only fifty-two and slated so soon to die, shuttled back and forth between hospitals and last-ditch experimental treatments. In Cathy's absence, George, who for many years had rented the basement space for his work, took over the care of Cathy's garden. Finally, all treatments failed, and as her brother put it, "Cathy came home to die." Neighbors on all sides welcomed her as best we could with cards and flowers. But Cathy's immune system was too weak to allow actual visits.

Cathy did call me once on the phone; she thanked me for my card. As we spoke, it occurred to me that if we each stepped out of our kitchen doors, we could see one another. So from the back landing, we continued our talk, noting how silly we felt clutching our two telephones.

In the following months, I would often look over across the yards to Cathy's bedroom window. Particularly at night, I was drawn by the glow of the lantern next to Cathy's bed, where she spent most of her time as she became more frail. I so wanted to lend support to this woman suffering beside us on our corner, someone I barely knew, but to whom—the cancer, the shared terrain, who knows what?—I felt an intangible bond.

It turned out, when I spoke with George about it, that he too had been trying to figure out how he could lend support. We decided that it might mean something to Cathy (and to us) if we sat together—offering our prayers from someplace close by but out of the way. So one evening we met in the basement right here, just where we neighbors sit now, underneath Cathy's bedroom. We set up a makeshift altar with some flowers George had been tending from the garden. He sat in a chair and I on my meditation cushion on the floor—just under where we imagined Cathy lay in her bed.

It was a week later, when Cathy seemed about to die, that her brother invited me upstairs to meditate in her room. I pulled my chair close to her as she lay beneath her white lace coverlet, and several days after that, close again as she lay there dead with the lace coverlet strewn with roses.

Right above where we neighbors now sit, the room where Cathy once slept is also where Carmen used to sleep. It was for sure right there where she kept her bed, where she read at night when she came home late from the emergency room. In the years that Carmen's old boyfriend lived here too, this is where he slept and where, I would imagine, the two made love. Indeed, in the master bedroom of this house, in the center of the room between the two windows, is the perfect—perhaps the only— spot for a double bed. So right above us, as well, is where Zoe and Michael keep their bed, perhaps where they conceived the new baby. And back through the generations of occupants here, this must have been the very spot where each couple had their bed—where Frederick and Annie Offe slept, made love, and (more than likely) died. Reflecting on that now, all the layers, I am deeply stirred.

It's still raining outside, thrumming on the pavement. For

some time I listen to the sound of the rain. Gradually my attention returns to the room above with its bed between the windows. Truly, no one owns this space. Depending on the map, this room could be a stand-in for anywhere and everywhere. From the time of the Ocean View settlement, the ranchos of the Spanish, the four and a half millennia of the shellmound, and long before that, all those who have lived and died and birthed here stream through. The whole universe—past, present, and future—is right here in this room.

In East Asia, we speak of the human body as a mini-cosmos. The cosmos is our home, and we can touch it by being aware of our body. Meditation is to be still: to sit still, to stand still, and to walk with stillness. Meditation means to look deeply, to touch deeply so we can realize we are already home.

—Thich Nhat Hanh

Epilogue

Already Home

In the front of our house, facing the street, I clear away dead leaves, uproot weeds. This patch of ground is long neglected; it's been many months since I took up rake and trowel or reached my fingers into the dirt. As I persevere, I discover hidden layers of garden, invisible yet here all along, ready to be revealed. This is the work of uncovering.

Last week, when the ugly hedge had a particularly mangy look (one of its bushes had actually died), Patrick turned to me. "What do you say we pull out the hedge?" Indeed! thought I. And so we did. This morning I've taken myself by the ear and dragged myself out to clean up the garden. Glowing with its new paint job, the face of the house is open to garbage trucks, teenagers in stolen cars, shouting fights, and screeches only audible to stray dogs. The house feels a bit naked, and I a bit vulnerable.

I begin along the sidewalk with the strip of soil over which the ugly hedge used to loom. As leaves and weeds are cleared, one brilliant red English primrose (*Primula vulgaris*) is first to be uncovered. This primrose is a survivor from my gardening attempts when I first settled here twelve years ago, having spent ten years running back and forth across the Bay and, before that, having run three thousand miles across the country—looking for home.

My neighbor Haddie had surveyed these initial gardening efforts and shaken her head. "Not much of a gardener, are you?" I now find a suave retort, 'No, I'm not!' And remembering the rear of the house—the broken lawn mower, the compost disaster—I fashion retorts to all projected critics, myself included: "And more than that! I'm a lapsed 'guardian,' front yard and back. But I do keep giving it a try."

This Sunday morning, I've plunged into garden cleanup with a spirit of vengeance. Mouth in a broad smiling grimace of stick-to-itiveness, I yank out weeds. Sniffing back a cold, I pry up stepping stones and heave them this way and that. I toss aside my new gardening gloves, tear out the early-blooming oxalis, and pull the soysia grass bare-fisted. As I wrench out these intransigents, I am thoroughly splattered, sprays of dirt stinging my eyes, coating my teeth.

Now for the more delicate work: teasing apart the quack-grass roots from those of the California poppies; extricating the full taproot of the dandelion, all the tiny hairs; sifting soil through tender fingers, searching out severed roots that might sprout into new weeds. This morning in our basement meditation hall, I refined my attention to just such delicacy: to the trembling of the breath; the rustling of incipient angers and griefs; to all the rumblings, cries, and bangings of the street.

In the front yard now, after hours of bagging leaves and pulling weeds, vestiges of our once-garden are uncovered. I salvage the dainty Mexican evening primrose (*Oenothera belandieri*), not even a cousin to the *Primula vulgaris* planted by the once-hedge. As the street trees grew tall, relegating our garden plot to shade, the whole bed of evening primrose fell prey to mildew. The memory of those tender-petaled flowers makes me think of Carmen—of the rose shimmer of evening primrose in her sunny corner garden, and of how years ago, she had helped me dig up some from her yard to transplant just here into ours.

The teenagers are beginning to gather out on the stairs next door by the boxes of boards and junk ready to be hauled off since Donna tore down the shed and fixed up her backyard. Now some of the teenagers come by in their own cars. A friend of Michelle's pulls up with the radio on full blast. Through pulsing music, cat excrement, tangles of sour grass and deep-rooted dandelions; through Cleo and Radio barking in the back and someone's coughing somewhere nearby—I keep dredging out the garden.

A tingle of mint pleases my nose. Transplanted to the front by mistake along with the iris once bordering the backyard fence, that hardy mint persists, offering leaves for Katy's tea and seasoning for salads. How mint propagates and invades. I'm guessing it first migrated to us under the fence from a neighboring yard. It could have been years ago (maybe even a century!), when Frederick and Annie Offe lived in the front house and perhaps planted the mint for young Lizzie and her husband, William Cleary, in the back.

Through my sniffs, I can't help noticing that the coughing nearby has intensified. The more I sniff, the louder the cough. A deep chest cough I've heard before. Maybe it's coming from the little alleyway between our house and Grandma Darlene's. It's got to be Dee, who has indeed been on the street of late, getting herself to AA meetings, she tells me. I give myself a shake. As if I'm the only one who has hardships, who struggles (with sometimes sparse results) to tend with kindness to myself, to my family, to the world.

A bell tolls down the block. It's the Pilgrim's Rest Church convening its service. I'm grateful for this presence right here on our corner—with its history of celebrating the cycles of life, of attending to loss. Just last fall, when a cataclysm shook our nation, the Pilgrim's Rest offered space allowing sixty neighbors to join together, exchange words, song, and silence. There's something that happens when people who live on shared ground come together in that home space to do even the most simple ritual. In our exchange that autumn evening (I think of the shell-mound dwellers), common aspirations and feelings found expression, and something was transformed. Truly we inhabited ourselves, our relations with one another, and our place. Give became receive, receive give.

Surveying the front patch now after a morning of weeding, I take stock. Through truck rumblings, coughs, shouts, and church bells, I appreciate this corner, see the history of this garden: English primrose, my first planting (was it vulgar?); Mexican primrose (truly elegant) from Carmen's; mint from unknown neighbors, perhaps even pioneers. As I uncover the layers, I see this garden new, a hologram of sorts, made up of fragments of the neighborhood.

Squatting here, I feel the dirt beneath my feet. I remember the ground-sensing methods of the archaeologists, tune my senses to moisture, heat, sound. Still damp from winter rains, the dirt cools the soles of my feet. Under this surface soil are alternate layers: sediments carried down by the creeks from the Berkeley Hills, then San Francisco Bay muds carried from the drainage of the Sacramento and San Joaquin Rivers, layer after layer of sediments from the hills, then bay muds again dating back thousands of years. Seeing the vast impermanence of time and space, insight can open. From this big view, there is no way to live in opposition to other things; there's only the challenge to rest in what's here—a continuous coming and going, arising and dissolving.

Breathing in, I am filled with scent: of mint, of excrement, of factory fumes, of my own sweat. Unaccountably, I am filled with a sense of completeness, that for this moment, nothing else is needed. What is here feels like fundamental ground—wide and peaceful. Deeply familiar. I recognize it as home. I give myself a pinch. Because of course I've been fuming and sniffing, struggling with discomforts, and all the while I've been right in this place with that stillness, a hidden possibility, here all along. I was already home.

Through the stillness comes the whistle of a train, a double hoot, then a long warble—loud, louder. At some imperceptible moment, it arrives and passes, softening until it disappears into the ongoing hum. I rest on my haunches in the dirt of this garden plot—now H and Willow (once H and Dover); in the Ocean View neighborhood of Berkeley, California; on the outskirts of what was, for forty-five hundred years, a village built on a shellmound and before that, marshland, mudflats, and bay. From this corner, where I am training myself to be a guardian, I hunker down and listen to the waning call of the train no longer audible to human ear.

acknowledgments

IN WRITING THE BOOK, I depended on research, insights, and editorial acumen from family and friends, from diverse creek walkers, tree lovers, map aficionados, from denizens of the back streets of the city and of the mind.

My deepest gratitude is to my husband, Patrick O'Donnell, my daughter, Caitlin O'Donnell, and our dog, Cleo—for being my family. Without the grounding within our small family, I could never have taken on the adventure with the larger family of the neighborhood. I extend gratitude as well to my neighbors, without whose friendships I could never have written the book: Amy Neiman, Bart Selden, Myriam Casimir, Emily Payne, John Heller, Olivia and Sammy Heller, David Hauer, Steve and Chia Haflich, Margaret Lee, Jane Diamond, Matt Haber, and Kathleen Van Sickle. I also thank those who no longer live on our corner: Cecilia Ramos, David Keiser, Amanda McCoy, Cathy Hall, Craig Reece, Nancy Weber, Morgan Weber, David Neidorf and Kateri Carmola, Roland Kanaar and Claire Wyman, and Tim and Bella Robbins. And thanks to the other neighbors who, in deference to their privacy, I am leaving unnamed.

Several members of my family read and commented on the manuscript: Patrick (meticulous in his care), Caitlin (fellow writer, tuning language), my mother, Nancy Spriggs (offering appreciation), and my sister, Julie Spriggs (raising key questions). I thank other family members as well: Mark Gates, Nicola Gates, Dillard Spriggs, Barbara Gallant, and Polly Fisher. And I thank the elders of my extended family: Jo Despres, Jane Shedlin, and Lizie and Ned Goldwasser. Thanks to my father, William Gates (1917–1975), with whom I wish I could share this book.

Many nonneighborhood friends have supported me through this writing. Dear friends who read and commented on the manuscript as a whole include Katherine Salazar-Poss and Antonio Salazar-Hobson (offering support throughout on matters of language—legal and heart) and kindred spirit Ellen Webb. I thank longtime companions Marie Wilson and Alan Miller (with insightful help on early chapters), Shelley and Ron Parlante, Shelly Fox and Matthew Rinaldi, Laurie Roberts, and Arie Shoshani, and reaching back still further, June Namais, Nancy Dyer, Nia Fliam, Bob Heilbroner, and Nancy Falk. I also thank Caitlin's friends Kyla Collins, Sarah and Ben Jelinsky, Emily Hecht, Lyla Weinstein, and Mariko Conner.

I extend great gratitude to meditation mentors: Kidder Smith (friend since age four), Jon Kabat-Zinn, Joseph Goldstein, Jack Kornfield, Sharon Salzberg, Ajahn Amaro, Ruth Denison, Thich Nhat Hanh, James Baraz, Reb Anderson, Norman Fischer, Swami Viganananda, and Gil Fronsdal (who generously read and commented on the whole manuscript).

I realized I was writing a book when Joanna Macy and Wendy Johnson invited me to join their three-woman writing group. Joanna asked, "You are writing a book, aren't you?" The breadth of Wendy's garden book—from the geologic formation of the Green Gulch valley to the evolution of the opposable thumb through hulling seeds—stirred my imagination. Joanna's brilliant articulation of the Buddhist teachings of dependent coarising—self with world, mind with body, knower with known—offered the foundational understandings for my book.

My dear friends on the staff of *Inquiring Mind* have also been essential to the birthing of this book. Wes Nisker, coeditor, kept me laughing (even when I was crying) and, through his own writing, kept reminding me of the teachings of the science of evolution. Alan Novidor, publisher, is a clear thinker whose understandings of systems theory provided key insights into the ecology of the whole. Dharma-sister Margery Cantor, designer, kept me company with her fine aesthetic and her love of poetry. Dennis Crean, managing editor, provided organizational skill and careful editing, thereby keeping the journal going, allowing me to write. With his characteristic meticulousness, he helped me put together the resource section of the book. Thanks to Joe Curran, Nancy Van House, and Lynne Prather, who helped me refine my language; Mindy Toomay for technical help; and Dewey and Kerry Livingston for support early on.

Thanks to my friends who walked and talked with me on the streets and trails: first, to my almost-brother, Peter Gradjansky, who, on early morning walks, introduced me to the neighborhood—to the trees in my yard and on the street, to Aquatic Park and the alley; and to Patrick McMahon, who, like Peter, has been teaching me to cherish the underworld of the city—the places generally forgotten and unloved. Special gratitude to other predawn walkers: Lucia Blakeslee (often laughing), Sue Bender (talking writing, taking heart), and Loie Rosenkrantz (who also offered me the gift of Rosen Work).

Gratitude, as well, to my daylight walking partners (or others who sat over tea): to Ida Landauer with whom I took on the fierce practice of walking for our lives, to Marilyn Rinzler and Pamplemousse, Nancy Bardacke, Alan Senauke, Susan Moon, Melody Ermachild Chavis, Anita Barrows, Diana Winston, Tova Green, Fran Peavey, Kaz Tanahashi, Terry Vandiver, Suzie Rashkis, Susie Stark, Mudita Nisker, Dan Clurman, Margie Neidorf and Giorgia Neidorf, Karen Rosenbaum, Ben McClinton, Susan Lydon, Phil Catalfo, and Phil Hutchings. And thanks to all the great moms (and dads, too) who walked with me: Pat Zambryski, Barbara Edwards, Craig Collins, Sharon Jelinsky, Arlene Suda, Ginger Parnes, Edie Jackson, Laura Natkins, Marti Green, Ellen Webb, Sandy Walker, Henry Hecht, Sue Juarez, Julie Wong, Beth Gorelick, Teri Tsuji-Mortimer, and Jennifer "Pooh" Medina (the most wonderful coach and mentor I can imagine for Caitlin).

I thank my bird-watching cohorts. First, my brother, Mark, bird-lover since childhood, who walked with me at Aquatic Park, teaching me the great and the snowy egrets, the bufflehead and pied-billed grebes. Many thanks to Brian Fitch, who imparted a love of bird-watching to Caitlin and then to me, and to Peter Dale Scott, who joined us for outings in the Delta to see the tundra swans and sandhill cranes.

I am grateful to the people who took care of my body and mind in healing from cancer during these seven years of working on *Already Home*. At the top on that list are Deeahna Lorenz (whose work with me is expressed in every layer of imagery in the book) and wonderful acupuncturist Robert Dreyfuss. Michael Broffman started me on the journey when he urged me to "take more risks." Great appreciation to Christine Ciavarella, Dave Irwin, David Teegarden, Elena Oakson, Michael Harrison, Katerina Lanner-Cusin, Janet Petroni, John Dyckman, and Jan Feldman. Saraswathi Devi kindly gave me acupressure massage and other more mysterious healings. Finally Sandy Eastoak sent me daily healings through the mail.

Several people generously offered financial help. Ellen Poss's substantial gift allowed me to take time off from my other remunerative work to focus on the book. I am also grateful for gifts from Meg Quigley, Jane Baraz, Genie Bird, and Ruth Denison. Burke Keegan and Pamela Michael gave me fund-raising advice. Peter Barnes provided me with a two-week stay at the Mesa Foundation, where the fertility of the wetlands seeped into my mind and permeated the writing. I also thank other writing hideaways: the guest house at Green Gulch Farm and Santa Sabina Center.

For help in doing research, first and foremost, gratitude goes to lay historian Stephanie Manning, who taught me how to study the history of my house and local streets, engaged me in the shellmound, and read through all the historical sections of the manuscript. Malcolm Margolin, orchestrator of the conferences on the local shellmounds, publisher of Heyday Books, and author of *The Ohlone Way*, provided inspiration and helpful information. Kent Lightfoot from the University of California Archaeological Research Facility and Ed Luby, formerly researcher/professor at the University of California at Berkeley, now at San Francisco State University, kindly reviewed the shellmound references in my manuscript.

Descendants of the native Ohlone Indians spoke at the shellmound conferences (1992, 2000, and 2001): Jakki Kehl, Linda Yamane, and Andrew Galvan. I would not have felt comfortable writing about this terrain without, on several occasions, hearing these native descendants speak—imparting understanding of the heritage of this place that only they could offer. I only wish I had been able to set up the further interviews I had hoped for.

I am grateful for help from Anthony Buffington Bruce and Lesley Emmington Jones of the Berkeley Architectural Heritage Association (BAHA) for assistance in studying the history of my Victorian house and others on my corner. I am also grateful to the Berkeley Historical Society for help in research and for the wonderful curriculum, "Victorian Berkeley: The Community of Ocean View" (1983) written by Karen Jorgensen-Esmaili. The "Industrial Walk through West Berkeley" led by Betty Marvin, the "Tour of Ocean View" led by Stephanie and Curt Manning, and the delightful memoir "Berkeley As I Knew It in Early Days" by Wilhelmine F. Bolsted Cianciarulo, offered in 1941 to the Berkeley Schools, gave me additional insights and information. Alan Acacia provided two informative presentations on Ocean

View history to the Sentral Ocean View Neighborhood Association (SONA).

Thanks to Dr. Howard E. Schorn, retired paleobotanist from the University of California at Berkeley, and Dr. Todd Dawson, professor of biology at the University of California at Berkeley, for reviewing my writing on the dawn redwood (*Metasequoia glyptostroboides*).

Doris Sloan, adjunct professor in the Department of Earth and Planetary Science at the University of California at Berkeley, generously offered her time and a meticulous review of my geologic reveries. Steve Edwards from the East Bay Regional Parks Botanical Garden gave time and thought in his consultations on local flora and suggestions for further research. At the shellmound conference, Beneath Our Feet (2000), Robin Grossinger from the San Francisco Estuary Institute made a fascinating presentation on the landscape of the East Bay before the Europeans arrived. Susan Schwartz, member of Friends of Five Creeks and active in restoration of creeks, native plants, and pathways, offered me a long informative conversation about Codornices Creek.

For information on, and insight into, the impact of toxic emissions on the local environment, I thank Barbara A. Brenner, executive director of Breast Cancer Action, and Joan Reiss from the Bay Area Breast Cancer Study Group of the Breast Cancer Fund. For investigations into pollution in West Berkeley, I thank Janice Shroeder, Terry Terteling, and LA Wood. For information on toxic discharges in the San Francisco Bay, I thank the International Bird Rescue Research Center.

For exploration of the history and meaning of homelessness, I am indebted to a long conversation with, and the writings of, Peter Marin, essayist and homeless advocate. For questions on Buddhist teachings, and novel perspectives on just about anything, thanks to Buddhist scholar and friend Steven Goodman.

Already Home benefited from the suggestions of many editors.

Shoshana Alexander generously walked me through the book proposal. Andy Cooper supported me through every word in the initial drafts, urging me to find my own voice and to cut sentimentality with a little vinegar. Later, Laura Tennen became a remarkable editorial muse, asking me essential questions until I knew myself how to cut and reshape. My Australian sister-writer Susan Murphy inspired me with her article "Feel Free to Look Around" (*Blind Donkey: Journal of the Diamond Sangha,* 18, no. 1 [Summer 1998]). She read through my first draft and urged me, as I rewrote, to descend into the dark.

Ronna Kabatznick buoyed me up whenever I stopped believing I could do it, read and commented on every version of the book, helped me clarify my understanding of some key Buddhist teachings, and generously connected me with my original agent, the marvelous Sharon Friedman. Judith Stronach (whose death last fall has left a great hole in many lives) read every draft, offering her particular brilliance in articulating the most subtle and elusive of thoughts. Another excellent editor, Barbara Self-ridge, helped me name my quest for home. Eloquent writers Annie Gottlieb and Charlotte Painter generously read the whole book. Rachel Markowitz did an amazing proofing job.

I am grateful to the staff at Shambhala Publications for their meticulous work. Peter Turner saw the potential of the book and worked closely with me through the early stages. Emily Bower's queries and careful reading led me to keep rewriting and clarifying what it was I truly wanted to say. Thanks to the cover designer, Jim Zaccaria, copy editor Karen Steib, and assistant editor Ben Gleason. Thanks to vice president Jonathan Green, who read the manuscript through several times as legal advisor.

Final thanks go to my agent from heaven, Christopher Schelling, of Ralph M. Vicinanza, Ltd., who read every draft, offered crucial editorial suggestions, and supported me through all the ups and downs with grace and humor.

resources

These are resources and sources that I drew on while writing *Already Home*. I list them with the hope that they'll prove useful to readers looking for more information about topics I explore in the book.

ARCHAEOLOGY

City of Berkeley Ordinance 4694 N.S. Landmark Documentation: The Site and Remnants of the West Berkeley Native Shellmound (CA-Ala-307), Willow Grove Park and Lower Strawberry Creek.

For information on the West Berkeley shellmound, read this extensive documentation recorded by Stephanie Manning, available at the Current Planning Division of the City of Berkeley, 2120 Milvia St., Berkeley, CA 94704.

Ingram, B. Lynn. "Differences in Radiocarbon Age between Shell and Charcoal from a Holocene Shellmound in Northern California." *University of Washington Quarterly Research* 49 (1998): 102–110.

Luby, Edward M., and Mark F. Gruber. "The Dead Must Be Fed: Symbolic Meanings of the Shellmounds of the San Francisco Bay Area." *Cambridge Archeological Journal* 9 (1999), no. 1: 95–108.

Manning, Stephanie. *Shellmounder News* (periodical). 2107 Fifth Street, Berkeley, CA 94710, sfbayshellmounds@yahoo .com.

Sher, Sandra. "Shell Mound Park: The Bay Area's Premier Amusement Resort." *Journal of the Emeryville Historical Society* 7, no. 3 (fall 1996).

——. "The Native Legacy of Emeryville." *Journal of the Emeryville Historical Society* 5 (1994), nos. 2 (summer) and 3 (fall).

Wallace, William J., and Donald W. Lathrap. "West Berkeley (CA-Ala-307): A Culturally Stratified Shellmound on the East Shore of San Francisco Bay." Department of Anthropology, University of California, Berkeley, November 1975.

The web address for the archaeological research facility within the department of anthropology is http://sscl.berkeley.edu/arf/.

BERKELEY HISTORY

Bancroft Library. University of California at Berkeley. (510) 642–6481, http://bancroft.edu/.

Berkeley Architectural Heritage Association (BAHA). *The BAHA Newsletter*. P.O. Box 1137, Berkeley, CA 94701, www.berkeleyheritage.com.

The Berkeley Historical Society Newsletter. P.O. Box 1190, Berkeley, CA 94701, www.ci.berkeley.ca.us/histsoc/.

Cerny, Susan Dinkelspiel. *Berkeley Landmarks: An Illustrated Guide to Berkeley, California's Architectural Heritage*. Rev. ed. Berkeley: Berkeley Architectural Heritage Association, 2001.

Manning, Stephanie. "Spenger's Fish Grotto: 1898 to 1998." *BAHA Newsletter* 96 (fall 1998): 8–9.

McArdle, Phil, ed. *Exactly Opposite the Golden Gate: Essays on Berkeley's History 1845–1945*. Berkeley: Berkeley Historical Society, 1983.

This informative anthology includes short essays on such topics as the land, the arrival of the Europeans, the beginnings of the university, and the 1906 earthquake.

Oakland Public Library. Oakland History Room. 125 Fourteenth Street, Oakland, CA 94612, oaklandlibrary.org/Seasonal/Sections/oakhr.html.

Paddison, Joshua, ed. *A World Transformed: Firsthand Accounts of California before the Gold Rush.* Berkeley: Heyday Books, 1999.

Pettitt, George A. *Berkeley: The Town and Gown of It.* Berkeley: Howell-North Books, 1973.

This delightful account of the early years of Berkeley—the linked stories of the town and the university—is full of fun-to-read anecdotes and vivid details.

Pitcher, Don. *Berkeley Inside/Out.* Berkeley: Heyday Books, 1989.

Schwartz, Richard. *Berkeley 1900: Daily Life at the Turn of the Century.* Berkeley: Richard Schwartz Books, 2000.

Newspaper articles from the *Berkeley Daily Gazette* and vintage photographs from family and other archives offer a sense of day-to-day life in Berkeley, circa 1900.

Temple Hill Family History Center. 4770 Lincoln Way, Oakland, CA 94602, (510) 531–3905, http://templehill.com/family_history_center.html.

The Oakland Family History Center is a branch of the Family History Library of the Mormon Temple in Salt Lake City. It is a wonderful resource for investigating local and family history. Its offerings include census, voting, and property records; passenger-ship lists; and military lists.

Wollenberg, Charles. "Berkeley, a City History." *Berkeley History Series.* Berkeley Public Library, 2002. 2090 Kittridge Street, Berkeley, CA 94704, (510) 981–6100, www.infopeople.org/bpl/system/historytext.html.

Read this informative and engaging history (including an excellent bibliography) online.

CREEKS

Aquatic Outreach Institute. 1327 South 46th Street, no. 155, Richmond, CA 94804, www.aoinstitute.org.

See especially *Creeks Speak: The Voice of Bay Area Citizens for Creek Restoration.*

Charbonneau, Robert, and Vincent H. Resh. "Strawberry Creek on the University of California, Berkeley Campus: A Case History of Urban Stream Restoration." *Aquatic Conservation: Marine and Freshwater Ecosystems* 2 (1992): 293–307.

Dury, John. "Biography of an Urban Creek." *Creeks Speak: The Voice of Bay Area Citizens for Creek Restoration* 6, no. 4 (winter 1995): 2, 8–9.

Friends of Five Creeks. www.fivecreeks.org.

Richard, Christopher M., ed. *Guide to East Bay Creeks.* Rev. ed. Oakland: Oakland Museum of California, 1995.

> Along with the *Creek and Watershed Map of Oakland and Berkeley* by Janet M. Sowers (also published by the Oakland Museum), this is a wonderful resource on East Bay Creeks, as well as an insightful description of the ecology of the local watershed.

Urban Creeks Council. 1250 Addison Street, no. 107C, Berkeley, CA 94702.

GEOLOGY AND NATURAL HISTORY

Alt, David, and Donald W. Hyndman. *Roadside Geology of Northern and Central California.* Missoula, Mont.: Mountain Press Publishing Company, 2000.

Earth Science and Map Library. University of California at Berkeley. (510) 643–6576, www.lib.berkeley.edu/EART/.

> This amazing map library offers the largest collection of maps in Northern California and one of the largest university map collections in the United States, including themes such as geology, soils, and climate, as well as city street maps from different eras.

Konigsmark, Ted. *Geologic Trips: San Francisco and the Bay Area.* Gualala, Calif.: GeoPress, 1998.

Martin, Glen. "Bay Today, Gone Tomorrow: S.F. Region's Defining Feature Is Just a Transitory Puddle in Geologic Time." *San Francisco Chronicle*, December 20, 1999.

McPhee, John. *Assembling California.* New York: Farrar, Straus and Giroux, 1993.

> An entertaining journey from Donner Pass in the Sierra Nevada to the San Andreas fault of the Bay Area, offering insight into geologic time.

Schoenherr, Allan A. *A Natural History of California*. Berkeley: University of California Press, 1992.

A rich compendium of diverse aspects of California natural history.

Tudge, Colin. *The Time before History: Five Million Years of Human Impact*. New York: Simon and Schuster, Touchstone, 1996.

NATIVE AMERICAN RESOURCES

Bean, Lowell John. *The Ohlone Past and Present: Native Americans of the San Francisco Bay Region*. Menlo Park: Ballena Press, 1994.

Margolin, Malcolm, ed. *The Way We Lived: California Indian Stories, Songs and Reminiscences*. Berkeley: Heyday Books and California Historical Society, 1981.

————. *The Ohlone Way: Indian Life in the San Francisco–Monterey Bay Area*. Berkeley: Heyday Books, 1978.

This is an imaginative and fun-to-read book on the life and customs of the Ohlone Indians before the coming of Europeans.

Milliken, Randall. *A Time of Little Choice: The Disintegration of Tribal Culture in the San Francisco Bay Area 1769–1810*. Menlo Park: Ballena Press, 1995.

News from Native California: An Inside View of the California Indian World. 2054 University Avenue, no. 400, Berkeley, CA 94704, http://heydaybooks.com/news/.

Each issue presents a range of articles by Native California Indians.

Teixeira, Lauren S. *The Costanoan/Ohlone Indians of the San Francisco and Monterey Bay Area: A Research Guide*. Menlo Park: Ballena Press, 1997.

PLANTS AND TREES

Clapperstick Institute. *Bay Nature*. P.O. Box 9145, Berkeley, CA 94709, www.baynature.com.

Edwards, Stephen W. "A Meditation on East Bay Natural History at First Contact." *The Four Seasons: Journal of the Regional Parks Botanic Garden* 10, no. 3 (1997): 10–35.

Flannery, Tim. *The Eternal Frontier: An Ecological History of North America and Its Peoples.* New York: Atlantic Monthly Press, 2001.

Gittlen, William. *Discovered Alive: The Story of the Chinese Redwood.* Berkeley: Pierside Publications, 1998.

Keator, Glenn, Linda Yamane, and Ann Lewis. *In Full View: Three Ways of Seeing California Plants.* Berkeley: Heyday Books, 1995.

In this beautiful book, a botanist, a Native American scholar, and an artist offer complementary perspectives on California native plants.

Raven, Peter H., Ray F. Evert, and Susan E. Eichhorn. *Biology of Plants,* 4th ed. New York: Worth Publishers, 1986.

SAN FRANCISCO BAY

Conradson, Diane R. *Exploring Our Baylands.* Fremont, Calif.: San Francisco Bay Wildlife Society, 1996.

Goals Project. *Baylands Ecosystem Habitat Goals: A Report of Habitat Recommendations.* San Francisco Bay Area Wetlands Ecosystem Goals Project. U.S. Environmental Protection Agency, San Francisco. Bay Regional Water Quality Control Board, Oakland, Calif., 1999.

Prepared by Bay Area environmental scientists, this study of the changing baylands includes comparative maps from 1800 and 1998 that show the layout of Bay/channel, tidal flats, salt ponds, sandy beaches, Bay fill, etc.

San Francisco Estuary Project. 2101 Webster Street, Suite 500, Oakland, CA 94612.

See especially Cohen, Andrew Neal. *An Introduction to the Ecology of the San Francisco Estuary,* 2d ed. Oakland: Save San Francisco Bay Association, 1991.

TOXINS AND THE ENVIRONMENT

Breast Cancer Action Newsletter. 55 New Montgomery Street, Suite 323, San Francisco, CA 94105, www.bcaction.org.

Council of Neighborhood Associations. *CNA Newsletter.* P.O. Box 1217, Berkeley, CA 94701.

Register, Richard. *Ecocity Berkeley: Building Cities for a Healthy Future.* Berkeley: North Atlantic Books, 1987.

Sustainable Energy Institute. *Auto-Free Times.* P.O. Box 4347, Arcata, CA 95518, www.culturechange.org.

Women's Cancer Resource Center Newsletter. 5741 Telegraph Avenue, Oakland, CA 94609, www.wcrc.org.

Wood, LA. "A Brief History of Strawberry Creek: Urban Runoff, Restoration, and Related Public Health Issues." *CNA Newsletter* 254 (1999): 5, 7.

See also LA Wood's website, www.berkeleycitizen.org, for many articles about environmental issues on topics including air quality, groundwater, toxics, hazardous waste, and environmental enforcements in the San Francisco East Bay.

OTHER RESOURCES

Altschuler, Stephen. *Hidden Walks in the East Bay and Marin: Pathways, Essays and Yesterdays.* Lafayette, Calif.: Great West Books, 2001.

American Friends Service Committee. *Street Spirit.* 65 Ninth Street, San Francisco, CA 94103.

This informative and well-written newspaper on homelessness is sold on street corners by the homeless of the San Francisco East Bay.

Hrdy, Sarah Blaffer. *Mother Nature: A History of Mothers, Infants, and Natural Selection.* New York: Pantheon Books, 1999.

A primatologist offers a brilliant and engagingly written work on the ways female strategies as mates and mothers have shaped the evolutionary process.

Marin, Peter. *Freedom and Its Discontents: Reflections on Four Decades of American Moral Experience.* South Royalton, Vt.: Steerforth Press, 1995.

This book of essays by an eloquent spokesperson for the down-and-out—welfare mothers, war-damaged veterans, and the homeless—includes several contemplations on homelessness.

Martin, Michael. "Back-Alley as Community Landscape." *Landscape Journal: A Journal of the Council of Educators in Landscape Architecture* 15, no. 2 (fall 1996): 138–153.

epigraph credits

Basham, A. L., trans. *Majjhima Nikaya*. Boston: Shambhala Publications, 1993.

Fischer, Norman. "The Sacred and the Lost." *Inquiring Mind* 14 (1997), no. 1: 5.

Nhat Hanh, Thich. *Going Home*. New York: Riverhead Books, 1999.

Nhat Hanh, Thich. *The Heart of the Buddha's Teaching*. Berkeley: Parallax Press, 1998.

Saddhatissa, H., trans. *The Sutta-Nipāta*. Surrey: Curzon Press Ltd., 1994.

Shimano, Eido T., Roshi, ed. *Like a Dream, Like a Fantasy: Zen Writings and Translations of Nyogen Senzaki*. Tokyo: Japan Publications, 1978.

Suzuki, Shunryu. *Zen Mind, Beginner's Mind*. New York: Weatherhill, 1970.